PACEMAKER®

Computer
Literacy

Globe
Fearon

Upper Saddle River, New Jersey
www.globefearon.com

We thank the following consultants and reviewers, who provided valuable comments and suggestions during the development of this book:

Consultants: **Martha C. Beech**, Research Associate, Center for Performance Technology, Florida State University. **John Ferro**, Director of Instructional Technology, Community School District Four, New York, New York.

Reviewers: **Patricia Brune**, Pine Forest High School, Pensacola, Florida; **Eileen Byman**, Harrington Park School, Harrington Park, New Jersey; **Tina Casale**, Voorhees Middle School, Blackwood, New Jersey; **Kimberly McClanahan**, Warren Alternative School, Garland, Texas; **Lena Murrill**, Guilford Middle School, Greensboro, North Carolina; **Suzie Oden**, Brownsboro High School, Tyler, Texas **Tim Flaherty**, Pearson Technology Centre, Old Tappan, New Jersey

Executive Editor: Eleanor Ripp; *Supervising Editor:* Stephanie Petron Cahill; *Senior Editor:* Douglas Falk; *Editors:* Dena Pollak, Gina Dalessio, Marilyn Sarch; *Production Editor:* Laura Benford-Sullivan; *Editorial Assistants:* Meredith Diskin, Jeff Wickersty, Kathy Bentzen; *Designers:* Susan Brorein, Jennifer Visco; *Market Manager:* Katie Kehoe-Erezuma; *Research Director:* Angela Darchi; *Cover Design:* Susan Brorein, Jennifer Visco; *Editorial Development:* WordWise, Inc.; *Electronic Composition:* Burmar Technical Corp., Linda Bierniak, Phyllis Rosinsky; *Manufacturing Supervisor:* Mark Cirillo

ACKNOWLEDGEMENTS

We would like to acknowledge the following companies for allowing the use of images and text referencing their products. **Apple Computer, Inc.** for allowing the reprinting of screen shots containing "Apple" copyrighted and trademarked materials. **Microsoft Corporation** for allowing the reprinting of screen shots containing Microsoft copyrighted and trademarked materials in reference to various Microsoft owned and copyrighted programs. *Microsoft® Windows®* is a registered trademark of Microsoft Corporation. Hereafter, every mention of Microsoft® Windows® refers to Microsoft® Windows® Operating System. **Netscape Communications Corporation (America Online, Inc.)** for allowing the reprinting of screen shots containing Netscape copyrighted and trademarked materials and images.

We would like to thank the following organizations for allowing the use of images of their Web sites and Web pages in our documentation.
U.S. Government Web sites: U.S. Environmental Protection Agency (EPA) at www.epa.gov; National Aeronautics & Space Administration (NASA) at www.nasa.gov; U.S. Department of Transportation at www.scitech.dot.gov
Private Web sites: The Ancient Egypt Site by Jacques Kinnaer at www.geocites.com; LLBean at www.llbean.com; The Rock and Roll Hall of Fame at www.rockhall.com

About the Cover: This book is about using personal computers to work with information. The keyboard (bottom left) shows one tool that we use to put information into the computer. The Edit menu (bottom right) has a list of commands that give information to the computer. The magnified processor chip in the background controls information flow through the computer. We use software, such as a Web browser (top left), a spreadsheet (top right), and desktop publishing (middle right), to work with information. The compact disks (bottom) are used to store information.

ISBN: 0-835-95474-9

Printed in the United States of America
1 2 3 4 5 6 7 8 9 10   04 03 02 01 00

Contents

A Note To The Student   viii

UNIT ONE	INTRODUCTION TO COMPUTERS	1
Chapter 1	**Understanding Computers**	**2-3**
1.1	What Is a Computer?	4–6
1.2	Parts of a Computer	7–9
1.3	Information and the Computer	10–13
▶	Computers In Your Life: Computers at Home	14
▶	Problem Solving: Find the Hidden Pointer	15
1.4	Applying: Using a Flowchart	16–17
▶	Chapter Review	18–19

Chapter 2	**Input & Output Tools**	**20–21**
2.1	The Mouse: An Input Tool	22–25
2.2	The Keyboard: An Input Tool	26–29
▶	Problem Solving: Resizing Windows Using a Mouse	30
2.3	Other Input Tools	31–32
2.4	The Printer: An Output Tool	33–34
▶	Computers On The Job: Message Board Operator	35
2.5	Applying: Organizing Icons	36–37
▶	Chapter Review	38–39

Chapter 3	**Giving Orders to the Computer**	**40–41**
3.1	What are Commands and Menus?	42–43
3.2	Using the Open Command	44–46
▶	Problem Solving: Why Menu Commands Sometimes Don't Work	47
3.3	Using the Save Command	48–51
3.4	Using the Print Command	52–53
3.5	Using Toolbars	54–56
▶	Computers In Your Life: Automated Teller Machines	57
3.6	Applying: Copy and Save Files	58–59
▶	Chapter Review	60–61

Chapter 4	**Managing Files**	**62–63**
4.1	Organizing A Computer	64–65
4.2	Viewing Files and Folders	66–67
4.3	Making New Folders	68–70
▶	Problem Solving: Files with Similar Names	71
4.4	Finding Files	72–74
▶	Computers On The Job: Account Assistant	75
4.5	Applying: Organizing Files	76–77
▶	Chapter Review	78–79

Chapter 5	**Inside the Computer**	**80–81**
5.1	Care of Personal Computers	82–83
5.2	The Computer System	84–86
▶	Computers On The Job: Computer Technician	87
5.3	What Is Storage?	88–90
5.4	Using Storage	91–92
▶	Problem Solving: A Computer Freezes	93
5.5	Applying: System Requirements	94–95
▶	Chapter Review	96–97
▶	Unit 1 Review	98

UNIT TWO	**WORD PROCESSING**	**99**
Chapter 6	**Basic Word Processing**	**100–101**
6.1	What Is Word Processing?	102–103
6.2	Making a Document	104–106
6.3	Editing Text	107–108
6.4	Selecting and Changing Text	109–110
▶	Computers On The Job: Customer Service Representative	111
6.5	Moving Text	112–114
▶	Problem Solving: Using Nonprinting Characters	115
6.6	Applying: Organizing a List	116–117
▶	Chapter Review	118–119

Chapter 7	**Checking Documents**	**120–121**
7.1	Why Do We Check a Document?	122–123
7.2	Finding Text	124–125
7.3	Replacing Text	126–128

▶   Problem Solving: The Word Cannot Be Found 129
7.4   Checking Spelling 130–132
7.5   Checking Grammar 133–134
▶   Computers In Your Life: Using the
         Spelling and Grammar Commands 135
7.6   Applying: Analyzing Errors 136–137
▶   Chapter Review 138–139

Chapter 8	Using Formats	140–141
8.1	What Are Formats?	142–143
8.2	Changing Text Style and Size	144–146
8.3	Using Fonts	147–149
8.4	Aligning Text	150–152
▶	Computers On The Job: Invitation Maker	153
8.5	Setting Up the Page	154–156
▶	Problem Solving: Fitting Extra Lines	157
8.6	Applying: Presenting a Poster	158–159
▶	Chapter Review	160–161
▶	**Unit 2 Review**	162

UNIT THREE	DATABASES AND SPREADSHEETS	163
Chapter 9	Using Databases	164–165
9.1	What Is a Database?	166–167
9.2	Planning a Database	168–170
9.3	Making Records	171–174
9.4	Changing Records	175–177
9.5	Finding Records	178–180
▶	Problem Solving: No Records Found	181
9.6	Sorting Records	182–184
▶	Computers In Your Life: Online Library Catalog	185
9.7	Working with Layouts	186–189
9.8	Applying: Communicate Your Data	190–191
▶	Chapter Review	192–193

Chapter 10	Making Spreadsheets	194–195
10.1	What Is a Spreadsheet?	196–197
10.2	Entering Data	198–200
10.3	Setting Up a Spreadsheet	201–203

	▶	Computers On The Job: Building Contractor	204
	10.4	Editing Data	205–207
	10.5	Using Formats	208–210
	▶	Problem Solving: Find the Best Cell Format	211
	10.6	Applying: Organizing a Budget	212–213
	▶	Chapter Review	214–215

Chapter 11	**Working with Spreadsheet Data**	**216–217**
11.1	Making Formulas	218–221
11.2	Making Formulas with Cell Names	222–224
11.3	Changing a Formula	225–227
11.4	Using a Function	228–230
▶	Problem Solving: Fixing an Error in a Formula	231
11.5	Making a Chart	232–234
▶	Computers In Your Life: Setting Up a Budget	235
11.6	Applying: Analyzing Time Spent	236–237
▶	Chapter Review	238–239

| | ▶ | Unit 3 Review | 240 |

UNIT FOUR	**PUBLISHING AND PRESENTING**	**241**
Chapter 12	**Desktop Publishing**	**242–243**
12.1	What Is Desktop Publishing?	244–245
12.2	Making Up a Page	246–249
▶	Computers On The Job: Desktop Publisher	250
12.3	Using Clip Art	251–253
12.4	Making Your Own Art	254–256
▶	Problem Solving: Pieces of Art Overlap	257
12.5	Applying: Presenting Page Layouts	258–259
▶	Chapter Review	260–261

Chapter 13	**Presentations**	**262–263**
13.1	What Is Presentation Software?	264–265
13.2	Planning a Presentation	266–268
13.3	Choosing Slide Layouts	269–270
13.4	Entering Text in Slides	271–273
▶	Computers In Your Life: Making a Presentation About Yourself	274
13.5	Adding Art to Slides	275–276

13.6	Showing a Presentation	277–278
▶	Problem Solving: Rearrange Slides in a Show	279
13.7	Applying: Presenting an Event Log	280–281
▶	Chapter Review	282–283
▶	**Unit 4 Review**	**284**

UNIT FIVE   **THE INTERNET**   **285**

Chapter 14   **Internet Communication**   **286–287**

14.1	What Is the Internet?	288–289
14.2	Sending E–mail	290–292
14.3	Reading and Answering E–mail	293–295
▶	Problem Solving: Undelivered E–mail	296
14.4	Newsgroups	297–298
▶	Computers On The Job: Sales Assistant	299
14.5	Applying: E–mail Communication	300–301
▶	Chapter Review	302–303

Chapter 15   **The World Wide Web**   **304–305**

15.1	What Is the World Wide Web?	306–307
15.2	Using Web Browsers	308–310
▶	Computers In Your Life: Online Shopping	311
15.3	Following Links	312–314
15.4	Using a Search Engine	315–317
15.5	Using Keywords to Search	318–320
▶	Problem Solving: A URL Cannot Be Found	321
15.6	Applying: Searching On The Web	322–323
▶	Chapter Review	324–325
▶	**Unit 5 Review**	**326**

Reference Page	**327**
Glossary	**328**
Index	**336**
Photo Credits	**344**

A Note to the Student

Computer Literacy will help you to understand how personal computers work and what their main parts are. The lessons in this book will teach you how to organize information as well as how to search for it, analyze it, and present it. To help you to perform these tasks, you will learn how to make a file, name it, and save it. You will also learn how to make folders for organizing and storing your files, and how to find your files and folders when you need them.

Computer Literacy will teach you to use different kinds of software. One kind of software—word processing—will help you to write, edit, and perform desktop publishing. Database software will help you to keep records. Spreadsheet software will help you to do math. You will learn about presentation software to present your ideas, and e-mail to communicate. Web browser software will help you to search for information on the Internet.

It is important to *use* computers, not just to read about them. For this reason, you will find **Lab Practice** pages in every chapter. Each Lab Practice gives you a chance to work on what you have learned. You will find a special feature in each chapter that shows you how computers are used in the workplace or how computers affect your everyday life. Every chapter also has a **Problem Solving** feature that can help you when you are having difficulty using a computer.

Throughout this book, you will find **Remember** notes in the margins of the pages. These notes will remind you of information you have already learned. You will also find study aids throughout this book. At the beginning of every chapter, there is a list of **Learning Objectives**. These objectives will help you to focus on the important points in the chapter. You will also find **Words to Know**, which is a look ahead at the vocabulary you will need to learn in each chapter. A **Summary** at the end of each chapter will help you to recall the concepts explained in the chapter. Finally, a **Chapter Quiz** will help you to prepare for—and succeed on—tests.

Everyone who put this book together worked hard to make it useful, interesting, and enjoyable. The rest is up to you. We wish you well in your studies.

Unit 1 ▶ Introduction to Computers

Chapter 1 **Understanding Computers**

Chapter 2 **Input and Output Tools**

Chapter 3 **Giving Orders to the Computer**

Chapter 4 **Managing Files**

Chapter 5 **Inside the Computer**

Music concerts use computers. What do you think the computers at a concert do?

Computers are everywhere—even on the concert stage. Your favorite song may sound about the same when it is live as it does on your CD player at home. This is because a computer is controlling the sound. The music review on this page is about a band that uses a computer onstage. Read it and answer the questions.

1. How can a computer help a band perform?

2. How do you think computers make concerts sound better?

HI-TECH CONCERT A HIT!

Last night's concert was a great show. The hi-tech band had almost as many computers as instruments. Their music sounded just like their newest CD. The sound effects and light show were timed perfectly by the computers. If you weren't there, you really missed something special.

1

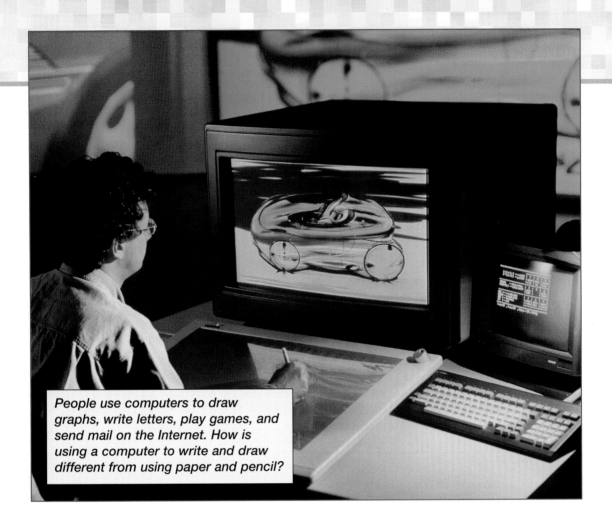

People use computers to draw graphs, write letters, play games, and send mail on the Internet. How is using a computer to write and draw different from using paper and pencil?

What You Need to Know

What *information* means

How to follow instructions

What data is

This chapter is about Understanding Computers.

What You Will Learn

Types of computers and their uses

Parts of a computer

How information moves through a computer

How to make a flowchart

Chapter 1

Understanding Computers

Words to Know

hardware	the equipment that makes up a computer
Central Processing Unit (CPU)	hardware that directs how information flows in, out, and through a computer
hard drive	a tool, built into the computer, for storing data and instructions
keyboard	the set of keys with numbers and letters used to type information into a computer
mouse	a pointing tool that you move with your hand
monitor	a screen that shows information on a computer
input	the information that is put into a computer
output	the information that comes out of a computer
software	a set of instructions that tells a computer what to do

Computer Search Project

Computers are often seen on TV. Look for computers during newscasts, sports events, TV movies, and others shows. Keep a journal for one week of how many computers you see and how they are used. Make a bar graph of the results.

Learning Objectives

- List types of computers and their uses.
- Explain the parts of a computer.
- Describe input, output, and types of software.
- Apply: Use a flowchart to organize information.
- PROBLEM SOLVING: Find the hidden pointer.
- COMPUTERS IN YOUR LIFE: Identify computers at home.

A computer is a machine that uses a set of instructions to do many kinds of jobs. A computer can do math. It can collect, store, and display information. It can help you write, draw, and play games. It also lets you communicate with people all over the world.

There are many types of computers. The type you use depends on what you want the computer to do.

Types of Computers

A *personal computer*, or *PC*, is a small computer made to be used by one person at a time. A personal computer can do a few jobs at one time. People often use personal computers at home, in school, or on the job. A personal computer can fit on a desk, small table, or countertop. Sometimes personal computers are linked together. This allows two or more people to use the same information at the same time.

Computer Fact

The term personal computer, or PC, has another meaning. It also can mean a type of computer that is not a Macintosh®. Macintosh computers were first made by Apple®. They operate differently from "PCs", which were made popular by IBM®. Today, "PCs"and "Macs" can be made by many different companies.

A *mainframe* is a very large computer compared to a personal computer. It can be as big as a refrigerator. Mainframes are used by many people at the same time. They can store huge amounts of information. They can also do many jobs at the same time. Look at the photograph on the bottom of the next page.

A *supercomputer* is a very fast mainframe computer. Supercomputers are used to do jobs at the fastest speed possible. In one second, they can do millions of math operations. They are often called "number crunchers." These large computers are very expensive. Governments, big businesses, and universities use mainframes and supercomputers. Look at the photograph on the top of the next page.

This photograph shows several supercomputers in one room.

Using Computers

Almost everything people do today involves some kind of computer. The type of computer that is used depends on who is using it and what needs to be done. Here are some ways to use different kinds of computers.

Personal Computers
- In school, students take computerized tests.
- In school, students present computerized reports.
- At home, people write letters on a computer.
- At home, children play video games.
- At home, shoppers buy things on the Internet.
- At home, friends chat on-line.
- At home and work, people send e-mail.
- On the job, managers make budgets on computers.
- On the job, assistants write computer memos.
- On the job, workers track inventory on computers.

Mainframes
- Telephone companies connect telephone calls.
- TV studios send shows to millions of homes.
- Transportation departments control traffic signals, railroads, and subways.
- Banks keep track of money on computers.
- Supermarkets keep track of goods and prices.
- Employers organize their workers' records.
- Electric companies print bills and track customer payments.

This man uses a mainframe that sits on the floor of his office.

Supercomputers

- Weather forecasters predict weather.
- Air traffic controllers locate and track airplanes.
- NASA launches rockets and guides the space shuttle.
- Researchers design new products and drugs.
- Artists make animated graphics.
- Sportscasters figure sport teams' statistics.

▶ **LESSON REVIEW**

1. How is a PC different from a mainframe? How are they alike?

2. Name at least five ways computers play a part in your life every day.

3. **CRITICAL THINKING** What type of computer would be the best choice for the home? Explain your answer.

On the Cutting Edge

THE ENIAC

One of the first electronic computers was named ENIAC—**E**lectronic **N**umerical **I**ntegrator **a**nd **C**omputer. It was built in 1945 by J. P. Eckert, Jr. and J. W. Mauchly.

ENIAC was much larger than today's computers. It was made up of 40 separate units. It weighed about as much as four adult African elephants. To give it information, users had to set thousands of switches and rewire the machine. However, ENIAC could add 5,000 numbers in 1 second. So it took ENIAC about 20 seconds to solve problems that took one person days to solve. Only one ENIAC was ever built. It worked for nine years.

ENIAC was the first modern electronic computer.

CRITICAL THINKING Why do you think ENIAC was so much larger than computers are today?

All the equipment that makes up a computer is called the computer's **hardware**. Look at the diagram below. It shows the basic pieces of computer hardware. Each piece of equipment serves one of these four functions:

1. It directs how information flows through the computer.
2. It puts in information.
3. It puts out information.
4. It stores information.

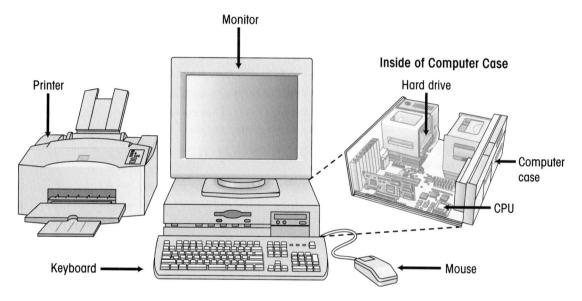

CPU

Inside the computer's case is the **CPU**, or **Central Processing Unit**. It directs how information flows in, out, and through the computer. It is also the part that does all the math and other jobs performed by the computer. The CPU is also called the *processor*.

Hard Drive

The **hard drive** is a tool for storing data and instructions. It is built into the computer's case. A hard drive is like a filing cabinet. It holds information until you need it.

Keyboard and Mouse

The **keyboard** is a set of keys with numbers and letters, used to type information into the computer. The **mouse** is a pointing tool that you move with your hand. You move the mouse on a flat surface, such as a desk or a soft pad. Both the keyboard and mouse let you tell the computer what you want it to do.

This is a computer keyboard.

Monitor

The **monitor** is a screen that shows information on a computer. When you move the mouse, you can see a pointer that moves across the screen.

Printer

A printer lets you make paper copies of the work you do on the computer. You can print all kinds of things, such as reports, letters, or pictures.

 LESSON REVIEW

1. What does the Central Processing Unit do?

2. What two tools are used to communicate with a computer?

3. What is a hard drive used for?

4. **CRITICAL THINKING** What are some things you would use a printer for?

1·2 Lab Practice

The diagram below shows the parts of a computer.
Follow the steps below.

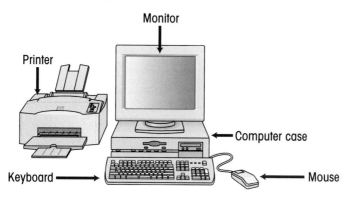

Monitor

Printer

Computer case

Keyboard

Mouse

STEP 1 On your classroom computer, locate the same parts as shown in the diagram above.

STEP 2 Check Your Work: How many different parts did you find on your classroom computer?

▶ **More Practice**

On a separate sheet of paper, name the parts labeled A, B, C, D, and E, shown below. Identify what each part does. Check your work. What are the parts labeled D and E used for? If you were to remove part A, what would probably happen?

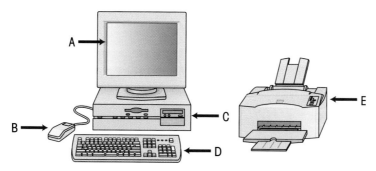

A

B

C

D

E

A computer is an information machine. You put information into a computer. Then the computer gives information back to you.

Input and Output

Input is the information that is put into a computer. Look at the diagram below. The computer receives input through the keyboard and the mouse. The CPU processes the information and sends back **output**. Output is the information that comes out of a computer. The monitor shows this output. The printer prints the output on paper.

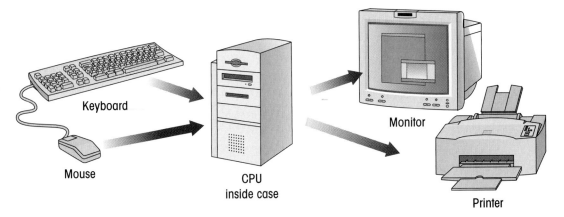

Keyboard

Mouse

CPU
inside case

Monitor

Printer

You can show input and output with a flowchart. A flowchart is a diagram that shows the steps needed to do a job. Compare the diagram above with the flowchart below.

Enter information with keyboard or mouse.

The CPU processes information.

The result is shown as output on a monitor or printer.

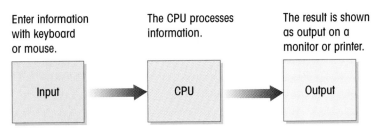

Input

CPU

Output

Computer Software

How does the hardware know what to do with input? When you put in information, a computer runs a program, or **software.** Software is a set of instructions that tells a computer what to do. When software is running, it tells the CPU how to process the information.

There are three main types of software:

1. *System software* keeps track of things, such as where the CPU stores data. It controls the way the hardware works together with other software. The two main kinds of system software are Microsoft® Windows® Operating System and Macintosh® OS.

2. *Applications software* lets you do a particular job with your input. Some jobs include writing a report, drawing a picture, and finding information. Examples of applications are Microsoft® Works® and Microsoft® Internet Explorer®.

3. *Utilities software* helps you keep a hard drive in order and a computer running smoothly. For example, it can help you find a virus. A *virus* is a program that stops your computer from working correctly. It can get into your computer accidentally. Examples of utilities software are Norton Utilities® and McAfee Antivirus™.

▶ **LESSON REVIEW**

1. How is input different from output?

2. What does system software do?

3. **CRITICAL THINKING** If you were using software to organize the names, addresses, and phone numbers of your friends, which type of software would you need?

1·3 Lab Practice

Look at your computer monitor. Study the screens below. Use the mouse to give the computer input. Follow the steps below.

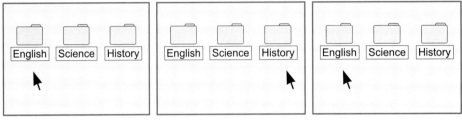

Screen 1   Screen 2   Screen 3

STEP 1 Look at Screen 1. It shows the pointer on the left side of the screen.

STEP 2 Look at Screen 2. Move the mouse slowly to the right. The pointer will move to the right.

STEP 3 Look at Screen 3. Move the mouse slowly to the left. The pointer will move to the left.

STEP 4 Check Your Work: What did you see when you moved the mouse left and right? Where is the pointer now?

You can also use the keyboard to give the computer input. First, locate the arrow keys. The arrow keys are on the right side of the keyboard.

Look at the picture below. It shows the four arrow keys. Each key points in a different direction.

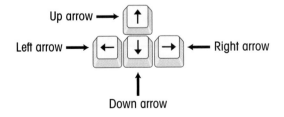

Look at the screens and follow the steps below.

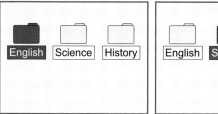
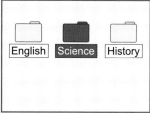
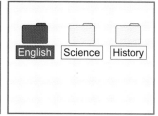

Screen 4   *Screen 5*   *Screen 6*

STEP 5 Look at Screen 4. One folder is *highlighted,* or darker than the other two.

STEP 6 Press the right arrow key once. A different folder is highlighted. Look at Screen 5.

STEP 7 Press the right arrow key once. Press the left arrow key twice.

STEP 8 Check Your Work: Which folder is highlighted now?

▶ **More Practice**

Move the mouse up and down on the mouse pad. See Steps 1 to 3.

Press the down arrow key one or more times. Press the up arrow key one or more times. See Steps 5 to 7.

COMPUTERS IN YOUR LIFE
Computers at Home

You might have more computers at home than you think. Many machines that are not personal computers have computers in them. Microwave ovens, VCRs, dishwashers, cell phones, answering machines, washing machines, and televisions can all contain computers.

The computers in these machines are not like personal computers. They are much smaller and they do only one job. For example, one might control how long a microwave heats food.

Like all computers, the computers inside machines must first receive input. They use the input to do a job. Then they give output. A microwave receives input through the keypad. The keypad is the area with numbered and lettered buttons. With the keypad, a person can enter the amount of time to heat food. The input goes into the tiny computer inside the microwave. The computer controls when the microwave turns on and turns off. The numbers that appear on the digital timer are output. The beep that sounds when the timer is done is output.

Many kitchen machines contain computers.

A television remote control contains a computer chip that controls the changing of channels.

1. How does a TV remote control receive input?

2. How does pressing the remote affect the TV's output?

3. **CRITICAL THINKING** How do you think computers have made people's lives better? Give two examples.

Sometimes your pointer may be hidden from view. You cannot see or find the pointer on the screen. Look at the screen below. See if you can find the pointer.

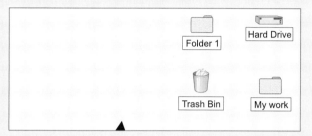

You can solve this problem by trying the following steps. If the first step does not help, try the next one. Keep doing this until you find the pointer.

- First, try moving the mouse around. This may bring the pointer into view.
- Second, check that the mouse is plugged into the computer. Sometimes the connection can get loose.
- Third, make sure the mouse is resting on a clean, flat surface.
- Fourth, if the mouse does not roll, you might try a *mouse pad*. This is a soft pad that helps the mouse roll smoothly.
- Fifth, be sure that the bottom of your mouse is clean. Sometimes dust or crumbs can cause problems.

Answer the following questions.

1. What is the input tool you use to move the pointer?

2. If you cannot find the pointer, what is the first thing you should do?

Critical Thinking

What should you do if everything checks OK and you still cannot find the pointer?

Applying: Using a Flowchart

A flowchart can be used to organize information. You can use a flowchart to show the steps of a job.

Example

John wrote a paragraph explaining how to make a ham and cheese sandwich. Make a flowchart showing each step.

Get bread, ham, cheese, and mayonnaise or mustard. Put the ham and cheese between 2 slices of bread. Spread on the mayo or mustard. Cut the sandwich in half.

STEP 1 GET READY What do you need to do first?
Make a list of steps and number them.

STEP 2 THINK What do you know about the information?
Decide how to order the steps. Decide which is the first step. Decide which is the last step.

STEP 3 APPLY Organize the information.
Draw a box for each step. Draw arrows between the boxes. This is how the flowchart might look.

Remember
A flowchart is a diagram that shows the order of events.

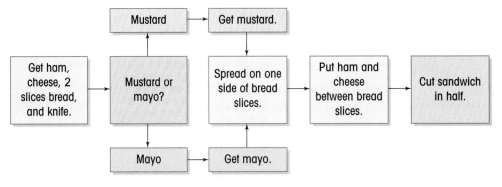

STEP 4 Check Does the information look correct?
Check the order in the flowchart.

1·4 Lab Practice

GET READY to organize each set of steps. Answer the questions under THINK. APPLY what you know to make each flowchart. CHECK your finished work.

1. Ray went to see a movie. The steps he followed once he got there are mixed up below. Organize them in a flowchart.

   watch movie   *sit down in theater*

   pay for ticket   *take money out of pocket*

   walk inside theater   *get ticket from clerk*

   THINK

   What is the first step?

   What is the last step?

2. Zakia wants to buy a computer. Brainstorm six steps she needs to take. Organize the steps in a flowchart.

   THINK

   What are some decisions she needs to make?

   What is the first step?

   What is the last step?

Making Connections

Write a paragraph explaining how to round a number to the nearest ten. Then make a flowchart showing the steps to follow. See if your classmates can follow your flowchart.

Summary

Understanding Computers
Almost everything in our lives depends in some way on computers.

- **Parts of a computer do different things.** The CPU processes information. The keyboard and mouse give input. The monitor and printer give output. The hard drive stores information.

- **There are different types of software.** Systems software controls the hardware, applications software does a particular job, and utilities software keeps computers in working order.

- **Information can be organized using a flowchart.** You can show the steps needed to do a job.

hardware

input

keyboard

monitor

output

personal computer

software

Vocabulary Review

Complete each sentence with a term from the list.

1. A set of instructions that tells a computer what to do is _____.

2. The equipment that makes up a computer is the _____.

3. A set of keys used to send information to a computer is the _____.

4. The _____ is the screen that shows output.

5. A computer made for use by one person at a time is a _____.

6. Information that is put into a computer is called _____.

7. Information that comes out of a computer is called _____.

Chapter Quiz

Answer the following questions.

LESSON 1·1

What is a Computer?

1. What are three types of computers?
2. What are three uses of mainframe computers?

LESSON 1·2

Parts of a Computer

3. What are the four functions of computer hardware?
4. Which parts of computer hardware do you move?
5. Which part of the computer does the math?

LESSONS 1·3 and 1·4

Computer Tip
Use a flowchart to show the order of events or the steps needed to do something.

Information and the Computer

6. What are input and output?
7. What are the main steps as information goes through a computer.
8. What are the three main types of software?
9. Why do computers need software?
10. How can a flowchart show the way information moves through a computer and its parts?

Group Activity

With your group, visit the computer lab. Look at the computer hardware. You already know about the CPU, keyboard, mouse, monitor, hard drive, and printer. What other kinds of hardware can you find? Decide what function each serves. Make a chart like the one on page 10 of your book. In the chart, list the hardware you find according to its function.

This graphic artist is adding a title to an illustration. How many different tools do you see that can be used to give input to the computer? Can you find any output tools?

What You Need to Know

Types of computers and their uses

Parts of a computer

What input and output are

What computer software is

This chapter is about Input and Output Tools.

What You Will Learn

How to use a mouse

How to use a keyboard

How to use a printer

About input tools

How to organize information

Words to Know

icon	a picture that stands for something else, such as a disk or a program
window	an area on the screen where information and icons appear
cursor	a blinking vertical line that shows the place on the computer screen where text is being entered
desktop	an area on the screen where icons and windows are shown on a background
character	a letter, number, word, punctuation mark, or symbol on a keyboard
trackball	an input tool that moves the cursor when rolled
joystick	an input tool with a lever and some buttons
stylus	an input tool, like a pen with no ink, used to draw on a special pad
scanner	an input tool used to input a picture of something

Input and Output Search Project

Many different tools are used to input information into a computer. Look for pictures in newspaper articles, magazine stories, and advertisements that show people using computers. Find different types of output tools. Use the pictures to make a poster about input and output.

Learning Objectives

- Explain how a mouse works.
- Use keyboard keys.
- Identify different input tools.
- Describe parts of a printer.
- Apply mouse skills to organizing a desktop.
- PROBLEM SOLVING: Solve a problem with resizing a window.
- COMPUTERS ON THE JOB: Post a message on a message board.

The Mouse: An Input Tool

Your computer is made up of many different parts. Most parts are found inside the computer. However, some parts are attached to the outside of the computer. One of these parts is the mouse.

How a Mouse Works

The mouse is a pointing tool that you hold and move by hand. Look at the diagram and the photo at the bottom of this page. On the underside of the mouse is a small ball. As you move the mouse on a flat surface, such as a desk, table, or soft pad, the ball rolls. This movement sends information through the mouse cable to your computer. The information makes a mouse pointer move across your computer screen. You move the mouse in order to place the pointer where you want it on the screen.

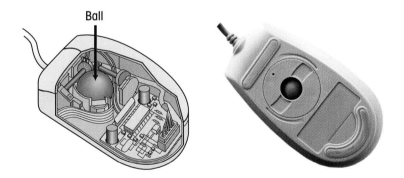

Ball

The diagram on the left shows the inside of a mouse. You can see the ball that moves as you move the mouse. The photo on the right shows the underside of a mouse.

The mouse also has one or more buttons. You can press, or click, a mouse button to choose an object on the screen. Since the mouse sends information to the computer, it is an input tool.

Remember
Input is information that is put into a computer.

A pointer on the screen can look different depending on the software you are using. This drawing shows you some pointers you may see when using different types of software. Pointers are also referred to as *cursors*.

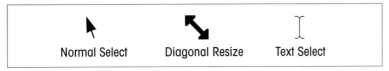

| Normal Select | Diagonal Resize | Text Select |

A pointer can look like a capital I,
a single arrow, or a double-headed arrow.

Clicking the Mouse

You click the mouse to choose an **icon**. An icon is a picture that stands for something else, such as a disk or a program. To choose an icon, place the pointer over the icon, and then click the mouse once.

Clicking a mouse can also open a **window**. A window is an area on the screen where information and icons appear. To open a window, you place the pointer over an icon and double-click the mouse. A double-click is two quick clicks in a row. The screen below shows an open window with two icons. At the top of the window is a bar with the window's name.

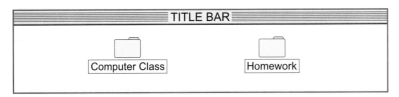

TITLE BAR

Computer Class   Homework

This window contains two icons.

You also click the mouse to put the **cursor**, or blinking vertical line, in place. A cursor shows the place on a computer screen where text is being entered. It is usually blinking on the screen. To set the cursor, you need to click the mouse. To do this, you press the mouse button and then release it. Clicking a mouse is one of the most important computer skills.

Using the Mouse to Move Things

The **desktop** is an area on the screen where icons and windows are shown on a background. You can use your mouse to move icons or windows around on the desktop. To move an icon or window, first place the pointer over the icon or the window's title bar. Then hold down the mouse button. As you continue to hold down the mouse button, *drag* the item to the place you want by moving the mouse. The moving mouse moves the selected item. When the item is where you want it, you can *drop* it by letting go of the mouse button.

Comparing "Mice"

The computer mouse you use depends on the type of computer system software you use. The two main types of systems are Macintosh® OS and Microsoft® Windows® Operating System. This chart shows you the difference.

For Macintosh® OS	For Microsoft® Windows® Operating System
The mouse has one button. Click the button using any finger you like.	The mouse has two (or more) buttons. The left button is the one needed most often. Click this button with your index finger. When you need to click the right button, instructions will tell you to right-click. Click this button with your middle finger.

▶ **LESSON REVIEW**

1. What tasks can you do with a mouse?

2. What do the terms *drag* and *drop* mean?

3. **CRITICAL THINKING** How are the two types of "mice" different? How are they similar?

2·1 Lab Practice

The diagram below shows what you should see on your monitor. You can use the mouse to drag and drop each icon. Follow the steps below to put the icons in alphabetical order.

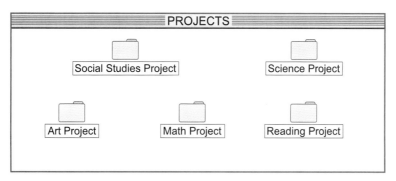

STEP 1   Use the mouse to place the pointer on the *Art Project* icon. Click and hold the mouse button.

STEP 2   Drag the *Art Project* icon to the top left corner. Let go of the mouse button to drop the icon in place.

STEP 3   Use the mouse to drag the *Math Project* icon. Put this icon after the *Art Project* icon.

STEP 4   Drag and drop the other three icons to put them in alphabetical order.

STEP 5   Check Your Work: How many icon names can you read? Where is the *Reading Project* icon?

 More Practice

Use the mouse to drag and drop each icon to create another list. Create a list that follows the order in which you have these classes. If you have Math class first, place the *Math Project* icon first.

The Keyboard: An Input Tool

A keyboard is made up of a set of keys for typing. Each key has a letter, number, word, punctuation mark, or symbol on it. When you press on the keys, you give the computer input. For example, some keys input letters.

Character Keys

The main part of a keyboard is made up of character keys. A character can be a letter, number, punctuation mark, or symbol. The character keys are used for typing words and numbers.

Number key   Symbol key   Backspace key

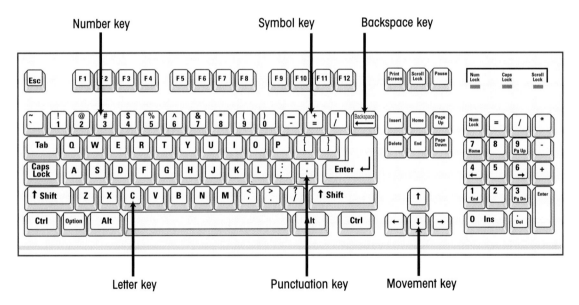

Letter key   Punctuation key   Movement key

The keys on a keyboard can look different depending on the computer. Some keyboards have more keys than others do. The keyboard shown above is based mainly on an IBM® PC. You can use it with the Microsoft® Windows® Operating System. Look on Reference page 327 to see a PC keyboard for Windows® and a Macintosh® keyboard.

Movement Keys

The movement keys are on the lower right of the keyboard. The arrow keys move the cursor up, down, left, and right.

The Home key moves the cursor to the top of the page. The End key moves the cursor to the bottom of the page. The Page Up (PgUp) key moves back one page. The Page Down (PgDn) key moves ahead one page. These keys are shown below.

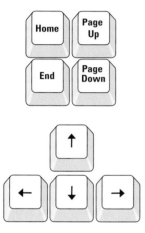

Numeric Keys

These keys are used to input numbers and do math. They can be used with the calculator that is built into the computer. The numeric keys are shown below.

Special Keys

In addition to character and movement keys, there are also special keys. The chart shows you some special keys and their uses in both Macintosh® and Microsoft® Windows®.

Some of the keys in the chart are used alone. Some are used together with other keys. This means that you hold down one special key, and press another key. For example, to type a question mark, you press and hold the Shift key while pressing .

For Macintosh® OS	For Microsoft® Windows® Operating System
Keys Used Alone Delete key — It removes characters after the cursor. Return key — It gives instructions to the processor. In word processing software, it tells the processor to start a new paragraph. **Keys Used Together** Shift key and a letter key — It types a capital letter. If the key contains two characters (instead of a letter), the top character will be typed.	**Keys Used Alone** Delete key — It removes characters in front of cursor. Backspace key — It removes characters behind cursor. Enter key — It gives instructions to the processor. In word processing software, it tells the processor to start a new paragraph. **Keys Used Together** Shift key and a letter key — It types a capital letter. If the key contains two characters (instead of a letter), the top character will be typed.

▶ **LESSON REVIEW**

1. What different types of character keys are there?

2. What are the different movement keys?

3. **CRITICAL THINKING** How can you type a capital *M*?

2·2 Lab Practice

Type the name **taylor jones**. Use all lowercase letters. To edit the name, follow the steps. The screens below show what you will see on your monitor.

Screen 1

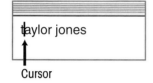

Cursor

Screen 2

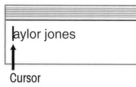

Cursor

Screen 3

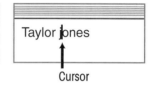

Cursor

STEP 1   Look at Screen 1. Point and click to place the cursor to the right of the letter **t**.

STEP 2   Press the Delete or Backspace key. This will delete the lowercase **t**. Look at Screen 2.

STEP 3   Press and hold the Shift key. Press the letter **t** one time to type an uppercase letter **T**. Release the Shift key.

STEP 4   Press the right arrow key seven times. The cursor will appear as in Screen 3.

STEP 5   Press the Delete key. This will delete the lowercase **j**. Press and hold the Shift key. Press the letter **j** one time to type an uppercase letter **J**. Release the Shift key.

STEP 6   Press the right arrow key four times, then press the Return or Enter key. This will create a new line.

STEP 7   Check Your Work: What is the first letter of the first name? What is the first letter of the last name? What does your screen say now?

 More Practice

Type your name. Use all lowercase letters. Correct your name using uppercase letters where needed.

PROBLEM SOLVING
Resizing Windows Using a Mouse

A window on your desktop is too small to show all the icons. You can solve this problem by using the mouse to change the size of the window. This is also known as resizing the window.

If you use a Macintosh®, use the mouse to place the pointer over the size box. Look at Screen 1. Click the mouse button and hold it down. Then drag the size box down and to the right until you can clearly see all the icons in the window. Let go of the mouse button.

If you use Microsoft® Windows®, use the mouse to place the pointer over any corner of the window. Look at Screen 2. The pointer will look like this ↘. Click the mouse button and hold it down. Then drag the corner down until you can clearly see all the icons in the window. See the resize arrow in Screen 2. Let go of the mouse button.

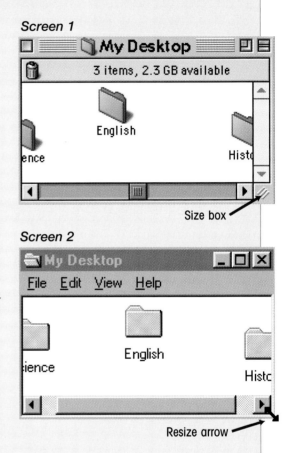

Screen 1

Size box

Screen 2

Resize arrow

Look at the screens above.

1. How is resizing a window with a Macintosh similar to resizing it with Microsoft® Windows®?

2. How is resizing a window with a Macintosh different from resizing it with Microsoft® Windows®?

3. **CRITICAL THINKING** What might you do to make the window smaller again?

Other Input Tools

You learned that the keyboard and mouse are input tools. They put information into a computer. Some computers can have other input tools. They are:

- a trackball
- a joystick
- a stylus and drawing pad
- a microphone
- a camera and video recorder
- a scanner

Trackball

One input tool is called a trackball. A **trackball** is a tool that moves the cursor when rolled. Some types of computers have a trackball instead of a mouse. You use the palm of your hand or your fingertips to roll the trackball. The cursor moves in the same direction you move the trackball.

Joystick

Another input tool is a joystick. A **joystick** is a tool with a lever and some buttons. Joysticks are most often used to control computer games.

Stylus and Drawing Pad

Another input tool is a stylus and its drawing pad. The **stylus** is like a pen with no ink. You use the stylus to draw on a special pad that is connected to the computer. The picture that you draw on the pad appears on the screen. This type of input tool is most often used with art software programs.

Microphone, Camera, or Video Recorder

Microphones and cameras are also input tools. Microphones input sounds. Cameras and video recorders input pictures. Some video recorders also input sounds.

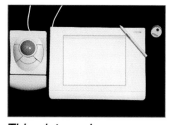

This picture shows some examples of different types of input tools.

You can use a scanner to copy a picture into your computer.

Scanner

A **scanner** is used to input a picture of something, such as a photo or newspaper article. A scanner works like a copy machine, but instead of printing a copy, it sends the copy to a computer screen or a file.

▶ **LESSON REVIEW**

1. Which input tool can you use in place of a mouse?

2. Which input tool can be used to input a photo?

3. **CRITICAL THINKING** What input tools would you use to present a scientific report? Why?

On the Cutting Edge

THE FIRST MOUSE

The mouse you use today is different from the first mouse ever made. Before there was such a thing as a mouse, input was given by touching a *light pen* to the computer screen. Computer scientists experimented to find an input tool that was easier to use than a light pen.

The first mouse was developed in 1965 by scientists at Stanford Research Institute. This mouse had two wheels on the bottom. As the mouse was pushed or pulled along a surface, it moved a pointer on the screen. Here is a photograph of the first mouse. It is turned upside-down to show its wheels.

The first type of mouse had wheels.

CRITICAL THINKING How was the first mouse similar to the mouse you can use today? How was it different?

The Printer: An Output Tool

A printer is an output tool. A printer is connected to a computer with a cord called a *printer cable*. Sometimes many computers are linked to the same printer. Output travels from a computer through the printer cable to the printer. The printer makes the output as printed pages.

Most printers have at least two buttons. One button is the on/off switch. The other is the *manual feed* button. When you press the manual feed button, you can add a sheet of stationery, other special paper, or an envelope into the printer by hand. Printed pages go into an output tray to keep them organized.

Remember
Output is the information that comes out of a computer. Computer monitors show output. Printers also make output as printed pages.

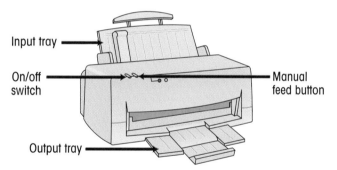

Input tray

On/off switch

Manual feed button

Output tray

This diagram shows the parts of a printer.

Printer paper is placed into an input tray. Some types of printers have a paper input tray that slides inside the bottom of the printer. The paper should be carefully placed in the input tray so that it lies flat.

Other types of printers have an input tray on top. The paper is placed upright in the tray. Paper should always be pushed gently into either type of input tray until it cannot go in any farther. Carefully examine any printer you plan to use to identify where the paper goes. The picture on the following page shows an example of each type of printer.

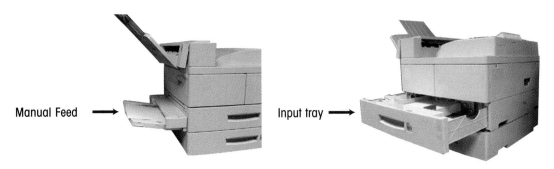

Manual Feed ➝   Input tray ➝

The photo on the left shows a manual feed tray. The photo on the right shows a paper input tray that slides inside the bottom.

If you try to print something when the printer is out of paper, a message will appear on your computer screen. It will say: *Printer is out of paper*. Some printers have a light that blinks when they are out of paper. To check the paper supply, look in the input tray. If there is no paper, add some. If there is some paper in there, try straightening out the sheets and putting them back in the tray. Be sure that the paper is pushed all the way in and that the tray is in correctly.

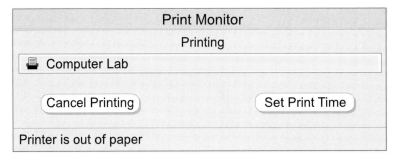

LESSON REVIEW

1. Where do you place the paper in a printer?

2. How will you know when your printer is out of paper?

3. **CRITICAL THINKING** How does a printer help get output to you?

COMPUTERS ON THE JOB
Message Board Operator

Natalie Hayes is a message board operator. On a message board, people can use a computer to read and post messages about certain topics. To *post* means to send a message to a message board.

Natalie reads everything sent to her message board. She makes sure that all the messages follow the rules. Natalie has to return messages that do not follow the rules.

Natalie works for the Dog World message board.

Look at Natalie's message board. It lists topics about Boxer dogs.

To post a message, you type onto a screen like the one shown above.

1. What are the two topics discussed on the board from June 2 through June 3?

2. Into which box would you type your message?

Critical Thinking

Natalie receives the following message: What is the best diet for my German Shepherd? What should Natalie do with this message?

Applying: Organizing Icons

You can use your mouse to organize icons on a desktop.
An organized desktop makes it easy to find files.

Example

Emma's icons are not organized on her desktop. Also, she
cannot see them all. The window is too small. Organize
the icons on the desktop.

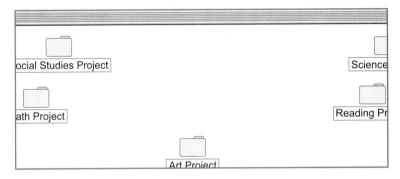

STEP 1 GET READY What do you need to do first?
Find the mouse and cursor.

STEP 2 THINK What do you know about the information?
Think about how you would organize the icons
within the window. Would you place them in
groups or organize them alphabetically? Also,
think about how to make the window larger so
you can easily see all the icons.

STEP 3 APPLY Organize the information.
Use the mouse to click on and drag a corner of
the window until it is large enough to see all
the icons. Then use the mouse to drag and drop
icons where you want them. Do this until the
icons are organized.

STEP 4 CHECK Does the information look correct?
The icons should be well organized within the larger
window. You should be able to find icons easily.

2·5 Lab Practice

GET READY to organize the icons in the window. Answer the questions under THINK. APPLY what you know to organize the icons and resize the window. CHECK your finished work.

1. Kentaro needs to organize the icons in a window like the one below. Organize the files in a logical order.

   THINK
   What is the best way to organize the icons?

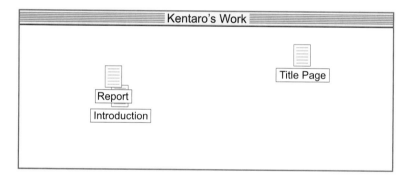

2. Now Kentaro wants to make the window smaller and still fit the organized icons. Resize the window so it is smaller.

   THINK
   What size window will fit <u>all</u> of the icons?

Making Connections

Think about other things to organize, such as school and homework supplies. Draw a sketch of what your schoolwork window might look like. Make up at least two icons for each of your classes. Organize them in a way that makes sense. Explain why you have put them in this arrangement.

Summary

Input and Output Tools
Different computer tools can be used to give input and output.

- **The mouse** is an input tool. You can use the mouse to select text or icons, move icons, and resize windows.
- **The keyboard** is an input tool for entering information. A keyboard has number keys, character keys, and special keys.
- **A window** is an area on a computer screen where output can be seen.
- **The printer** prints documents made with software.
- **Other input tools** include: trackball, joystick, stylus, microphone, camera, and scanner.
- **To organize icons,** use a mouse to move them where you want them.

character

cursor

desktop

icon

stylus

window

Complete each sentence with a term from the list.

1. A picture that stands for something, such as a disk or program, is an _____.
2. A letter, number, punctuation mark, or other symbol is called a _____.
3. The area on the screen in which information and icons appear is the _____.
4. The area on the screen where you work with software is the _____.
5. A blinking vertical line that shows where text is being entered is the _____.
6. An input tool, like a pen with no ink that is called a _____, is used to draw on a special pad.

Chapter Quiz

Answer the following questions.

LESSON 2·1

Test Tip
Picture your keyboard and mouse. Think about how you use them.

The Mouse: An Input Tool

1. How do you select an icon using a mouse?
2. How do you open a window using a mouse?
3. How can you move things on your desktop?

LESSON 2·2

The Keyboard: An Input Tool

4. How do you type a capital letter?
5. Which keys can you use to move the cursor?
6. What are some special keys that are used alone to do a task?

LESSON 2·3

Other Input Tools

7. What are five other input tools?

LESSON 2·4

The Printer: An Output Tool

8. What does the manual feed button do?
9. What is an input tray used for?

Applying: Organizing Icons

LESSON 2·5

10. How can you use an input tool to organize icons?

Group Activity

With your group, draw a computer. Be sure to include the different input and output tools you learned about in this chapter. Label each part with its name. Then identify and label each part as either an input tool or an output tool. Display your drawing. Compare your drawing with other drawings made by your classmates. How are they similar? How are they different?

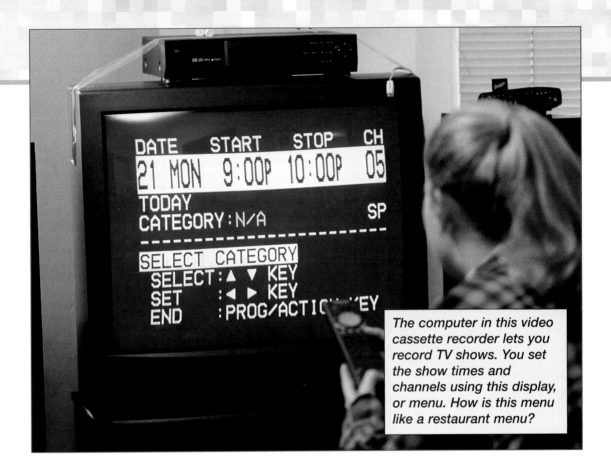

The computer in this video cassette recorder lets you record TV shows. You set the show times and channels using this display, or menu. How is this menu like a restaurant menu?

What You Need to Know

How information moves through a computer

How to make a flowchart

How to use a mouse

How to use a keyboard

How to use a printer

This chapter is about Giving Orders to the Computer.

What You Will Learn

Computer commands and menus

How to use the Open command

How to use the Save command

How to use the Print command

How to use toolbars

How to copy and save files

Chapter 3

Giving Orders to the Computer

Words to Know

command	an order you give to a computer to do a job
menu	a list of commands for doing different jobs on the computer
file	a set of information or instructions that is named
dialog box	a window that asks for more information, then finishes the command
folder	a place where you can save and organize files
scroll bar	a bar along the edge of a window that moves what is in the window up and down, or left and right
title bar	a bar across the top of a window that shows the file's name
toolbar	a row of buttons you click to give commands to a computer

Flowchart Project

In this chapter, you will learn ways to give commands to a computer. Choose one of the commands. Think about the steps you follow to give the command. Draw a flowchart that shows the steps.

Learning Objectives

- Explain commands, menus, and toolbars.
- Use dialog boxes and scroll bars.
- Use the Open, Close, Save, Save As…, and Print commands.
- Apply the use of commands to saving a copy.
- PROBLEM SOLVING: Solve problems with "gray" commands.
- COMPUTERS IN YOUR LIFE: Describe how an ATM works.

3·1 What are Commands and Menus?

You can use the parts of a computer to give orders to the computer. An order you give to a computer to do a job is called a **command**.

Menu in Microsoft® Windows®

A **menu** is a list of commands for doing different jobs on the computer. The diagram on the left shows a menu called the File menu. Read the words listed there. These are commands that can do a job with a **file**. A file is a set of information or instructions that is named.

Notice the top row of words to the right of the word *File* in the diagram. These are the names of other menus, such as the Edit menu, View menu, and Help menu.

Using a Mouse

You can use your mouse to open a menu. Click on the menu name you want. This opens the menu. To choose a command, place the pointer over the command. It will be highlighted. Click the mouse once to give that command.

Using a Keyboard

You can also use your keyboard to choose a command. In Microsoft® Windows®, the Alt key helps open menus. Look at the File menu again. The letter *F* in File is underlined. You can use an underlined letter and the Alt key together to open a menu. For example, the Alt key and the *F* key can open the File menu. In the File menu, the letter *O* in Open is underlined. When the menu is open, press the *O* key to give the Open command.

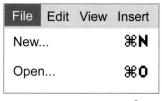

Menu on a Macintosh®

In a Macintosh®, notice the symbols and letters in the File menu. You can see them to the right of the commands. Two examples are shown at the left. The symbol ⌘ stands for the Command key on the Macintosh keyboard. If you press the Command and letter keys together, you will give the command.

▶ LESSON REVIEW

1. What do you see when you open a menu?

2. How can you make the File menu appear?

3. **CRITICAL THINKING** How might using the keyboard give faster commands than using the mouse?

On the Cutting Edge

GIVING COMMANDS USING SPECIAL TOOLS

Today people can give computers commands even if they cannot click a mouse or type on a keyboard. One way is by giving voice commands. Words are spoken into a microphone. Software takes the words and turns them into commands.

This boy moves an input tool with his mouth.

People who cannot use their hands may give commands using special tools attached to a joystick or trackball. Commands can even be given by puffing air through a tube. Each pattern of breath stands for a different command.

Braille keyboards have raised dots that stand for letters and numbers. People with problems seeing can feel the symbols. A computer voice tells them what is on the screen.

CRITICAL THINKING Why is it important to develop different ways for people to use computers?

The Open command opens files and software. To open a file, double-click on the icon or name. Opening a file also opens the software application that was used to make the file.

In applications, some commands are followed by three dots. This means that more information is needed in order to finish the command. Look at the example on the left. For example, to use the Open command you need to tell the computer which file to open.

| File | Edit | View | Insert |
| New... |
| Open... |

Three dots

What are Dialog Boxes?

When you click on a command with three dots, a **dialog box** appears. A dialog box is a window that asks for more information, and then finishes the command.

Look at the Open dialog box below. It appears when you choose Open from the File menu. This dialog box shows a list of **folders** in the window. A computer folder is a place where you can save and organize your files. In the screen on below, the *History* folder is selected, or highlighted. If you click the Open button, it opens that folder.

Click here for pop-up menu.

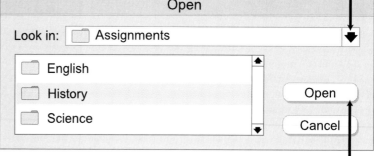

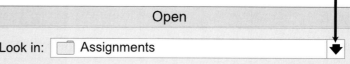

Open

Look in: Assignments

English
History
Science

Open
Cancel

Click here to open folder.

The dialog box below shows the files inside the *History* folder. The file, *George Washington* is selected. If you clicked Open, the file on George Washington would open. To close the dialog box without opening a file, click the Cancel button.

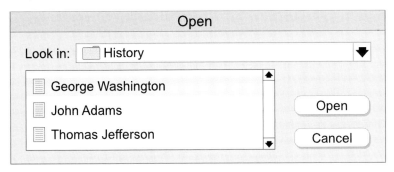

You can find and go back to other folders. To do this, click on the pop-up menu button. The screen at right shows a pop-up menu. The *History* folder is inside the *Assignments* folder. The *Assignments* folder is on the Desktop. Click on the *Assignments* folder to go back to it.

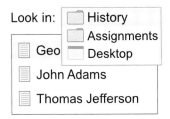

Scroll Bars in Dialog Boxes

Sometimes you cannot see all the files or folders in the Open dialog box. When this happens, you can use a **scroll bar**. A scroll bar is a bar along the edge of a window that moves whatever is in a window up and down, or left and right. Look at the scroll bars in the dialog box above.

Use your mouse to move the scroll bar. Click on one of the arrows or use the slider. To use the slider, click on it and hold the mouse button as you move it.

▶ **LESSON REVIEW**

1. What input do you have to give in the Open dialog box?

2. **CRITICAL THINKING** What might be in the dialog box if you selected the *Science* folder and clicked Open?

3·2 Lab Practice

Follow the steps below to open folders and files.

STEP 1 Find and select the *Assignments* folder. Use the scroll bar if needed. Click once to select it.

STEP 2 Open the File menu and click on the Open command. The *Assignments* folder will open.

STEP 3 Find and select the *Science* folder. Double-click on the folder icon. The *Science* folder will open.

STEP 4 Open the *Plants* file. You can double-click on the icon, or use the Open command in the File menu.

STEP 5 To close the *Plants* file, open the File menu and click on the Close command.

STEP 6 Your application software should still be open. Choose the Open command. An Open dialog box like the one below will appear. Select the *Animals* file. Click on the Open button.

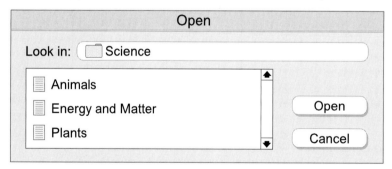

STEP 7 Check Your Work: How many files did you open? How many times did you use the Open button in the Open dialog box?

 **More Practice**

Look in the *Assignments* folder for the *English* folder. Open the *English* folder. Open and close the *Essay* file. Check your work.

Sometimes a menu item is tinted gray. A gray command means it is not active. It will not work when you try to select it. To solve this problem, you must find the reason a command is not active.

Look at the File menu shown below. Notice that the Open and Print commands are not bold like the other command. Look carefully at the icons on the desktop. Notice that none of the icons is selected. If an icon on your desktop is not selected, the Open command cannot be used.

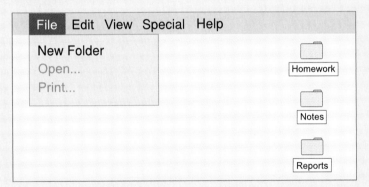

Gray commands can become active. Just find the reason it is gray and do something about it.

Look at the menu above. Use it to answer the questions.

1. Which command is gray?

2. What must you do to be able to use the Print command?

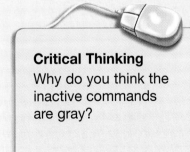

Critical Thinking
Why do you think the inactive commands are gray?

3·3 Using the Save Command

You can make a new file if you are in an application. Click on the File menu and choose the New command. A new file will be created. After working in the file, you should save it. When you save a file, you are giving the computer a command to store the file. You need to save any changes you make to an older file. If you do not, all the changes will be lost.

The Save Command

Remember
You learned how to use a dialog box to choose and open folders in Lesson 3.2.

To save a new file or to save changes to an old file, you need to use choose the Save command. This is found in the File menu. Click on the Save command to save the file. Look at the diagram below.

File
New...
Open...
Close
Save
Save As...

When you have a file open, and you want to close it, you should always save it. This way you will have it later. If you do not save it, it will be lost. If you forget to save before closing, a reminder will come up to ask you if you want to save. The reminder may look like this:

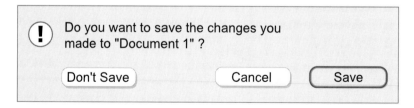

> ① Do you want to save the changes you
> made to "Document 1" ?
>
> Don't Save   Cancel   Save

If you click on the Save button, it is like choosing the Save command.

Saving and Naming a New File

Once you select the Save command, the Save dialog box appears. Look at the diagram below. It shows you an example of a Save dialog box. It has a place that shows where the file will be saved. In the example below, the file will be saved in the folder called *My Work*. To choose a different folder, you can point and click on it with the mouse.

The dialog box also has a place for you to enter the file's name. You can enter a name that you choose. You can choose any name. However, the best name tells you what the file is. A party invitation might have the name *My Invitation* or *Pam's Party*. After you enter the file name, click on the Save button.

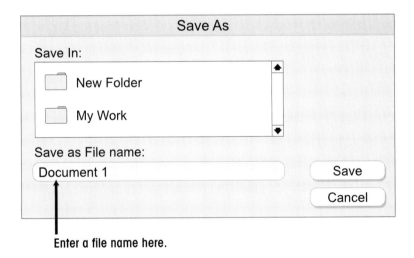

Enter a file name here.

If you do not enter a file name, the computer will give it a name. This is called a *default name*. A default name might be *Untitled 1, Document 1,* or *Workbook 1.* Do not use default names when you save files. They can be confusing when you try to find a file later.

Every file on your computer needs to have a name. Look at the diagram of an open file below. Notice that the file's name, *Sue's Birthday*, appears at the top of the window. The bar across the top of a window that shows the file's name is called the **title bar**. Also notice that this file's name is only two words. Try to keep file names short.

```
══════════════════ Sue's Birthday ══════════════════

     IT'S A PARTY!
     FOR        Sue
     WHEN       October 15th
```

Saving Changes to an Existing File

Sometimes you need to save changes that you made to an existing open file. Since the file already has a name, you do not need to give it a new one. Select the Save command. This saves all the changes you have made up to this point.

Making a Copy of a File

Suppose you want to make a copy of a file named *Book Report*. Select the Save As command from the File Menu. When the Save dialog box opens, enter a new name, then click on Save. This allows you to make a copy of the file under a new name, such as *Book Report 2*. You can make your changes in the new file and still keep a copy of the original.

▶ **LESSON REVIEW**

1. Which menu command do you use to save a file?

2. What can happen if you forget to name a file?

3. **CRITICAL THINKING** Why is it important to save a file?

3-3 Lab Practice

To make and save a new file, follow the steps below.

STEP 1 Use the mouse to open the File menu. Choose New. A new file will appear.

STEP 2 Open the File menu. Choose Save or Save As. The Save dialog box will appear.

STEP 3 A window in the dialog box will show a list of folder names. Scroll or click on the pop-up menu to find the *Assignments* folder.

STEP 4 Click on the Assignments folder, then click on the Open button.

STEP 5 Point and click in the naming box. Type **Class Notes** as the name of the new file.

STEP 6 Click on the Save button. The file name will appear in the title bar of the window.

STEP 7 Close the file by choosing Close from the File menu.

STEP 8 Check Your Work: What menu did you use to get the Save command? What name appeared in the title bar of the file you saved?

▶ **More Practice**

1. Make another new File. Name it *Journal Ideas*. Save it in the *English* folder. Check your work.

2. Use the file named *Journal Ideas*. Use the Save As command to make a copy of the file. Give the copy a new name, such as *Journal Ideas 2*.

3·4 Using the Print Command

When you **print** a file, you are giving the computer a command to put your file on paper.

To print a file, you need to choose the Print command. This is found in the File menu. Look at the diagram on the left. Click on the Print command to print the file.

Once you choose the Print command, the Print dialog box will appear. Look at the Print dialog box below. You can choose to print all the pages. Select the All button. You can also print some pages. This is called printing a range of pages. For example, you can just print pages 3 to 4.

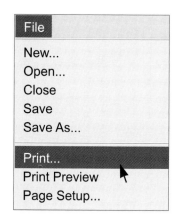

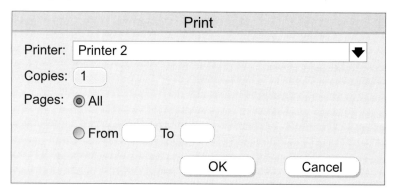

Look for the OK or Print button near the bottom of the dialog box. When you click it, you give the computer the command to print.

▶ **LESSON REVIEW**

1. In what menu do you find the Print command?

2. After the Print dialog box appears, what do you click to make the computer print your file?

3. **CRITICAL THINKING** Why is it a good idea to save your file before you print it?

3-4 Lab Practice

To print pages from the *Poems* file, follow the steps below.

STEP 1 Open the *Assignments* folder. Open the *English* folder. Open the *Poems* file.

STEP 2 Use the mouse to click on the File menu. Choose the Print command. A Print dialog box will appear.

STEP 3 Use the mouse to click in the circle next to the word *From*. Type the number **2** in the first box after the word *From*.

STEP 4 Click in the circle after the word *To*. Type the number **2** in the box after the word *To*.

STEP 5 Click on Print or OK.

STEP 6 Repeat Step 2. Then use the mouse to click on the All button. Click on Print or OK.

STEP 7 Check Your Work: What number did you type in the **To** box in the Print dialog Box?
How many pages did you print?
Do they match the file on the screen?
When you printed all the pages in the file, what did you click after the word pages?
Close the file.

▶ **More Practice**

1. Print page 2 of the *Essay* file. Check your work.
2. Print all the pages in the *Essay* file. Check your work.

You learned how to give different commands using menus. Commands can also be given to a computer without using menus or even the keyboard.

What is a Toolbar?

Another way you can give commands to a computer is to use a **toolbar**. A toolbar is a row of buttons you click to give commands.

Look at the diagram below. You can see a toolbar at the top of the screen under the names of menus. Most buttons on a toolbar have an icon. The icon shows what the button does. It takes only one mouse click to give a command using a toolbar button.

There can be several toolbars on a screen. Some toolbars have words and numbers on them. Other toolbars have special uses, such as drawing. Here are more examples of toolbars.

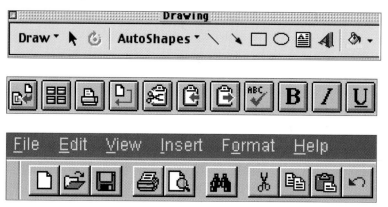

Icons for Toolbars

On each button is an icon that tells you what the button does. Different programs use different icons for the same commands. Look at the icons and the commands they each do.

Remember
An icon is a picture that stands for something, such as a disk or program. See Lesson 2.1.

Icon	What it Does
	It opens a file in Microsoft® Office.
	It opens a file in ClarisWorks®.
	It saves a file in Microsoft® Office.
	It saves a file in ClarisWorks®.
	It prints a file in Microsoft® Office.
	It prints a file in ClarisWorks®.

You can find out the command for which an icon stands. Move the mouse pointer over the icon but do not click. This makes a small label appear. The label tells you the command's name.

▶ LESSON REVIEW

1. How does a toolbar work?

2. How can you find out what a toolbar icon stands for?

3. **CRITICAL THINKING** Why might someone choose to use a menu rather than a toolbar icon?

3·5 Lab Practice

You can use the toolbar buttons to open, save, and print a file. To do this, follow the steps below.

STEP 1 Use the mouse to click on the Open toolbar button. The Open dialog box will appear.

STEP 2 Choose the *Class Notes* file from the *Assignments* folder.

STEP 3 Enter your name and today's date in the file. Click on the Save toolbar button.

STEP 4 Click on the Print toolbar button. Print the file.

STEP 5 Close the file.

STEP 6 Check Your Work: When you clicked on the Save button on the toolbar, what happened? When you clicked on the Print button on the toolbar what appeared on the screen?

▶ More Practice

1. Open the *Journal Ideas* file and enter your name. Then save and print the file. Use the toolbar buttons. Check your work.

2. Open the *Journal Ideas* file and enter the date and time. Then, save and print the file. Use the toolbar buttons. Check your work.

COMPUTERS IN YOUR LIFE
Automated Teller Machines

Today, most banks have automated teller machines, or ATMs. An ATM is a computer. It is connected to the computer of a bank. The ATM holds information about bank customers' accounts. This allows people to do their banking even when the bank is closed.

To use an ATM, a person puts a special plastic card into the machine. Then the computer connects the user with the bank's supercomputer. Next, a main menu appears on the ATM's screen. This menu lets customers choose commands that tell the ATM what to do. Usually the commands include "Get Cash", "Deposit Money", or "Move Money from one Account to Another." The user can push buttons on a keypad or touch the screen to make the selection.

You can get money anytime, by using an ATM card.

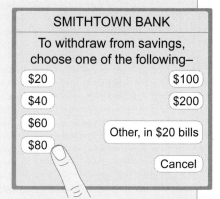

Suppose the person selects *Get Cash* from the menu. The next menu asks which account to take the money from—savings or checking. Then it asks for the amount of money. When the person pushes enter, the money comes out of the machine.

1. Look at the ATM menu above. What command is being sent to the computer?

2. How is an ATM menu like a command menu on your computer?

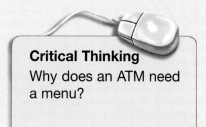

Critical Thinking
Why does an ATM need a menu?

3·6   Applying: Copy and Save Files

You sometimes need to make a copy of a file. Suppose you need to make a change in your work without losing the original work. You can use the Save As command to make a copy of a file. You can give the copy a new file name using the Save As command. The original file does not change.

Example

Keisha wants to change a poem she wrote. She also wants to keep the original poem. She saved the poem with the file name *Sailing*. It is in the *English* folder. Copy and save Keisha's file.

STEP 1   GET READY What do you need to do first?
Open the *Sailing* file in the *English* folder.

STEP 2   THINK What do you need to know?
Decide on a new name for the copy of the *Sailing* file.

STEP 3   APPLY Copy the file, name it, then make a change to it.
Use the Save As command to make a copy of the file *Sailing*. Choose Save As from the File menu. In the dialog box, find the Save As field. Enter the name you decided on in Step 2. Then click on the button called OK or Save.

Make a change to one word in the poem. Then save the file.

STEP 4   CHECK Does the information look correct?
Check to see that you have saved the change you made to the poem. Print the *Sailing* file and the file with the new name. Read the two copies. Find the change you made.

3·6 Lab Practice

GET READY to use the Save As command to copy a file. Answer the questions under THINK. APPLY what you know. Copy the files. CHECK your finished work.

1. Jonathan wants to change a recipe file he has. It has the file name *Chocolate Chip Cookies*. The file is in a folder named *Cooking Class*. In the new file, Jonathan wants to change **chocolate chips** to **raisins**. He also wants to keep the original recipe. Save the new file with a new name.

   THINK
   What name should he give the new file?

2. Jonathan wants to change the new recipe and keep the original recipe. In the new file, he wants to add $\frac{1}{2}$ **cup of quick oats**. Save the new file with a new name.

   THINK
   What name should he give the new file?

Making Connections

Think about how you would organize files and folders on the computer for your school projects and assignments. Across the top of a piece of paper, write all the folder names. Under each folder, write the name of each file you could put in that folder. How could you use the Save As command to make copies of some of the files?

Summary

Giving Orders to the Computer
Several tools are used to give orders to the computer. The same orders can be given to a computer in different ways.

- **Use a menu** to give the computer a command.
- **Choose file names** that help identify a file's contents.
- **Use a dialog box** to give more information when opening, closing, and printing a file. Scroll bars move the contents of a dialog box.
- **Use toolbars** to give commands more quickly.
- **Make a copy** of a file using the Save As... command.

command
dialog box
file
folder
menu
scroll bar
title bar
toolbar

Vocabulary Review
Complete each sentence with a term from the list.

1. A bar along the edge of a window that moves the text in the window is a _____.

2. A _____ is a list of commands for doing different jobs on the computer.

3. A _____ is a box that asks the user for input, then does the command.

4. An order given to a computer to do a job is a _____.

5. A row of buttons you click to give commands to a computer is a _____.

6. A place where you can save and organize files is called a _____.

7. The bar across the top of a file that shows the file's name is called the _____.

8. A set of information or instructions that is named is called a _____.

Chapter Quiz

Answer the following questions.

LESSON 3·1

What Are Commands and Menus?

1. What is a computer menu used for?

2. How can you give commands using the keyboard?

LESSONS 3·2 to 3·4

Computer Tip
Check the File menu for commands that are followed by three dots. They have dialog boxes.

Using Open, Save, and Print Commands

3. How do you use a dialog box to open a folder or file?

4. What should you do when saving a new file?

5. What can happen if you forget to save?

6. How can you print all the pages in a file?

LESSON 3·5

Using Toolbars

7. What is the difference between using toolbars and menu commands?

LESSON 3·6

Copying Using Save As...

8. How do you use the Save As... command to copy and name a new file?

9. When you use the Save As command to copy a file, what happens to the original file?

Group Activity

With your group, create new icons that could stand for Open, Print, and Save. Make a presentation poster for each icon. Write what each one means. Explain why it is a good icon for that command.

Organizing your folders and files makes it easier to find and use them. Why is organizing files important?

What You Need to Know

- The parts of a computer
- How to use a mouse
- How to use a keyboard
- How to use menus and commands
- How to use the Open command

This chapter is about Managing Files.

What You Will Learn

- How to organize a computer
- How to view and rename files and folders
- How to make new folders
- How to find files
- How to organize files

Chapter 4 ▶ Managing Files

Words to Know

path	the address that tells you where to find a file on a computer drive
drive	a part of the hardware that stores data and instructions
list view	a way to view files and folders with their names listed in alphabetical order
icon view	a way to view files and folders shown as icons with their names

Organization Project

Make at least ten different files. Include personal letters, invitations, class notes, reports, and anything else you like. Write the name of each file on an index card or small piece of paper. Next, organize, or sort, the cards into groups. Write a name for each group on a folder. Tape each file's index card into the folder you would keep the file in. How many types of folders did you create? Make a list to share with your class.

Learning Objectives

- Describe how to organize files on a computer.
- View and rename files and folders.
- Make new folders.
- Explain how to find specific folders and files.
- Apply the making and naming of new folders to organizing files.
- **PROBLEM SOLVING:** Solve problems by reading details about files and folders.
- **ON THE JOB:** Explain how computer files can keep track of billing customer accounts.

4-1 Organizing A Computer

If you just toss all your school papers into your school bag, you will probably have a mess of papers. Trying to find one paper becomes very difficult. However, you could easily find it if you organized your papers into folders.

You can think of a computer like your school bag. Just as your bag holds all of your papers, the computer holds all of your files. If you don't organize your computer, your files will be hard to find. Computers can arrange files in alphabetical order by name. This makes finding files easier.

Remember
A folder is a place where you can save and organize files.

A good way to organize files is to put them in folders. Folders have names so that users can tell them apart. A good folder name is short and tells what is inside. This makes a folder easy to find and recognize.

Look at the screens below. Screen 1 shows files arranged alphabetically in a folder called *Assignments*. You can organize these files even more by putting folders inside the *Assignments* folder. Screen 2 shows the five folders that are inside the *Assignments* folder.

Assignments
Civil War report
Columbus report
Geography report
Microscopes report
My Vacation
Picasso report
Water cycle

Screen 1

Assignments
Art
History
Language Arts
Science
Social Studies

Screen 2

A computer finds the files by following a **path**. A path is the address that tells you where to find a file on a computer **drive**. A drive is part of the hardware that stores data and instructions. A computer can have more than one drive. The path shows the drive name and folder names in a file's address. You can show a path in a picture or in words. Look at the diagram below.

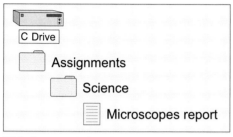

C:\Assignments\Science\Microscopes report

This is a path in pictures.   *This is a path in words.*

▶ **LESSON REVIEW**

1. How do folders help keep a computer organized?

2. **CRITICAL THINKING** What might be a good name for a folder in which you keep your school homework?

On the Cutting Edge

MINI-COMPUTERS THAT HELP YOU STAY ORGANIZED

Today, many people use mini-computers because they can be easily carried around. They are great tools to organize information. A person uses a stylus and an electronic keyboard on the screen to input and organize data such as reminder notes, phone numbers, and addresses. People also use these computers to keep track of schedules. It is like having a telephone book, calendar, and filing cabinet all in the palm of your hand!

CRITICAL THINKING Do you think you would find a mini-computer useful? Explain your answer.

Mini-computers help people stay organized.

4·2 Viewing Files and Folders

Files and folders in a window can appear in two basic ways. You can choose the way you view files and folders using the View menu. One way to view is by name. This is called **list view**. This is a way to view files and folders with their names listed in alphabetical order. In Microsoft® Windows®, users can also use *details view*.

The other way to view is called **icon view**. This view shows files and folders as icons with their names. The icon names appear under the icons. In this view, you can arrange the icons any way you want. Look at the examples in the diagram below.

Remember
The desktop is the screen where you work with icons and windows. An icon is a picture that stands for something, such as a file, disk, or program.

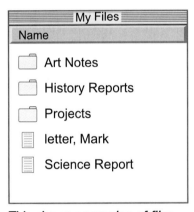

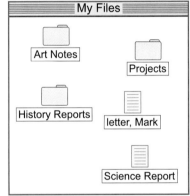

This shows examples of files and folders in list or details view.

This shows examples of files and folders in icon view.

You can rename any folder or file in a window or on the desktop. Changing a name is the same in both list view and icon view.

▶ **LESSON REVIEW**

1. What are the two different ways files and folders can be viewed on the desktop?

2. **CRITICAL THINKING** Compare viewing files and folders in list view and icon view. When might you choose one or the other?

4·2 Lab Practice

To rename a file, follow the steps below.

STEP 1   Choose Icon view from the View menu.

STEP 2   Find the name of the file or folder you want to change. Click on the icon to select it. Both the icon and name will be highlighted. Look at the diagram below.

STEP 3   Click again on the name. The name will be outlined in a box.

STEP 4   Type the new name. Then press the Enter (or Return) key.

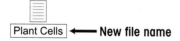

STEP 5   Check Your Work: Choose List view from the View menu. Where does the renamed file or folder appear in List view?

▶ More Practice

Choose list view from the View menu. Rename a file or folder. Check your work.

Sometimes when you are organizing your files, you need to make a new folder. There are several steps to take to make a new folder. The steps for making a new folder are different depending on whether you are using Macintosh® or Microsoft® Windows®.

The steps below tell you how to make a new folder. The new folder will appear where you are working. For example, if you are working on the desktop, the folder will appear on the desktop. If you are working in a folder, it will appear within that folder.

You must name a new folder. If you do not, the computer will name it. In Windows, it will be named *New Folder*. In Macintosh®, it will be named *untitled folder*.

Making a New Folder Using Macintosh®

Remember
See Lesson 2.1 to read about right-clicking a Microsoft® Windows® or PC mouse.

1. Click on File menu on the desktop.

File	Edit	View
New Folder		⌘N
Open		⌘O
Print		⌘P

2. Click on the New Folder command. A folder icon named *Untitled Folder* will appear.

untitled folder

3. Type in a new name of your choice. Press the Return key. The folder will have a new name.

New Name

Making a New Folder Using Windows®

1. Right-click the mouse on the desktop. The shortcut menu will appear.

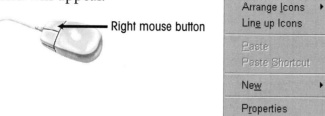

2. Move the mouse pointer on the New command. Another menu will pop up. Click on Folder.

3. A folder icon named New Folder will appear.

4. Type in a new name of your choice. Press the Enter key.

▶ **LESSON REVIEW**

1. In which menu do you find the New Folder command?

2. What would happen if you did not type a new name for a new folder?

3. **CRITICAL THINKING** Give two reasons you might want to make a new folder.

4·3 Lab Practice

You can make a new folder inside another folder. Use the *Lesson 4-3* folder. Follow the steps below.

STEP 1   Use icon view. Open the *Lesson 4-3* folder. You will see a window with the name *Lesson 4-3* in the title bar.

STEP 2

For Macintosh®	For Microsoft® Windows®
Click on the File menu. Then click on the New Folder command. Go to Step 3.	Right-click the mouse to open the shortcut menu. Point at the New command, then click on Folder. Go to Step 3.

STEP 3   Type the folder name **Math**, then press the Enter (or Return) key.

STEP 4   Check Your Work: Close the *Lesson 4-3* folder, then open it again. Is the *Math* folder inside? If you open the *Math* folder, what is inside?

▶ **More Practice**

1. Make another new folder within the *Math* folder. Name this new folder *Fractions*. Check your work.

2. Make another new folder within the *Fractions* folder. Name this new folder *Adding Fractions*. Check your work.

PROBLEM SOLVING
Files with Similar Names

You need to find a letter you wrote and saved on April 7th. Your letter files have very similar names. The file names do not tell you when they were written. Look at the *Letters* folder shown in the screen below. It shows the files in a folder named *Letters*. The files are in icon view.

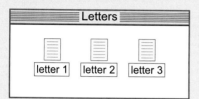

Use the View menu to choose List view in Macintosh® or Details view in Microsoft® Windows®. Study the diagram below. Look to the right of the file names. You can see the last date a file was saved. This information is in the column called Date Modified.

If you cannot see all the information shown, resize a window to make it as large as needed.

Critical Thinking
Suppose you wanted to find the longest letter you had written. Which file details would help you?

Look at the window below.

Name	Size	Date Modified
letter 1	1 KB	4/7/2001
letter 2	2 KB	4/8/2001
letter 3	3 KB	4/9/2001

1. What is the name of the letter written on April 7?

2. How do you know?

It is easy to forget where a file you want is saved. People often have many files saved on a computer. To help you find a file, you can use the Find command. This will open a Find dialog box.

The screen below shows an example of a Find dialog box. It has a place for you to type the file's name. Look at the words *Find File*. Notice the box to the right of these words. In this example, you would type the file name in the box. If you cannot remember the full name, you can input parts of the name that you remember.

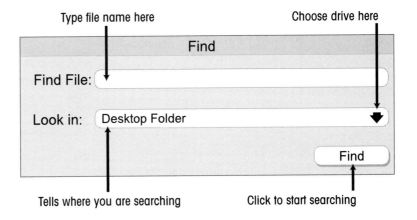

Type file name here   Choose drive here

Find

Find File:

Look in: Desktop Folder

Find

Tells where you are searching   Click to start searching

Next, choose the drive you need to look in. In the example above, you would choose the drive from a pop-up menu. Notice the arrow on the right side of the dialog box. Clicking on the arrow makes the pop-up menu appear. Then click the Find button to start finding a file.

The table below tells you how to find files for both Macintosh® and Microsoft® Windows®.

For Macintosh®	For Microsoft® Windows®
Click on the File menu on the desktop.	Click on the Start button on the desktop.
Click on the Find command.	Click on the Find command. Then click on Files or Folders.
Enter a file name.	Enter a file name.
Choose the drive next to *Find Items*	Choose the drive next to *Look In.*
Click the Find Button	Click the Find Now button.

When the computer is done finding a file, you will see a window. This window shows the location of the file or its path. The file you find may be on your desktop. It may be in a folder or in a folder within another folder.

Look at the Microsoft® Windows® example below. The *Letters* folder is inside a folder named *Desktop*. The *Desktop* folder is inside a folder named *Windows*. The *Windows* folder is in the C: drive.

Windows®

Look at the Macintosh® example on the right. The *Letters* folder is inside the *Desktop Folder*. The *Desktop Folder* is in the *Mac Hard Drive*.

Macintosh®

▶ **LESSON REVIEW**

1. What command do you need to select to help you find a file?

2. **CRITICAL THINKING** Look at the Microsoft® Windows® diagram above. Suppose that a folder named *Letters* is also in the *Windows* folder. What will happen if you enter *Letters* in the Find dialog box and press the Find button?

4·4 Lab Practice

Find the folder called *Letters*. Follow the steps.

STEP 1   Click on the Find command. The Find dialog box will appear.

STEP 2   Select the drive to search on.

STEP 3   Type in the name **Letters**.

STEP 4   Click on the Find or Find Now button to begin the search.

STEP 5   Study the window that appears. It will tell you where to find the folder.

STEP 6   Check Your Work: What information did you enter into the Find dialog box? Describe where the folder was located.

▶ More Practice

1.   Find the file named *letter-1*. Describe where the file is located.

2.   Find another folder or file of your choice. What information did you enter into the Find dialog box?

Describe where the file or folder is located.

Teresa works for a home heating oil company. It is her job to organize all of the customers' accounts. She keeps track of each customer's name, address, and account number. Teresa also keeps track of how much oil each customer orders and how much it costs. She then records how much each customer has paid and how much each customer owes.

Teresa uses a computer to do her work. Each customer has a main folder with his or her last and first name. Within that folder are other folders. These folders hold every year's bills. Each bill in these folders is a separate file.

Theresa uses a computer to keep customers' accounts in order.

Look at the window below. It shows information from Teresa's computer.

Save As
Save in
📁 Smithson, Tom
📁 1997
📁 1998
📁 1999
📁 2000

Critical Thinking
Why is it easier for Teresa to keep track of her accounts on a computer than in paper folders?

1. In which folder will Teresa save a bill to Tom Smithson, dated May 3, 1999?

2. What will she do with a bill from the same customer, dated March 23, 2000?

3. What will she do with a bill from the same customer, dated January 5, 2002?

4-5 ▶ Applying: Organizing Files

To help you organize files, you can move them from one folder to a new folder.

Example

Sumana saved letters that she wrote to friends in a folder called *Sumana's Letters*. She wants to put the letters in different folders. Organize the letters into new folders.

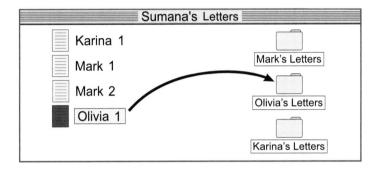

STEP 1 **GET READY** **What do you need to do first?**
Open the folder called Sumana's *Letters*.

STEP 2 **THINK** **What do you know about the information?**
Decide how you will organize the files into new folders.

STEP 3 **APPLY** **Organize the information.**
Make a new folder called *Olivia's Letters*. Select the file *Olivia 1*. Drag it to the new folder. Make two new folders for Sumana's friends Mark and Karina. Move Sumana's other files to these new folders.

STEP 4 **CHECK** **Does the information look correct?**
Check that the files have moved. Open the *Olivia's Letters* folder. The file *Olivia 1* should be inside. Check inside the two other new folders.

4·5 Lab Practice

GET READY to organize the following files. Answer the questions under THINK. APPLY what you know to organize the files. CHECK your finished work.

1. Look at the list of file and folder names below. Organize the files into the folders.

File Name	Letters	Party	School
Guest list			
History report			
Invitation			
Letter-to-Abdul			
Science notes			

THINK
What do the folder names tell you about the files inside?

2. Suppose you wrote a new report on dinosaurs. You named it *dinosaurs*. Decide which folder to put it in.
THINK
In which folder would you look for the file *dinosaurs*?

Making Connections

Look at the names of files and folders you created for the chapter project and other classes in school. Decide if you need to divide the files into new folders to organize them better. Create the new folders on the computer. Then move any computer files into the folders.

Summary

Managing Files
There are several ways to organize your computer and manage your files. You can:

- **Use folders** to organize files on your computer.
- **Name folders** with short names that tell what is inside.
- **Rename files and folders** from the desktop.
- **View folders and files** as large icons or as a list in alphabetical order.
- **Make new folders** using the New Folder command.
- **Find a file** on the desktop using the Find command.
- **Organize information** by moving files from one folder to another.

list view

icon view

drive

path

Vocabulary Review

Complete each sentence with a term from the list.

1. The address of a file in your computer is its _____.

2. Files and folders that are shown with large icons and their names on the desktop are in _____.

3. Files and folders that are arranged in alphabetical order are in _____.

4. A piece of computer hardware that stores data and instructions is a _____.

Chapter Quiz

Answer the following questions.

LESSONS 4·1 and 4·5

Computer Tip
The easiest way to organize your files on a computer is to use folders.

Organizing Your Computer

1. Why are folders good places to save and store your files?

2. What are two things to remember when naming a folder?

LESSONS 4·2

Viewing and Renaming Files and Folders

3. What is the difference between viewing files and folders in list view and icon view?

4. What are the steps in renaming a file?

LESSON 4·3

Making New Folders

5. What happens when you right-click a Windows® mouse?

6. Suppose you are working inside a folder. If you use the New Folder command, where will the new folder appear?

LESSON 4·4

Finding Files

7. Which dialog box do you use to locate a file from the desktop?

8. What information should you put into the dialog box to find the file?

Group Activity

With your group, look for six newspaper articles. Divide the articles into groups by subjects. Make folders with names for each group. Then make up a file name for each article. Organize the articles into the folders.

This microscope view shows the tiny circuit that runs a computer. What other machines are run by circuits?

What You Need to Know

The parts of a computer

How to use a mouse and keyboard

How to use menus, commands, and toolbars

How to save files

This chapter is about hardware and software Inside the Computer.

What You Will Learn

How to care for a personal computer

The CPU, system software, and memory

About built-in and portable storage

How to use storage

How to analyze system requirements

Words to Know

hard disk	a thin, flat, round metal plate on which data can be stored magnetically
computer virus	a small program that can make copies of itself and be spread from one computer to another
memory	the part of a computer system where information and instructions are held for use by the CPU
ROM	Read-Only Memory; a permanent area in the memory
RAM	Random-Access Memory; a temporary area in the memory
byte	the amount of memory or space one character takes up
storage	a place where data and software can be held or saved
storage capacity	the number of bytes that a disk can hold

Computer Hardware Project

Collect at least five ads about computers from newspapers, magazines, and catalogs. In each lesson, look at the ads. Circle the parts of the ads that describe the features you have learned about. Explain to a partner what is described in the ads. Keep your ads to use with the Group Activity.

Learning Objectives

- Describe caring for a computer.
- Describe computers.
- Explain types of storage.
- Use storage to backup files.
- Apply analyzing RAM to choosing software.
- PROBLEM SOLVING: Solve the problem of a frozen computer.
- COMPUTERS ON THE JOB: Use software memory needs to plan an upgrade.

Taking care of a computer starts with taking care of the hardware. There are utility programs and steps you can follow that can help you with this task.

Caring for the Hard Disk

Remember
A hard drive is a tool for storing data and instructions. You learned about the hard drive and utility software in Chapter 1.

A disk is a thin, flat, round plate on which data can be stored. Inside a computer's hard drive is the **hard disk**. The hard disk is a metal plate on which data can be stored magnetically.

Over time, problems can develop with information stored on a hard disk. You can use utility software to scan the hard disk and repair any file or folder problems. Another kind of software is used to *defragment* the hard disk. Defragment means rejoin parts of files that are stored in different places on the hard disk. This can help a computer perform better.

Preventing Viruses

Another way to take care of a computer is to protect it from a **computer virus**. A computer virus is a small program that can make copies of itself and then be spread from one computer to another. Many viruses are harmful. They can damage or erase files and cause the hard disk to have problems.

You can use antivirus utility software to scan the computer for viruses. It can remove viruses and repair any damage that was done.

Always use antivirus software to check files you receive from someone else. Update your antivirus software every month. New viruses are being created all the time.

Caring for Portable Disks

You also need to take care of portable disks, such as floppy disks and CDs. Always store portable disks in a protective box. Keep them away from magnets, direct sunlight, high heat, and dirt. Never remove a disk while it is in use. Wait for the disk drive light to go off before taking out a disk. Remove any portable disks before shutting off the computer.

Shutting Down

Follow the proper shut-down steps when you turn off the computer. The table shows the commands to use.

For Macintosh®	For Microsoft® Windows®
Choose Shut Down from the Special menu. Or, press the power key on the keyboard. Click Shut Down in the dialog box that appears.	Choose Shut Down from the Start menu. Click on Shut down the computer? from the list. Click Yes in the dialog box that appears.

Other Good Habits

- Use a *surge protector* to protect all your hardware from electrical damage.
- Keep food and drink away from your keyboard and other hardware.
- Keep your computer clean. Use a soft, lint-free cloth when dusting.
- Wash your hands before handling disks and working at the computer.

▶ **LESSON REVIEW**

1. What are three things you can do to take care of your computer?

2. **CRITICAL THINKING** Why is it important to take care of your computer?

The Computer System

The system inside a computer is made up of the CPU, the memory, and the system software.

The CPU

The CPU is a computer *chip*. It is a very thin piece of material that contains an electronic circuit. A chip is usually made of the element silicon. It is put in a plastic case to protect it.

Inside the plastic case is a tiny silicon chip.

There are many electrical pathways on a chip. The greater the number of pathways, the greater the speed of the CPU.

The speed of a CPU is measured in *megahertz* (MHz). The greater the speed, the faster the CPU carries out its jobs. For example, a 750-MHz CPU chip is faster than a 600-MHz CPU chip. A computer with a greater CPU speed can work faster than one with a slower CPU.

Remember
The CPU or processor does all the math and other jobs, as well as controls the flow of information in a computer.

Memory

Memory is the part of the computer system where information and instructions are held for use by the CPU. A computer has two kinds of memory, ROM and RAM.

ROM, or read-only memory, is a permanent area in the memory where instructions are stored. The CPU can read instructions on a ROM chip, but cannot change them. ROM tells the CPU how to operate. The information in ROM stays there when a computer is shut down.

RAM, or random-access memory, is a temporary area in the memory where information is stored. It is where information is kept while the CPU does its jobs. For example, when you write a report, information about the document is sent to RAM. If you shut down the computer, all the information in RAM can be lost. Always remember to save your work.

A **byte** is the basic unit for measuring memory and stored data. It is the amount of memory one character of information, such as a letter or a number, takes up. Computers can store millions of characters. This table shows different units for counting bytes.

The amount of RAM a computer has determines how much information the CPU can process at one time. It also determines what applications software a computer can run. The amount of RAM that comes with a computer goes up as computer makers improve their machines.

Units of Memory
Kilobyte   KB or K
Exactly 1,024 bytes
Kilo means one thousand
About 1,000 bytes
Megabyte   MB
Exactly 1,048,576 bytes
Mega means one million
About 1,000,000 bytes
Gigabyte   GB
Exactly 1,073,741,824 bytes
Giga means one billion
About 1,000,000,000 bytes

System Software

Almost all personal computers use either Microsoft® Windows® or Mac® OS as the system software. Software packages list the system needed to run the software. Before you buy an application, you need to know what version of system software your computer uses.

The diagrams below and on the next page tell you how to find the system software and amount of RAM for your computer.

Remember
You learned about system software and applications software in Lesson 1.3.

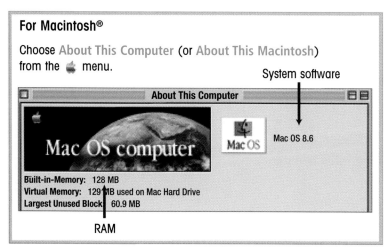

For Macintosh®

Choose About This Computer (or About This Macintosh) from the menu.

System software

About This Computer

Mac OS computer

Mac OS   Mac OS 8.6

Built-in-Memory: 128 MB
Virtual Memory: 129 MB used on Mac Hard Drive
Largest Unused Block   60.9 MB

RAM

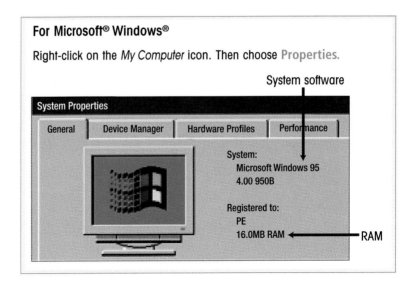

For Microsoft® Windows®

Right-click on the *My Computer* icon. Then choose Properties.

System software

System Properties

| General | Device Manager | Hardware Profiles | Performance |

System:
Microsoft Windows 95
4.00 950B

Registered to:
PE
16.0MB RAM ← RAM

▶ **LESSON REVIEW**

1. What are two ways RAM is different from ROM?

2. About how many bytes are in 32 MB of RAM?

3. **CRITICAL THINKING** Why might you want to add more RAM to your computer?

On the Cutting Edge

PROCESSOR TIMELINE

The processors listed in the timeline below are examples of changes in CPU speed since the 1980s. Notice that the first CPUs had very slow speeds compared to more recent CPUs.

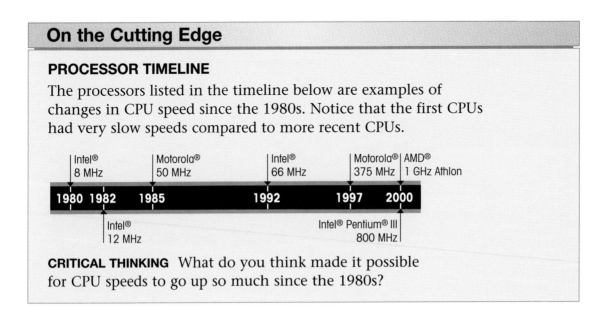

| Intel®
8 MHz | Motorola®
50 MHz | Intel®
66 MHz | Motorola®
375 MHz | AMD®
1 GHz Athlon |

1980 1982   1985   1992   1997   2000

Intel®
12 MHz

Intel® Pentium® III
800 MHz

CRITICAL THINKING What do you think made it possible for CPU speeds to go up so much since the 1980s?

COMPUTERS ON THE JOB
Computer Technician

Frederick Pearson is a computer technician. He knows how to install hardware and software. One way Frederick helps people is by upgrading the RAM in their computers.

Most RAM chips come in groups mounted on a small circuit board. To add more RAM, Frederick plugs new RAM boards into the *motherboard*. This is the main circuit board of the computer.

A customer wants to use software with the system requirements shown below. The About This Computer screen shows information about the customer's Macintosh® computer.

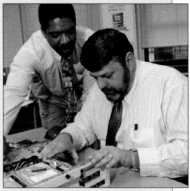

A technician upgrades the RAM in a personal computer.

System Requirements *Macintosh®*
- Macintosh® or 100% compatible computer
- PowerPC or later model
- Mac® OS 8.0 or higher
- minimum 64 MB RAM

```
About This Computer
Mac OS computer                Mac OS      Mac OS 8.6
Built-in Memory: 32 MB
Virtual Memory: Off
Largest Unused Block: 25.3 MB       ™ & © Apple Computer, Inc.
```

Use the information above to answer the questions.

1. How much RAM is needed to run the software on the computer?

2. Does Frederick need to add RAM? How much RAM should he add?

Critical Thinking

If Frederick's customer had Mac® OS 7.0, what else would the customer need Frederick to do in order to run the new software?

Storage is a place where data and software can be held or saved. A computer may use built-in storage or *portable storage*. Portable storage means a disk that can be removed from the computer.

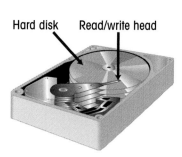

Hard disk   Read/write head

The read/write head is part of the hard drive.

Built-in Storage

Most computers come with a built-in hard disk like the one in the photo at the left. The hard disk is sealed inside the hard drive to protect it from dust. Files saved to a hard disk remain there even when the computer is not using them.

Look at the table below. It shows the icons for the different kinds of disks you might find in computers.

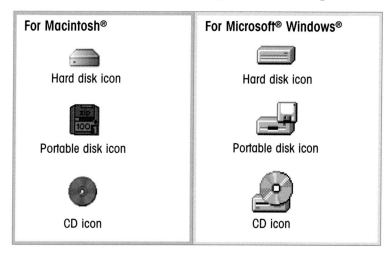

For Macintosh®	For Microsoft® Windows®
Hard disk icon	Hard disk icon
Portable disk icon	Portable disk icon
CD icon	CD icon

The **storage capacity** of a disk is the number of bytes that it can hold. Computer makers continue to increase the capacity of hard disks. In the early 1990s, the storage capacity of hard disks was measured in megabytes. By the late 1990s, it was measured in gigabytes. A half page of text in a word processing document takes up about 1 KB of storage. A color photograph can take up more than 1 MB of storage.

Portable Storage

Sometimes you may need to take information stored on your computer to another computer. Then you need some kind of portable storage disk. The table at the right lists portable disks and their storage capacities.

You may already be familiar with *floppy disks*. The name "floppy" was first used to describe a thin, bendable $5\frac{1}{4}$-inch plastic disk. These disks were used with personal computers from the 1980s. The smaller $3\frac{1}{2}$-inch disk is in a hard plastic case.

The table below tells how to find the storage capacity of any kind of disk.

Type of Disk	Capacity
$5\frac{1}{4}$-inch floppy	1.2 MB
$3\frac{1}{2}$-inch floppy	1.44 MB
CD-R (recordable)	650 MB
CD-RW (rewritable)	650 MB
ZIP	100 MB, 250 MB
JAZ	1 GB, 2 GB

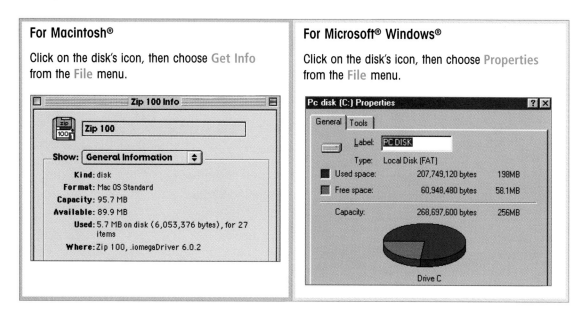

For Macintosh®

Click on the disk's icon, then choose Get Info from the File menu.

Zip 100 Info

Zip 100

Show: General Information

Kind: disk
Format: Mac OS Standard
Capacity: 95.7 MB
Available: 89.9 MB
Used: 5.7 MB on disk (6,053,376 bytes), for 27 items
Where: Zip 100, .iomegaDriver 6.0.2

For Microsoft® Windows®

Click on the disk's icon, then choose Properties from the File menu.

Pc disk (C:) Properties

General | Tools

Label: PC DISK
Type: Local Disk (FAT)
Used space: 207,749,120 bytes 198MB
Free space: 60,948,480 bytes 58.1MB
Capacity: 268,697,600 bytes 256MB

Drive C

▶ **LESSON REVIEW**

1. Why do you need a hard disk in a computer?

2. What are three kinds of portable storage disks?

3. **CRITICAL THINKING** Suppose you wanted to store a file that was 60 KB. What kind of portable storage disk would you use? Why?

5·3 Lab Practice

You have a word processing document file that is 950 KB (972,800 bytes) in size. Follow the steps below to see if a portable disk has enough free space to store the file.

STEP 1 Place a $3\frac{1}{2}$-inch disk into its slot in the computer.

STEP 2

For Macintosh®	**For Microsoft® Windows®**
Click on the floppy disk icon on the desktop.	Open the *My Computer* window. Click on the floppy disk icon.
Choose Get Info from the File menu.	Choose Properties from the File menu.

STEP 3 Find the amount of available (or free) space on the floppy disk.

STEP 4 Compare the size of the word processing document file with the amount of available (or free) space on the floppy disk.

STEP 5 Decide if the file will fit on the floppy disk.

STEP 6 Check Your Work: Is the amount of available (or free) space on the floppy disk larger than or equal to the size of the file?

▶ **More Practice**

1. You have a file that is 560 KB (573,440 bytes). Decide if the file will fit on a different floppy disk. Check your work.

2. One file has a size of 133 KB (136,192 bytes). Another file has a size of 427 KB (437,248 bytes). Decide if both files will fit on the floppy disk you used for the above exercise. Check your work.

Using portable storage can serve two purposes. First, you can protect important files by copying them to a portable disk. This gives you a backup, or extra, copy of your files in case something happens to the hard disk.

Second, you can free up hard disk space by copying files you no longer use to a portable disk. Then you can delete the files from the hard disk to make more room.

Look at the screens below. They show you how to copy a file onto a portable disk using Macintosh® and Microsoft® Windows®.

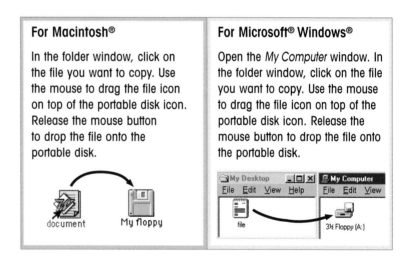

For Macintosh®

In the folder window, click on the file you want to copy. Use the mouse to drag the file icon on top of the portable disk icon. Release the mouse button to drop the file onto the portable disk.

document   My floppy

For Microsoft® Windows®

Open the *My Computer* window. In the folder window, click on the file you want to copy. Use the mouse to drag the file icon on top of the portable disk icon. Release the mouse button to drop the file onto the portable disk.

My Desktop   My Computer
File Edit View Help   File Edit View
file   3½ Floppy (A:)

▶ **LESSON REVIEW**

1. What is a backup file?

2. What are two reasons to use portable storage?

3. **CRITICAL THINKING** Suppose you kept your address book on the computer. Why would you want to backup this file?

5·4 Lab Practice

Place a blank portable disk into the computer. Follow the steps below to Copy a file from the hard disk to the portable disk.

STEP 1   Locate the file called *Math Homework*.

STEP 2

For Macintosh®	For Microsoft® Windows®
Look for the portable disk icon on your desktop.	Open the *My Computer* window. Look for the portable disk icon.

STEP 3   Resize or move any windows as needed so that the icon for the *Math Homework* file and the icon for the portable disk are both visible.

STEP 4   Use the mouse to select the *Math Homework* file.

STEP 5   Drag and drop the file onto the icon for the portable disk.

STEP 6   Check Your Work: Double-click the portable disk icon to see its contents. Check to see if the *Math Homework* file has been copied.

▶ **More Practice**

Make a backup copy of the file called *Computer Homework* by dragging and dropping it onto a portable disk. Check your work.

Sometimes, when you are working on a computer, it freezes. An application or the computer stops responding to commands from the mouse or the keyboard.

If an application freezes, first try to close the application. If you are using Mac® OS 7 or higher, you can force an application to close by pressing the Command-Option-Esc keys together. A dialog box appears. Click Force Quit to close the application.

If you are using Microsoft® Windows®, press the Ctrl-Alt-Delete keys together. This opens the Close Program dialog box like the one shown. Use the arrow keys to select the application. Then press Alt-E or the End Task button.

After closing the application, save any work in any other open applications. Then restart the computer.

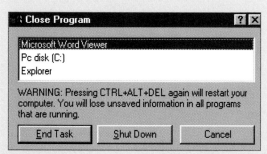

If both the keyboard and mouse are no longer working, you will have to use the power switch to turn it off. You will lose any work that was not saved. Wait at least 10 seconds, then turn the computer on again.

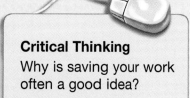

Critical Thinking
Why is saving your work often a good idea?

1. What should you do if your screen freezes?

2. What else can you do if a computer freezes?

Applying: System Requirements

It is important to know about your computer system. It can help you decide whether a software product will run on your computer.

Example

You want to install a new software program on your computer. The software lists the system requirements shown below. Decide if you can run the software on your computer.

To install this software, you will need the following minimum system requirements:

IBM® PC Software Requirements
- Microsoft® Windows®95/98
- 8 MB RAM
- CD-ROM drive

Macintosh® Software Requirements
- Macintosh system software version 7.01
- 8 MB RAM
- CD-ROM drive

STEP 1 GET READY What do you need to do first?
Find out what kind of information you need to know about your computer system.

STEP 2 THINK What do you know about this information?
Think about how you can find the information. You need to know the system software version and RAM (memory) size.

STEP 3 APPLY Find the information on your computer.
For Macintosh®, use About This Computer.

For Microsoft® Windows®, right-click on the *My Computer* icon. Then choose Properties.

STEP 4 CHECK How does the information look?
Compare the information about your computer with the information on the package. Decide if the software will run or if you need to first upgrade your computer.

5·5 Lab Practice

GET READY to make a decision. Answer the questions under THINK. APPLY what you know to analyze the information. CHECK your finished work.

1. Thomas wants to know whether the software with the system requirements shown below will run on your computer system.

IBM® PC Software Requirements	Macintosh® Software Requirements
• Microsoft® Windows®95/98	• Mac OS 8.1, 8.5, or 8.51
• 16 MB RAM	• 8 MB RAM (12 MB recommended)

THINK

Does your computer have the right version of system software?

Does your computer have enough RAM (memory)?

2. Thomas finds out that the software will need 8.9 MB of storage when it is installed on the hard disk.

THINK

How can you find out if you have enough free space on your hard disk to install the software?

Making Connections

Look in the library or in a computer store for software that might help you in science, social studies, math, or language arts class. For example, you might look for an encyclopedia on CD or math practice software. Write the system requirements needed to run the software. Compare those requirements with information about your school or home computer. Decide whether you could run the software.

Summary

Inside the Computer
Inside the computer is system software and the hardware that helps the computer carry out its tasks.
• **Take care of a personal computer** using hard disk utilities and antivirus software on a regular basis. Shut down properly. Use a surge protector.
• To find information about the computer system, use About This Computer (Macintosh®) or System Properties (Microsoft® Windows®).
• To find **storage capacity,** click on the icon for a disk. From the File menu, choose Get Info (Macintosh) or Properties (Windows) to find storage capacity.
• **Use storage** when you drag–and–drop a file from the hard disk to a portable disk to make a backup copy of the file.
• **Make an informed decision** by comparing system information with system requirements on a software package.

byte
computer virus
disk
hard disk
memory
storage

Vocabulary Review

Complete each sentence with a word from the list.

1. A thin, flat, round plate on which data can be stored is a _____.

2. The part of a computer system where information or instructions are held for use by the CPU is its _____.

3. A place where data and software can be held or saved permanently is _____.

4. The amount of memory or space one character takes up is a _____.

5. A small program that can make copies of itself and be spread from one computer to another is a _____.

6. A thin, flat, round metal plate on which information can be stored magnetically is a _____.

Chapter Quiz

Answer the following questions.

LESSON 5·1

Care of Personal Computers

1. What are four ways to take care of your computer?

LESSONS 5·2

Computer Tip
The About This Computer or System Properties windows tell you the system software and amount of RAM.

The Computer System

2. Which CPU chip is faster, one with a speed of 400 MHz or one with a speed of 550 MHz? Why?

3. What is the difference between RAM and ROM?

4. What are the two operating systems in most personal computers?

LESSON 5·3 and 5·4

Understanding and Using Storage

5. A group of files takes up 4,194,304 bytes of space on a hard disk. About how many megabytes do the files take up?

6. What are two reasons for using portable storage disks?

7. How can you find the amount of free space on a disk?

LESSON 5·5

System Requirements

8. Why is it important to know the system requirements for software before you buy it?

Group Activity

Have your group combine all the computer ads they collected for the chapter project. Use the ads to research the features of different computers. Make notes on the type and speed of the CPU, the amount of RAM, the storage capacity of the hard disk, and the types of portable storage that can be used with the computer. As a group, compare the features of all the computers. Decide which computer has the best features. Explain your decision to the class.

Unit 1 **Review**

Choose the letter of the correct answer.

1. What are two functions of computer hardware?
   A. Design and point to new information
   B. Store and put out information
   C. Copy and collect information
   D. Make a chart and send information

2. What are two ways to give input to a computer?
   A. Press keyboard keys and print a page
   B. Click a mouse and read information on the monitor
   C. Read a printed page and use a scanner
   D. Move icons with a mouse and press keyboard keys

3. Which of the following actions gives a command to the computer?
   A. Choose Open from the File menu
   B. Point the mouse at an icon
   C. Move the desktop
   D. Read a file name

4. What information can you get by reading the system requirements on a software package?
   A. How to use the hard disk
   B. RAM needed to use the software
   C. The size of ROM
   D. How to upgrade RAM

5. How can you find the storage space needed by a folder?
   A. Copy it onto a floppy disk
   B. Open it to see how many files it has
   C. Click on it and use the Properties or Get Info command
   D. Open it and use the Find command

Critical Thinking
You decide to store your homework files in folders. Make a list of the names of the folders. Explain why the folder names will help you organize information.

Unit 2 ► Word Processing

Chapter 6 **Basic Word Processing**

Chapter 7 **Checking Documents**

Chapter 8 **Using Formats**

Sammy Sosa and Mark McGwire were the topic of many baseball articles written in 1998.

During the 1998 baseball season, newspaper reporters wrote many articles about Mark McGwire, Sammy Sosa, and their home runs. Reporters used word processing software to write their stories about the players. The article shown was made using word processing software.

1. How does the title stand out from the text?

2. How can you tell when a new paragraph starts?

3. **CRITICAL THINKING** How do computers help writers and newspaper reporters do their jobs?

HOME RUN RECORD BREAKERS!

The 1998 baseball season will be known as the year a home run record was broken—twice! Mark McGwire hit 70 home runs. Sammy Sosa hit 66 home runs.

Both players broke the major league baseball record for home runs in one season. The old record was 61 home runs. Roger Maris set the old record in 1961.

This TV newswriter is typing last-minute changes to news copy that will be read on air. Word processing software helps them make changes quickly. Why is it important to make these changes fast?

What You Need to Know

How to point and click with a mouse

How to use a keyboard

How to open a menu

How to choose a command

This chapter is about Basic Word Processing.

What You Will Learn

About Word Processing

How to make a document

How to edit and replace text

How to move text

How to organize a list

Chapter 6 ▶ Basic Word Processing

Words to Know

word processing	computer software, or program, used to type and change text
document	any work done on a computer with applications software, such as a letter, report, budget, newsletter, or presentation
edit	to change text that is already entered
cursor	a blinking vertical line that shows the place on the computer screen where text is being entered on the screen
indent	the extra space at the start of a paragraph
word wrap	the automatic movement of text to the next line after filling the current line
delete	to remove something from a document, such as text as art

Word Processing Project

Word processing is a tool for computer users. Look around your school, your library, an office, stores, your home, and shows on TV. Look anywhere that people are using computers to type. How many uses of word processing can you find? Make a list. Share what you find in class.

Learning Objectives

- Identify uses of word processing.
- Enter new text.
- Edit text by adding, deleting, or replacing.
- Move and copy text from one place to another.
- Apply word processing skills to organizing information.
- **PROBLEM SOLVING:** Solve a problem by showing nonprinting characters.
- **COMPUTERS ON THE JOB:** Use word processing to make a business form.

Computers use software to do special jobs. One kind of software is called word processing. **Word processing** is computer software that helps you type and change text.

Using Word Processing

You can use word processing software to type letters, reports, or text. With word processing, you can easily fix mistakes and make changes. You can save your work at any time. If you stop your work before it is done, you can finish it another time.

When you use word processing, you can do some basic jobs, or *tasks*. Tasks are pieces of work to be done. One task you can do is enter text. To enter text, you type words into a **document**. A document can be any work made with software. Letters and reports are examples of documents made using word processing.

You can also **edit** text. When you edit, you change the text you have already entered. You can move text from one place to another. The lessons in this chapter will help you learn and practice these tasks.

Word processing tasks can be done on any kind of computer. Word processing tasks can be done on any kind of computer. The skills you learn in this unit can be used with any word processing software.

Word processing skills are also needed in other kinds of software. You will use word processing skills when you learn to use the following kinds of software:

- spreadsheet and database software
- desktop publishing and presentation software
- electronic mail

Choosing a Word Processing Program

In order to use word processing, you need to choose a word processing program for your computer. All word processing programs do the same basic tasks, but some programs can do more than others.

A simple program lets you do basic tasks such as entering and editing text. A complex program can do more. For example, it can help you make tables, draw pictures, do math, and make graphs. Look at the chart to the right.

Kinds of Word Processing Programs	
Simple Programs	Complex Programs
Enter text	Enter text
Edit	Edit
Move	Move
Format	Format
Save	Save
Print	Print
	Make tables
	Draw pictures
	Do math
	Make graphs

▶ **LESSON REVIEW**

1. How will word processing help you type a letter, report, or text?

2. **CRITICAL THINKING** Why might you want to buy a complex word processing program instead of a simple one?

On the Cutting Edge

THE FIRST PRINTING PRESS

Today, word processing is used in the same way as a printing press. The first printing press was invented in 1436 by Johannes Gutenberg. This press had many metal letters that could be moved around to form different words. To print words, the printer had to put ink on the metal letters, then press the letters against paper. Printers could also print pictures this way.

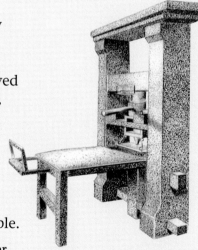

Before Gutenberg, most books were copied by hand. Gutenberg's invention made printing much faster. In 1455, Gutenberg printed the Bible.

CRITICAL THINKING Why do you think it is easier to change documents on a computer than on a printing press?

This is a Gutenberg press.

6·2 Making a Document

You enter text to start a new document. A document can be a letter, report, or any text you are writing. You can also enter new text in a document that has already been created.

Starting a Document

Remember
To review using toolbars, see Lesson 3.5.

Look at the screen below. It shows the row of buttons called the toolbar. The buttons let you choose commands quickly. You can click them with the mouse. Look for these buttons on the toolbar in the screen.

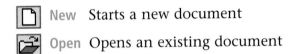

New   Starts a new document

Open   Opens an existing document

New document button   Open button

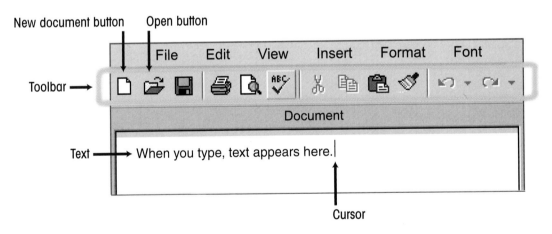

Toolbar →

File   Edit   View   Insert   Format   Font

Document

Text → When you type, text appears here.|

Cursor

Look at the screen above. It shows a new document window. The white part of the screen is for text. The **cursor** is the vertical line that shows where the text is being entered. It is usually blinking on the screen. In a new document, the cursor is at the top left corner of the screen. After you type, you can put the cursor anywhere with the mouse.

Entering Text

You can use your keyboard to enter text. When you enter a paragraph, use the Tab key first. This will put an **indent** in your text. An indent is the extra space at the start of a paragraph. The Tab key is on the left side of the keyboard. Look for the Tab key in the picture below.

Tab key ➞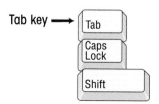

Remember
To review the entire keyboard, see Lesson 2.2.

The Tab key moves the cursor to the right. Then you can begin to type. As you type, the text will fill the line. Words that do not fit on that line will move to the next line. This is called **word wrap**. Word wrap moves text to the next line after filling the current line. You do not have to tell the computer to do this. You do have to tell the computer when you want to start a new paragraph. The chart below tells you which key to use.

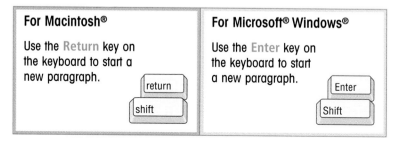

For Macintosh®	For Microsoft® Windows®
Use the Return key on the keyboard to start a new paragraph.	Use the Enter key on the keyboard to start a new paragraph.

▶ **LESSON REVIEW**

1. List two things that you can do by using the buttons of the toolbar.

2. How do you move the cursor?

3. **CRITICAL THINKING** Why does word wrap make word processing easier to use?

6·2 Lab Practice

Make a new document. Look at the screen.
Then follow the steps.

Paragraph 1 ——→ The morning was bright and sunny. The temperature was warm.
Paragraph 2 ——→ The afternoon turned cloudy. It began to rain.

STEP 1   Find the cursor on your screen.

STEP 2   Press Tab to indent the paragraph.

STEP 3   Enter the text for paragraph 1.

STEP 4   Press Return (or Enter) to begin the second paragraph.

STEP 5   Press Tab to indent the paragraph.

STEP 6   Enter in the text for paragraph 2.

STEP 7   Check Your Work: How many times did you press the Tab key? How many times did you press the Return (or Enter) key?

 More Practice

Make another new document. Look at the screen below.
Enter the text shown. Check your work.

> The ocean breeze blows across an empty boardwalk.
> It is a nice day at the beach.
> The streets off Ocean Drive are clear. Let's go!

Selecting Text

Sometimes, after entering text, you need to change it. To replace text, you select it and edit it. Use the mouse to select text. First, point and click at the start of the text you want to select. Next, drag the mouse moving the cursor over the text. Hold the mouse button down as you drag. As you select text, it will become highlighted. Then let go of the mouse button when you get to the end of the text you want to select.

Look at the screen below. Notice the selected text highlighted in blue.

> To edit text easily, you should know how to select text.
> Use the mouse to select text.
> Selected text appears in a highlight of color.

Remember
To review dragging with the mouse, see Lesson 2.1.

Click and drag to select any amount of text. To select only one word, you can point at the word and double-click.

Changing Selected Text

There are several ways to edit selected text. You can delete selected text just by pressing the Delete key. You can change selected text by entering a new word. You can replace any text if you select it and enter new text.

▶ **REVIEW**

1. How do you replace text?

2. **CRITICAL THINKING** Suppose you want to remove a paragraph. Why is it a good idea to select the paragraph first?

Make a new document. Enter the following text.

> The home team bleachers at the field are full of cheering students.

To edit the text, follow the steps below.

STEP 1   Replace text. Select the word **home**. Enter the word **visiting**.

STEP 2   Delete text. Select the words **at the field**. Press Delete (or Backspace).

STEP 3   Replace text. Select the words **cheering students**. Enter the words **fans from Central High School**.

STEP 4   Check Your Work: Which words did you delete? Which words did you replace?

This is the finished document.

> The visiting team bleachers are full of fans from Central High School.

 More Practice

Make another new document. Enter the following text.

> The school dance is next week. Tracey wants to shop for a new outfit.

To edit the text, do the following. Then check your work.
Replace **dance** with **party**.
Delete the word **a**.
Replace **new outfit** with **fancy clothes**.

COMPUTERS ON THE JOB
Customer Service Representative

Diane Thomas is a customer service representative. She works in the office of a music store. She likes her job because she gets to talk to people about music.

Part of Diane's job is typing letters to her customers. She sends letters about special sales and new music. She also answers customer questions and complaints.

Sometimes Diane follows a form letter. This means that most of the letter is already typed. She just fills in the blanks. Here is a form letter she uses for a special sale.

Diane works at a computer.

Dear Valued Customer,

  We are having a sale on __(A)__ ! Everything is marked down to __(B)__ % off.

  Bring in your Music card and get a prize. We will give you a free __(C)__ with your purchase.

  This sale will start on __(D)__ and end on __(E)__. We hope you can make it!

      From your friends at Music World

Diane's manager gave her the following information about a big sales event.

 (A) all Compact Discs
 (B) 25
 (C) carrying case
 (D) May 1
 (E) May 15

1. What should the first sentence say?

2. What will be given away for free?

Critical Thinking
Diane's manager gave her the information on May 5. Why is this a problem? What should Diane do?

Sometimes you need to move text from one place to another when you are editing a document. In this lesson, you will learn about moving text with the Cut, Paste, and Copy commands.

Cutting and Pasting

Remember
Click and drag the mouse
to select text.

One way to move text is by using the Cut and Paste commands. First, select the text you want to move. In Screen 1 below, the light blue color shows the text that will be cut. Next, choose the Cut command from the Edit menu. Screen 1 shows the Cut command in dark blue. When you choose Cut, the text is not lost. It is stored by the computer.

Screen 1

| Edit | View | Insert | Format | Font | Tools | Table | Window | Work | Help |

Undo Typing
Repeat Copy

Document1

Cut
Copy
Paste

You can move text from one place in a document to a new place.

Selected text to be cut

Now, put the cursor where you want the text to be. Then use the Paste command. Screen 2 shows the Paste command in dark blue. When you choose Paste, the text appears at the cursor. Screen 2 shows where the four words "to a new place" are pasted. If you do not choose Paste, the text you cut will be deleted.

Screen 2

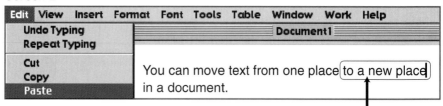

| Edit | View | Insert | Format | Font | Tools | Table | Window | Work | Help |

Undo Typing
Repeat Typing

Document1

Cut
Copy
Paste

You can move text from one place to a new place in a document.

Text cut in Screen 1 pasted here

Copying and Pasting

Another way to move text is to copy and paste.

First, select the text you want to copy. In Screen 3 below, the light blue color shows the text that will be copied. Next, choose the Copy command from the Edit menu. Screen 3 shows the Copy command in dark blue. When you choose the Copy command, a copy of the text is stored by the computer.

Screen 3

Edit	View	Insert	Format	Font	Tools	Table	Window	Work	Help

Undo Paste	Document1
Repeat Paste	
Cut	You can move text from one place in a document
Copy	to a new place.
Paste	

Now, put the cursor where you want the copied text to go. Then use the Paste command. Screen 4 shows the Paste command in dark blue. When you choose Paste, the text appears at the cursor. Screen 4 shows where the copied text is pasted. You can copy the same text to more than one place.

Screen 4

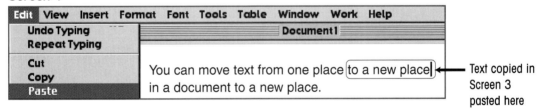

Text copied in Screen 3 pasted here

▶ **LESSON REVIEW**

1. How do the Cut and Paste commands help you edit text?

2. **CRITICAL THINKING** What is the difference between the Cut and Copy commands?

6·5 Lab Practice

Make a new document. Enter the following text.

> The bleachers are full of students. The game has started.

To edit the text, follow the steps below.

STEP 1 Move text. Select the second sentence. Choose Cut from the Edit menu. Put the cursor to the left of the first sentence. Choose Paste from the Edit menu.

STEP 2 Copy text. Select the two words **The game**. Choose Copy from the Edit menu.

STEP 3 Paste text. Put the cursor after the second sentence. Choose Paste from the Edit menu. Finish the third sentence in your own words.

STEP 4 Check Your Work: How many times did you use the Copy command? How does your text read now?

This is the finished document.

> The game has started. The bleachers are full of students. The game [your own words].

 More Practice

Make another new document. Enter the following text.

> We plan to watch the fireworks in the park. We will celebrate Independence Day soon.

To edit the text, do the following. Then check your work.
Move the second sentence in front of the first sentence.
Copy the phrase **Independence Day**.
Paste **Independence Day** after the second sentence.
Finish the sentence in your own words.

PROBLEM SOLVING
Using Nonprinting Characters

There is a mistake in the text below. One of the paragraphs is indented too far.

> The weather for tomorrow will be hot. It will be cloudy in the morning. It will be humid.
> By late afternoon, the clouds will clear away. The sun will be out. It will be less humid.

You can solve this problem by turning on, or showing, *nonprinting characters*. Nonprinting characters show where you have pressed the Tab key, the Enter key, and the space bar. You can hide or show nonprinting characters. To do this, click the ¶ button on the toolbar. The screen below shows what the nonprinting characters look like.

Means Tab   Means one space

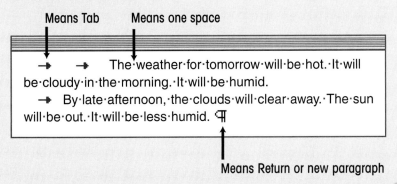

→　　→　　The·weather·for·tomorrow·will·be·hot.·It·will be·cloudy·in·the·morning.·It·will·be·humid.
　　→　By·late·afternoon,·the·clouds·will·clear·away.··The·sun will·be·out.·It·will·be·less·humid. ¶

Means Return or new paragraph

Look at the nonprinting characters in the picture above.

1. What is the problem with the text?

2. How would you fix this problem?

Critical Thinking
What key might you use to remove a Tab?

Applying: Organizing a List

Word processing can be used to organize information. You can organize a list of things you need to do.

Example

Joe wants to use word processing to organize his list of jobs. Put Joe's list in order of importance.

Call Lucy about a concert.   Buy a CD for a gift.
Take out the garbage.   Rent a video game.
Wash the car.   Finish my science project.

STEP 1   GET READY   What do you need to do first?
Make a new document. Type each job above on a separate line. Press the Return (or Enter) key after each job.

STEP 2   THINK   What do you know about the information?
Decide which is the most important job on the list. Decide which is the least important job.

STEP 3   APPLY   Organize the information.
Move the most important job to first on the list. Move the least important to last. Put the middle jobs in order of importance too. Number the jobs from 1 to 6. Press the Tab key after each number. This is how the list might look.

1. Take out the garbage.
2. Finish my science project.
3. Call Lucy about a concert.
4. Wash the car.
5. Buy a CD for a gift.
6. Rent a video game.

Remember
You can save and print from the menu or toolbar.

STEP 4   CHECK   Does the information look correct?
Read the list. Fix any errors. Save and print.

6·6 Lab Practice

GET READY to organize each list. Answer the questions under THINK. APPLY what you know to put each list in order. CHECK your finished work.

1. A librarian needs a list of the favorite books for the week. Put the list below in alphabetical order. Do not use the word *the* to put the list in order. Then number it from 1 to 5.

> *Wuthering Heights*   *Macbeth*
> *Lord of the Flies*   *The Great Gatsby*
> *The Red Badge of Courage*

THINK
Which title starts with the letter closest to the beginning of the alphabet?
Which title starts with the letter closest to the end of the alphabet?

2. A receptionist needs a list of steps to make a letter. Put the steps below in order. Then delete the question marks and number the steps.

> *Step ? Print the letter.*
> *Step ? Type the letter.*
> *Step ? Make a new document.*
> *Step ? Save the letter.*

THINK
What is the first step? What is the last step?

Making Connections

Make a list of things you need to do this week in math, science, social studies, or language arts. Use the computer to put them in order from most important to least important. Number them. Print the list and post it where you'll see it.

✓ Check off each item after you have completed it.

Summary

| **Basic Word Processing** |
| *Word processing software is used to write and edit text.* |

- **To start a new document** choose New or Open from the toolbar.
- **To enter text** use the keyboard.
- **To add text** type letters or words where you want new text.
- **To delete text** use the Backspace key or the Delete key.
- **To move text** select it, remove it with the Cut command, then place it somewhere else with the Paste command.
- **To make a copy of text** use the Copy and Paste commands.
- **To organize information** use word processing to put a list in order.

cursor

delete

document

edit

indent

word processing

word wrap

Vocabulary Review

Complete each sentence with a word from the list.

1. _____ is a computer program that helps you type and change text.

2. When you take something out of a document you _____ it.

3. A _____ is a blinking line that shows where text is entered on the screen.

4. The space at the start of a paragraph is an _____.

5. _____ moves text to the next line after filling the current line.

6. A letter or report are examples of a _____.

7. When you _____ a document, you change text that is already entered.

Chapter Quiz

Answer the following questions.

LESSONS 6·1 and 6·2

Word Processing

1. What are three basic tasks that you can do with word processing?
2. Which key do you use to indent the start of a paragraph?

LESSONS 6·3 and 6·4

Editing and Replacing Text

3. Name one way to edit text.
4. Which keys can be used for removing text?
5. How can you replace a word using the mouse and the keyboard?

LESSON 6·5

Computer Tip
The Edit menu has commands for moving text.

Moving Text

6. What are two commands you can use to move text from one paragraph to another?
7. In which menu do you find the Cut, Copy, and Paste commands?

LESSON 6·6

Applying: Organizing a List

8. What are two reasons to organize a list?

Group Activity

With your group, create a new document. Type a list of your favorite musicians. Put the list in alphabetical order. Then have group members take turns typing one sentence about his or her favorite musician. Decide the order of the sentences to make one paragraph. Remember to indent the first sentence of the paragraph. Check the list and paragraph for mistakes. Fix any errors.

This computer operator is typing messages. The messages will appear on the scoreboard. The computer checks the spelling before the messages appear in front of the fans. Why is this important?

What You Need to Know

How to use a mouse

How to use a keyboard

How to use menus and toolbars

How to use a dialog box

How to make a document

This chapter is about Checking Documents.

What You Will Learn

About checking documents

How to find and replace text

How to check spelling

How to check grammar

How to analyze errors in a document

Words to Know

case sensitive	this indicates that the computer will recognize the case (uppercase or lower case letters) of a word or phrase
ignore button	a dialog box button that gives a command to skip past highlighted text
resume button	a dialog box button that gives a command to start again

Journal Project

Start a journal named *Technology Journal.* Use word processing to write the journal for one week. Write about all the things you use that have computers inside. Describe the effects that these computers have in your life. An example is shown below. Do these computers make tasks easier or faster to do? Then share your observations with your classmates.

Monday, May 7: I used my calculator to do math homework. Without it, long division would take me a long time to do. The calculator helped me do these problems in less time.

Learning Objectives

- Explain the purpose of checking a document.

- Find words and phrases using the Find command.

- Change words and phrases using the Replace command.

- Find and correct spelling errors.

- Find and correct errors in grammar.

- Apply Spelling and Grammar commands to edit a journal.

- PROBLEM SOLVING: Solve problems by using the Find command.

- COMPUTERS IN YOUR LIFE: Use the Spelling and Grammar commands to check a letter.

It is important to check for mistakes in spelling and grammar. Grammar is the correct use of language. In school, spelling and grammar mistakes can make your writing confusing to read. It can also mean a lower grade.

Remember
A document is a letter, report, or other text you type with word processing. See Lesson 6.1.

When you make a document, you should check and edit it. When you check a document, you look for mistakes. When you edit a document, you make changes to it. Word processing software can help you check and edit documents quickly.

Look at the document below. It has several spelling and grammar mistakes. Try to find them.

Document with mistakes

> Mr. Henry Jones hass taught science in the high school for 20 years. Now he are about to retire. Henry made science an adventures. All of us have graet storys to tell about his class.

Now look at the finished document below. The writer used the Spelling and Grammar commands to check the work. These commands helped the writer find and fix the spelling and grammar mistakes. The writer also used the Find and Replace commands to change a name. The writer then saved the finished document as *Mr. Jones*.

Finished document

> Mr. Henry Jones has taught science in the high school for 20 years. Now he is about to retire. Mr. Jones made science an adventure. All of us have great stories to tell about his class.

The table below shows the commands the writer used to check and edit the document named *Mr. Jones*. You can use these commands to check and edit your documents.

Checking and Editing Commands	
Command	What It Does
Find	It finds a word or phrase in a document.
Replace or Find/Change	It finds a word or phrase in a document. Then it changes that word or phrase to another.
Spelling or Spell Check	It compares words in the document to words in a dictionary. Highlights spelling mistakes. Then it suggests corrections.
Grammar or Grammar Check	It finds mistakes in punctuation, grammar, and capitalization. Then it suggests corrections.

 LESSON REVIEW

1. What are two commands that a writer can use to check a document?

2. **CRITICAL THINKING** What should you do before you give a document to your teacher?

On the Cutting Edge

A WORD PROCESSING STAR

The first word processing application for personal computers that was widely sold was WordStar. It was made by Bob Barnaby and Seymour Rubinstein, who formed the company Micropro International. They released WordStar in 1979.

WordStar users did not have a mouse to point and click on commands. Users had to give commands using the keyboard. Many editing commands were given using the Shift or Control key with a letter key. For example, to make a Tab indent you would have typed Shift + I.

Seymour Rubinstein was one inventor of WordStar.

7·2 Finding Text

Suppose you want to find a word or phrase in a document. You do not have to read the whole document. You can use the Find command to quickly locate any word or phrase each time it appears.

Select the Find command in the Edit Menu to open the Find dialog box. Look at the Find dialog box below.

Remember
See Lesson 3.1 to review selecting commands and menus. See Lesson 3.2 to review how to use a dialog box.

Type the word or phrase you want to find here.

Click on this button to find the word in another place.

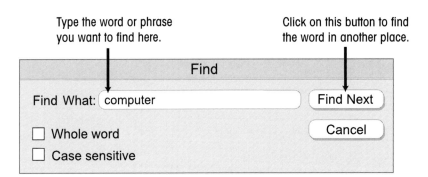

You type the word or phrase you want to find next to Find What. Then click on the Find Next button. The first place that the word appears in the text will be highlighted. Then click Find Next in the dialog box. The next place the word appears in the document will be highlighted. If you keep pressing Find Next, your computer will check the whole document.

▶ **LESSON REVIEW**

1. How do you tell the computer which word or words to find?

2. **CRITICAL THINKING** Why is using the Find command useful for finding words in a long document?

7·2 Lab Practice

Open the document named *Actor*. To find the word *actor,*
follow the steps below. Count the number of times this
word is found.

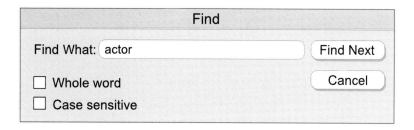

Find		
Find What: actor		Find Next
☐ Whole word		Cancel
☐ Case sensitive		

STEP 1   Place the cursor at the beginning of the document.
Select the Find command in the Edit menu.

STEP 2   Enter **actor** next to Find What in the Find dialog box.

STEP 3   Click on the Find Next button. The first place *actor*
appears will be highlighted.

STEP 4   Click on the Find Next button to find the next place
actor appears. Continue to click Find Next until you get to
the end of the document.

STEP 5   Check Your Work: How many times did you find the
word *actor*? What else did you find?

▶ **More Practice**

Use the document named *Actor*. Find the word **movie**.
Count the number of times this word appears. Check
your work.

Suppose you wrote a story about Will Smith. The first place you use his name, you write his full name. Then you write only *Will*. You decide to change *Will* to *Smith*. It would take a long time to find and change each *Will* to *Smith*. The Replace or Find/Change command can help.

The Replace or Find/Change command finds every place that a word or phrase appears. Then you can replace the word or phrase with a new word or phrase automatically.

Select Replace or Find/Change from the Edit menu. A dialog box appears. It may be called a Replace dialog box or a Find/Change dialog box. Look at the example below.

First, type the word or phrase you want to replace next to Find What or Find. Then, type the new word or phrase next to Replace With or Change. Last, click on the Find Next button. The computer finds and highlights the word or phrase the first place it appears.

Suppose that your story includes the name William. If you type *Will* into the Find dialog box, it will find the *Will* in *William*. It will also find the letters *will* in such words as *willing*. To find only the four letters W-i-l-l, check the whole word box before you click the Find button or Find Next button.

Click here to begin.

Now you have three choices about what to do next.

Using the Replace or Find/Change Dialog Box		
What you want to do	How to do it	What happens next
To change the highlighted word at that place in the document,	click the Replace or Change Button.	The next place the word or phrase appears will be highlighted.
To change the highlighted word at all places where it appears,	click the Replace All or Change All Button.	You see a message box telling you that replacements have been made.
To skip past the highlighted word,	click the Find Next Button.	The next place the word appears will be highlighted.

Suppose you want to replace the name *Will* in a document. You can type *Will* with a capital *W*. The computer will then find the words *will* and *Will*. To find only the name *Will*, you have to tell the computer to look for *Will* with a capital *W*. To do this, you must check Match case or Case sensitive in the dialog box. This is shown in the lower left corner of the diagram on page 126.

Capital letters are uppercase. The case means whether or not a character is capitalized. **Case sensitive** means that the computer will only recognize the case of the word or phrase you want to find or replace.

▶ **LESSON REVIEW**

1. What does the Replace or Find/Change command do?

2. What do you click to skip past a highlighted word?

3. **CRITICAL THINKING** Why would you use Match case or Case sensitive in the Replace dialog box?

7·3 Lab Practice

Open the document named Actor. Then follow the steps below.

STEP 1 Select the Replace or Find/Change command from the Edit menu. The dialog box appears.

STEP 2 Type the word **movie** in the Find What or Find box. Click on the whole word box to check it.

STEP 3 Type the words **motion picture** in the Replace With or Change box.

STEP 4 Click on the Find Next button.

> I like to see a movie about once a week.

STEP 5 Click on Replace or Change. Then click on Find Next.

> I like to see a motion picture about once a week.

STEP 6 If you do not want to replace *movie* now, just click on Find Next.

STEP 7 Check Your Work: How many times did you click on the Replace or Change button? How many times does the phrase *motion picture* appear in the text now?

▶ **More Practice**

Use the document named *Actor*. Replace the word **clothes** with the word **costume**. Check your work.

PROBLEM SOLVING
The Word Cannot Be Found

After writing your science report, you find out that the word *petri* is a lowercase word. You know that you made it uppercase. You decide to find and replace *Petri* with *petri*. You use the Replace or Find/Change dialog box to make this change.

The computer gives you this message: "The search item was not found." To solve this problem, read your document until you find the word you want to replace. Part of it is shown below.

I checked each *Petrie* dish. In the first *Petrie* dish, no mold had grown. In the second *Petrie* dish, a lot of mold had grown.

The first time the word appears, it is spelled *Petrie*. Now use the Replace command again. Enter **Petrie** next to *Find What* in the dialog box. Replace it with the correct spelling and capitalization.

When a computer cannot find a word you want to replace, look for a spelling mistake.

Look at the diagram below.

What should you type next to Replace With in the dialog box?

Critical Thinking

You try several times. The computer still cannot find the word you want to replace. What might you try?

Find/Change		
Find What: Petrie		Find Next
Replace With:		Replace
☑ Whole word		Replace All
☑ Case sensitive		Cancel

Word processing programs can scan a document to find spelling mistakes. This is called a **spell check**. The spell check compares all the words in the document against a built-in dictionary. It can find misspelled words like *ti*, incorrect capitalizations like *joHn* and repeated words like *to the the moon*.

Remember
See Lesson 3.1 to review selecting commands and menus, and Lesson 3.2 to review how to use a dialog box.

Select the Spelling command to get the Spelling dialog box. An example is shown below. The dialog box shows the mistakes found in the text.

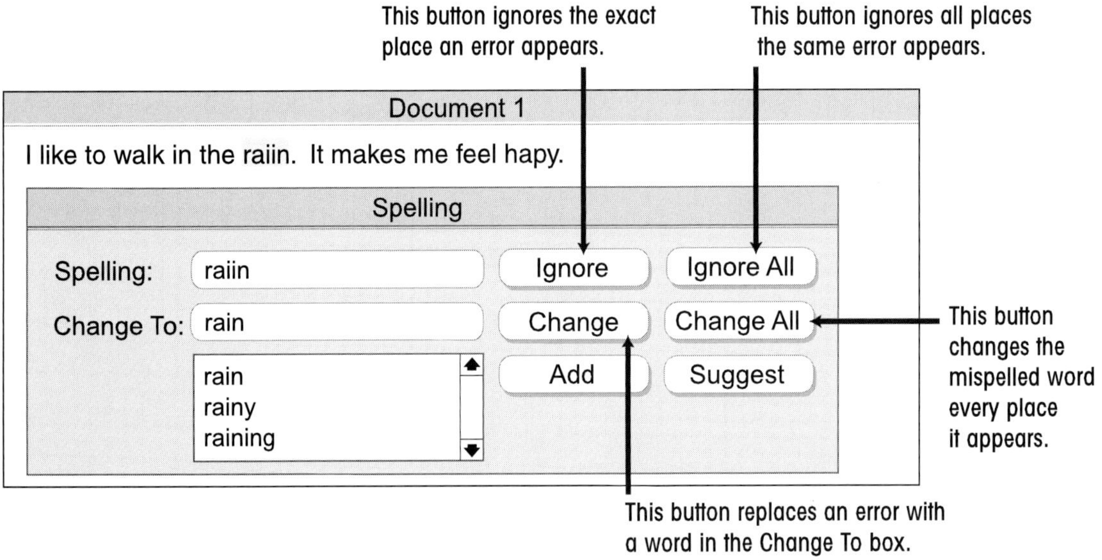

This button ignores the exact place an error appears.

This button ignores all places the same error appears.

Document 1

I like to walk in the raiin. It makes me feel hapy.

Spelling

Spelling: raiin   Ignore   Ignore All

Change To: rain   Change   Change All

            rain   Add   Suggest
            rainy
            raining

This button changes the mispelled word every place it appears.

This button replaces an error with a word in the Change To box.

The spell check usually suggests a correction. Click on the correction you want from the suggestions. To fix the mistake, click on the Change button. The next mistake is highlighted automatically. If you want to fix the mistake every place it appears, click the Change All button.

Sometimes the change you want is not suggested. If you typed *softar* instead of *software*, suggestions might include *soft*, *softer*, and *softly*. To correct the error, place the cursor in the highlighted word. Then change it to the word you want, *software*. Click the Change button to replace *softar* with *software*.

Look at the diagram below. The spell check has highlighted a repeated word. When this happens, click the Delete button. The repeated word will be deleted.

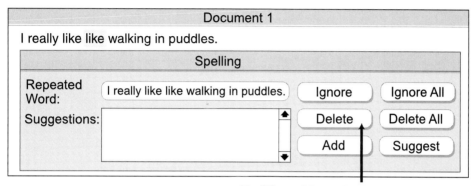

The "Change" button becomes a "Delete" button.

Sometimes, the spell check may suggest a change you do not want. If so, click the Ignore button. The Ignore button means to skip the text. The spell check will move to the next error. If you think the mistake will appear often, you can click on the Ignore All button. The spell check will not highlight the mistake again.

Suppose you click into the document window while the Spelling dialog box is open. When you click back on the dialog box, it may have a Resume or Start button. The Resume button means to start again. Click on the Resume or Start button to continue the spell check.

▶ **LESSON REVIEW**

1. What types of mistakes does the Spelling command find?

2. What can you do if you want to accept a change suggested by the computer?

3. **CRITICAL THINKING** Why do you think the Change button becomes a Delete button when spell check finds a repeated word?

7·4 Lab Practice

Open the file called *Science Report.* To correct the spelling, follow the steps.

> The microscoope is an important scientific tool. In 1665, English scientist Roberte Hooke used a simple microscoope. He examined cork. What he saw looked like like little boxes. He named them cells.

STEP 1   Select the Spelling command from the Edit menu or the Tools menu. The Spelling dialog box will appear and highlight the first mistake, *microscoope.*

STEP 2   To correct the spelling of *microscope,* click on the Change button. To correct the mistake every place it appears, click on the Change All button.

STEP 3   To correct the spelling of *Roberte,* type **Robert** into the Change To box. Click the Change button.

STEP 4   To skip the word *Hooke,* click on the Ignore button.

STEP 5   To remove the repeated word *like,* click on the Delete button.

STEP 6   Check Your Work: How many mistakes did you find in the document?

▶ **More Practice**

Open the file called *More Practice 7-4.* Use the Spelling command to find and correct the misspelled words.

> The hoome team bleeachers are ful of chering students.

Word processing programs can look through a document to find grammar mistakes. This is called a *grammar check*. The grammar check can find mistakes in grammar, punctuation, and capitalization.

Select the Grammar command from the Edit menu or Tools menu. The Grammar dialog box opens. It shows the mistakes and suggestions. Look at the example below. The labels tell you what to do.

Highlighted sentence   Mistake appears here   Click to leave the highlighted sentence as is

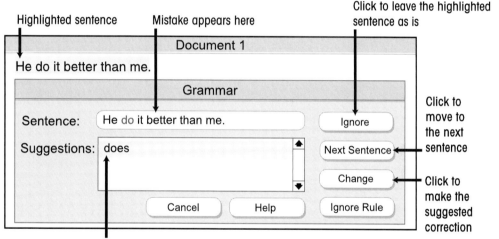

Suggested correction appears here

The Grammar dialog box works like the Spelling dialog box. It will tell you how to fix the mistake in the Suggestions box. To make a change, click on the Change button. To leave the sentence or word as it is, click on the Ignore button.

 LESSON REVIEW

1. What types of errors does the Grammar command find?

2. **CRITICAL THINKING** Compare the Spelling and Grammar commands. How are they similar?

7·5 Lab Practice

Open the file called *Practice 7-5*. It has the text shown below. To correct the grammar, follow the steps.

> The family have ten member.

STEP 1   Select the Grammar command from the Edit menu or the Tools menu. The Grammar dialog box will appear.

STEP 2   The computer begins to check the grammar. It highlights the errors and makes the following suggestions:
- Use *has* instead of *have*.
- The word *ten* does not agree with *member*. Consider *members* instead of *member*.

STEP 3   Click on the Change button to make the suggested correction.

STEP 4   Check Your Work: How can you double-check that you have corrected all errors?

▶ More Practice

Open the file called *More Practice 7-5*. Correct the grammar. Check your work.

> There is five person in the family.

COMPUTERS IN YOUR LIFE
Using the Spelling and Grammar Commands

Don is applying for a new job. He just wrote his cover letter. The cover letter explains why he wants the job. It also explains why he thinks he is the best person for the job.

The person reviewing applications reads the cover letter first. It is very important that Don's cover letter not have any spelling or grammar mistakes. Don is about to use the Spelling and Grammar commands to check his letter before he sends it. Here is part of the letter he wrote.

Carefully read the part of Don's letter shown below. Look for spelling and grammar errors. List the corrections.

Dear Mrs. Bailey,

     I am applying for the position in slaes. I am verry interested in the open position. I has five years of experience in this field. My work includs decreasing costs and increasing sales. I fell that I would make a good addition to you company.

              Sincerely,
              Don Reese

Critical Thinking
Why does the person reviewing applications care about spelling and grammar mistakes?

When you use the Replace, Spelling and Grammar commands, you need to analyze information to correct the errors.

Example

Lee used these commands to edit the Technology Journal he made for the chapter project. He followed the steps below.

> Mondey, June 7: I used my calculator to do the math homewrk. Before, Nick helped me. I needed a lot of time to do cross products an long division. now the calculator help me completed word problems in less time.

STEP 1   GET READY   What do you need to do first?
Open your journal.

STEP 2   THINK   What do you know about the information?
Think about how to select commands and use dialog boxes.

STEP 3   APPLY   Analyze the information.
Decide which word or words to change. Use the Replace command. Analyze suggested corrections made by the Spelling and Grammar dialog boxes. Make the best choices.

This is how Lee's journal might look.

> Monday, June 7: I used my calculator to do the math homework. Before, Nicholas helped me. I needed a lot of time to do cross products and long division. Now the calculator helps me complete word problems in less time.

7·6 Lab Practice

GET READY to analyze information from the Replace, Spelling and Grammar commands. Answer the questions under THINK. APPLY what you know to correct the errors. CHECK your finished work.

1. Open the file called *Video log*. Choose the Spelling or Grammar command from the Edit or Tools menu. Check the document.

THINK What spelling or grammar mistakes will you change? What mistakes will you ignore?

VIDEO LOG
By using the VCR, I can go to socerr practice. Then I can wathc the program when I get home. Here is my log of videos:
Wednesday: I used the VCR to record a program about fish. The most interesting fish are in the Class Agnatha.
Thursday: I used the VCR to record a programs about tigers.
Friday: I used the VCR to record a program about the baseball and Yogi Berra.
Saturday: I used the VCR to record a program about surfing

2. You want to change *VCR* to *videocassette recorder* in the whole document. Use the Replace or Find/Change command to make the changes.

THINK What words do you type in the Find What or Find box? What do you type in the Replace With or Change box? Which button will you click to make the change?

Making Connections

Print your journal from the chapter project. Check and edit it on the print out. Then use the Replace, Spelling and Grammar commands. Make the corrections. Print the document again. Then compare the two. Did the commands find all the mistakes you did? Did you find any that the commands missed?

Summary

Checking Documents
Most word processing programs have commands that help you find and correct mistakes in a document.

- **Find** specific words and phrases using the Find command and dialog box.
- **Replace text** using the Replace or Find/Change command and dialog box.
- **Check and correct spelling** using the Spelling command and dialog box.
- **Check and correct grammar** using the Grammar command and dialog box.
- **Analyze information** and decide which corrections suggested by the computer to use to correct mistakes.

case sensitive

ignore button

resume button

Vocabulary Review

Complete each sentence with a term from the list.

1. _____ indicates that the computer will be sensitive to the case of the word or phrase you want to replace.

2. When you want the Spelling command to start checking a document again, you click the _____.

3. The dialog box button that means to skip past highlights text is the _____.

Chapter Quiz

Answer the following questions.

LESSON 7·1

Why Do We Check a Document?

1. When you finish entering text in a document, what should you do next?

LESSONS 7·2 and 7·3

Computer Tip
The names of the commands studied in this chapter tell you what they do in a document.

Finding Text and Replacing Text

2. How can the Find command help you check a document?

3. What does the Replace or Find/Change command let you do with a word or phrase in a document?

4. What does checking the Case Sensitive option in the Replace dialog box tell the computer?

LESSONS 7·4 to 7·6

Checking Spelling and Grammar

5. What types of mistakes does the Spelling command find?

6. What does the Ignore button in the Spelling dialog box do?

7. How does the Grammar command help you with a document?

8. Why is it important to analyze the information a spelling or grammar check gives you?

Group Activity

Work in pairs. Exchange the *Techology Journal* that you created for the chapter project. Be sure that you have checked the spelling and grammar using the Spelling and Grammar commands. Proofread each other's report. List any mistakes that the computer missed. Tell how to correct them. Why is it important to read and check a document after the computer has checked it?

People all over the world use computers to design documents. What gets your attention when you look at the documents in this photo?

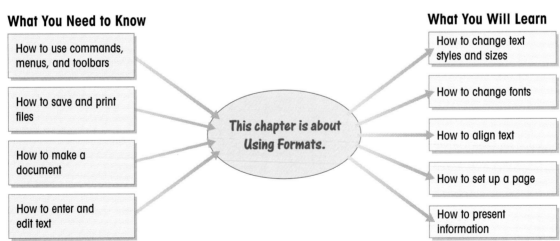

What You Need to Know

- How to use commands, menus, and toolbars
- How to save and print files
- How to make a document
- How to enter and edit text

This chapter is about Using Formats.

What You Will Learn

- How to change text styles and sizes
- How to change fonts
- How to align text
- How to set up a page
- How to present information

Chapter 8 — Using Formats

Words to Know

format	the way text looks on a page
style	the way text characters look—regular, **bold**, *italic*, or <u>underline</u>
bold	a style that makes characters look darker or thicker
italic	a style that makes characters slant to the right
point size	a measure of the height of characters
font	the design of text characters
margin	the space from the edge of the paper to the text area
alignment	the way text lines up with the margins

Formatting Poster Project

Look for examples of how formats are used in newspapers and magazines. Cut out four examples from different newspapers and magazines. Paste them on posterboard to create a Format Poster. Label the kinds of formatting used. Explain how the formatting makes the page more interesting or conveys a message.

Learning Objectives

- Explain the use of formats.
- Change the style and size of text in a document.
- Change fonts in a document.
- Set up tabs and alignment.
- Apply formats to making a poster.
- PROBLEM SOLVING: Solve problems by using formatting to fit an extra line.
- COMPUTERS ON THE JOB: Use formatting to make an invitation.

8·1   What Are Formats?

Word processing programs have features that let you change the **format** of a document. The format of a document is the way the text looks on a page.

Using Formats

Formats can make text more interesting to read. They can help organize a document. Formats can draw attention to different parts of your document. Here are some of the things you can do with formats.

- make text larger or smaller
- make text darker
- make text slanted
- underline text
- change the design of the characters in a document
- line up text at the left, right, or in the center
- change the amount of blank space in your document

Look at the two business cards below. Notice how use of text formats makes each one look different.

Remember
Characters are the letters, numbers, and symbols that appear on the screen and in a printed document.

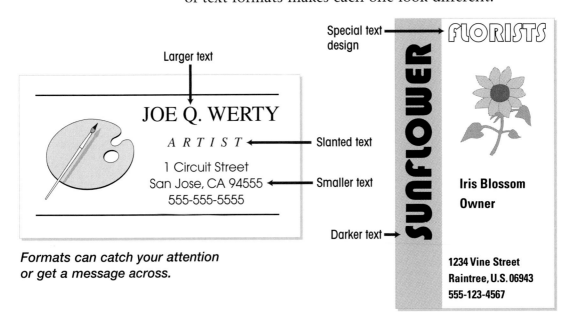

Larger text

JOE Q. WERTY

A R T I S T ← Slanted text

1 Circuit Street
San Jose, CA 94555 ← Smaller text
555-555-5555

Formats can catch your attention or get a message across.

Special text design → ꟻⳑORIꟳꞔꙊ

SUNFLOWER

Iris Blossom
Owner

Darker text →

1234 Vine Street
Raintree, U.S. 06943
555-123-4567

Commands for Formats

You can find the commands for formats in the Format menu. You can also find many of the format commands on the toolbar. Look at the diagram below. You will learn to use these commands in this chapter.

Style buttons

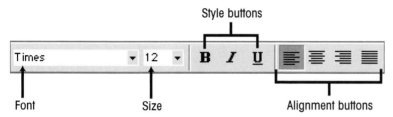

Font   Size   Alignment buttons

▶ **LESSON REVIEW**

1. What are three things you can do with formats?

2. **CRITICAL THINKING** Why would you use different formats in a document?

On the Cutting Edge

TYPING WITH YOUR VOICE

Voice recognition software lets you use your voice to type! This kind of software can work with word processing and other programs. You speak into a microphone and tell the computer what to do. For example, you can say "Open" to open a document. Or you can tell the computer what words to display on the screen. You can even tell the computer how to format text by speaking the commands.

Voice recognition software lets you display text with formats on your screen.

You start by training the computer to understand your words. As you use the program, the computer learns to understand more of your words. This kind of software can be of help to people who cannot type.

CRITICAL THINKING How could this kind of software be helpful to someone who is physically not able to type?

You may want part of your text to look different from the rest. One way to do this is to change its size and **style**. Style is the way the text characters look. Regular text or plain text is the basic style.

Changing Text Style

Style buttons

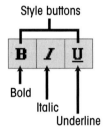

Bold
Italic
Underline

Remember
See lesson 6.4 to review how to select text.

Look at the toolbar buttons on the left. You can use these buttons to change text styles. These styles make text look different. If you select text that already has a style, the toolbar button for that style will look like it has been pressed.

Bold characters are darker or thicker than regular or plain text. Bold style tells you the text is important. *Italic* characters slant to the right. You use italic style for special words, such as the titles of books and plays. Underlined characters have a line below them. You can use underline style to set words apart or for names of columns in a list.

To change the style of text, first select the text you want to change. Then choose the menu command or click the toolbar button for the style you want to use. You can also use the Style menu or the Font command in the Format menu. The Font command opens a Font dialog box like the one below.

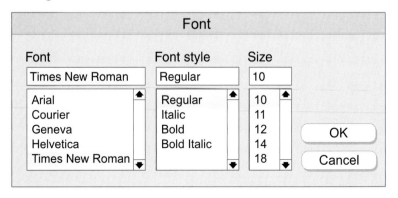

Changing Text Size

Another way to make text look different is to change its **point size**. The point size is a measure of the height of the characters. One point equals $\frac{1}{72}$ of an inch. You can see three different text sizes in the screen below.

> The size of this text is 10 point.
>
> The size of this text is 14 point.
>
> The size of this text is 20 point.

To change the size of text in a document, first select it. Then change the point size in one of the three ways:

- You can use the size list in the toolbar. Look at the example on the right. Click on the Size button to make the size list appear. Some software programs have a Size menu.

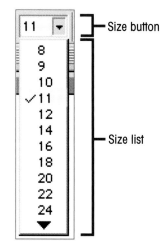

When you click on the down arrow, the Size list drops down.

- You can use special toolbar buttons that change the size by one point. These buttons are called Grow Font and Shrink Font buttons. Look at the examples shown below.

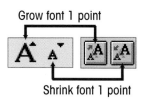

- You can use the Font dialog box. Look at the example on page 144. It has a size list.

example on page 144.

▶ **LESSON REVIEW**

1. Explain how bold and italic text styles can be used.

2. **CRITICAL THINKING** Suppose you make the point size of text larger. Will the text take up more space or less space on the page?

8·2 Lab Practice

Open the *Technology Journal* file you created in Chapter 7. Choose the entry you wrote for *Monday*. To change the style and size of the text, follow the steps below. When you are done, your screen may look something like the one shown.

Monday, May 7

I used my *calculator* to do math homework. Without it, long division would take me a long time to do. The *calculator* helped me do these problems in less time.

STEP 1   Select the word **Monday** and the date. Use the toolbar or menus to make the words bold.

STEP 2   Select the rest of the text in the *Monday* entry. Use the toolbar or menus to change the point size to 14.

STEP 3   Select the name of one item of technology. Use the toolbar or menus to change the style to italic. Save your work.

STEP 4   Check Your Work: Select the word **Monday**. Look at the toolbar. Which button looks like it has been pressed?

 More Practice

Use the *Technology Journal*. Choose the entry for *Tuesday*. Change the style of the day and date to bold.

Change the point size of all the text to 16.

Change the style of the first sentence to italic. Check your work.

Another way to format text is to use a specific **font**. The font is the design of the text characters.

Choosing Fonts

Look at the table below. Notice the names of the four different fonts. They are in the first column. The letters in the word *Computer* look different in each font. You can change the way text looks by changing the font.

Examples of Fonts			
Font Name	**Regular**	**Bold**	**Italic**
Times	Computer	**Computer**	*Computer*
Helvetica	Computer	**Computer**	*Computer*
Courier	Computer	**Computer**	*Computer*
Futura	Computer	**Computer**	*Computer*

The fonts you use can create a mood or feeling. Look at the fonts shown below. Some fonts are friendly or fun-looking. Some are easier to read than others. Some have special uses.

Friendly

Easy to read

Harder to read

SPECIAL

Look at the diagrams below. You can choose a font from a **Font** list. When you click the arrow, a list of fonts drops down. You can scroll through the list to find different fonts. Then you can choose a font by clicking on it. In some word processing programs, you can also choose a font from a Font menu.

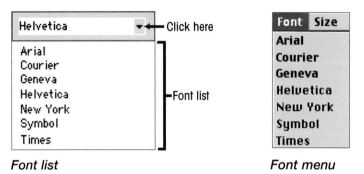

Font list   *Font menu*

Changing Fonts

You can change the font of text you have already entered. First select the text you want to change. Then you can choose the font. Only the font of the selected text will change.

You can also change the font before you enter text. First put the cursor where you want a new font to be. Choose the font you want to use. Then enter text. The text you enter will be in the font you chose.

 **LESSON REVIEW**

1. Where can you find a list of fonts to choose from?

2. What are two ways to change the font using the Font command?

3. **CRITICAL THINKING** Would you use the same font for a letter to your best friend and a report for your class? Explain your answer.

8·3 Lab Practice

Open your *Technology Journal* file. Choose the entry for *Wednesday*. To change the fonts used, follow the steps below.

STEP 1 Select the day and date. Change the font using the Font list in the toolbar or the Font menu.

STEP 2 Select the rest of the text. Choose another font from the Font list or Font menu.

STEP 3 Put the cursor at the end of the text in your file. Press the Enter (or Return) key.

STEP 4 Choose a third font. Enter today's date.

STEP 5 Add the following text:

Today I learned how to format text by changing fonts.

STEP 6 Save your work.

STEP 7 Check Your Work: Compare the fonts in the *Wednesday* entry to the fonts used in the *Monday* entry. Do they look different?

▶ More Practice

Use your *Technology Journal*. Choose the entry for *Thursday*. Change the font of the day and date.

Change the font of the rest of the text.

Use a different font to add a new line of text at the end. Check your work.

Word processing software usually lines up text along the left **margin**. The margin is the space from the edge of the paper to the text area. The **alignment** of text is the way it lines up with the margins.

Using Alignment Commands

You can use commands to change the text alignment. The diagram at the left shows toolbar buttons that are used for alignment.

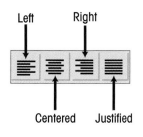

Left   Right

Centered   Justified

The table below shows four examples of text alignment. The word **justified** means that the text lines up along both the left margin and the right margin.

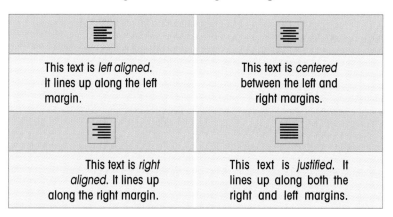

This text is *left aligned*. It lines up along the left margin.	This text is *centered* between the left and right margins.
This text is *right aligned*. It lines up along the right margin.	This text is *justified*. It lines up along both the right and left margins.

You can change the alignment before you enter text. Click on an Alignment button. Then enter text. All the paragraphs will have the alignment you choose until you change it again.

You can also change the alignment after you have entered text. Place the cursor anywhere in the text you want to change. Then click on an Alignment button. Only that paragraph will have the new alignment.

Using Tabs

You can indent text by pressing the Tab key. The cursor or text moves to the right. Most word processing software is set up so that text indents $\frac{1}{2}$ inch each time you press the Tab key. You can control the amount of indent by changing the Tab settings.

Look at the screen below. It shows the horizontal ruler at the top of a document window. To set a tab, click on the ruler where you want the tab to be. A tab symbol will appear on the ruler. You can click and drag the tab symbol to move it. In the example below, a tab is set at the 1-inch mark.

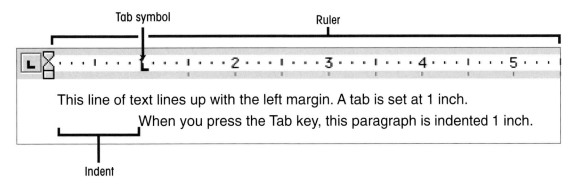

Tab symbol   Ruler

This line of text lines up with the left margin. A tab is set at 1 inch.
When you press the Tab key, this paragraph is indented 1 inch.

Indent

▶ **LESSON REVIEW**

1. What are two ways to change how text lines up?

2. How is left-aligned text different from justified text?

3. **CRITICAL THINKING** How might you use alignment to help make text stand out?

8·4 Lab Practice

Open your *Technology Journal* file. Choose the entry for *Thursday*. To change the text alignment, follow the steps below.

STEP 1 Place the cursor at the beginning of the first paragraph. Point your mouse on the 1-inch mark in the ruler at the top of your screen. Look at the diagram below.

Point here

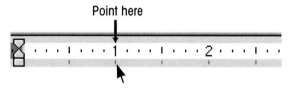

STEP 2 Click on the 1-inch make on the ruler. This will set a new 1-inch tab.

STEP 3 Press the Tab key to indent the first line of the paragraph. The cursor will be at the 1-inch mark.

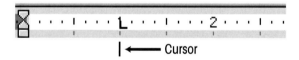

|◀—— Cursor

STEP 4 Place the cursor anywhere in the paragraph. Click on the Justified button to align the text. Save and print your work.

STEP 5 Check Your Work: On your printout, measure the tab indent of the first line with a ruler. How many inches is the indent?

▶ More Practice

Use the *Technology Journal*. Align the day and date with the center of the page.

Indent the next line of text $1\frac{1}{2}$ inches.

Right-align the rest of the text. Check your work.

COMPUTERS ON THE JOB
Invitation Maker

Marco Crane is an invitation maker. He creates invitations for special occasions. He likes his job because he gets to use his sense of design and word processing skills.

Marco uses his computer to format the invitations. He chooses fonts to match the occasion. He also chooses the size, style, and alignment for different parts of the invitation. Here is one invitation he is working on.

Marco is making an invitation for a birthday party.

IT'S A PARTY!

Join Me For My Birthday.

Who: Enrique Martinez
Date: Saturday, April 25
Time: 12:00 to 2:00 P.M.
Place: Bowlmore Lanes, 42 Main Street
For: Bowling and Pizza!

Use the invitation to answer the questions.

1. What would make the first line stand out more?

2. What's wrong with the text *Time:?*

3. How should the text *Time:* be formatted? Why?

Critical Thinking
Suppose Marco is making an invitation for a wedding. Do you think it should look similar to the one shown here? Why or why not?

Another way to change format is to change the way a page is set up. The Page Setup command lets you change
- the page length and width
- the size of a margin

Changing Page Margins

A margin is the space from the edge of the paper to the edge of the text area. There are four margins: top, bottom, left, and right. By changing the margins, you make more or less space around the text area. The screen below shows a dialog box for setting up margins. You can set each of the four margins separately.

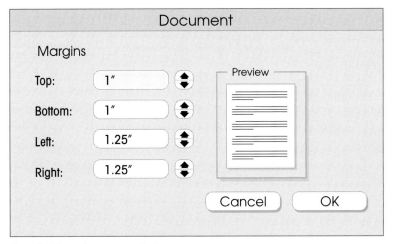

By clicking the up and down arrows, you can make a margin larger or smaller.

To format the page margins, click in the box for the margin you want to change. You can click on the arrows at the side of the box. Or you can select the measurement that is already there to highlight it. Then type in a new measurement. You may have a **Preview area** that shows you how your document will look as you change the margins.

Changing Paper Size

You can change the size of the paper when you print a document. The diagram below shows a Page Setup dialog box. Notice the arrows near the top. You can click on the arrows to show a list of paper sizes. Then, you can choose the paper size.

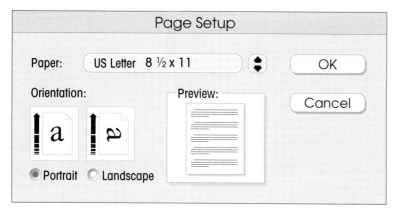

You can also use the Page Setup command to change the *orientation*. This means which edge of the paper will be the top of your printed page.

Look at the diagrams on the right. When you print a document with the short edge of the paper at the top of the page, it is called a *portrait orientation*. If the long edge of the paper is at the top of the page, it is called a *landscape orientation*.

portrait orientation

 **LESSON REVIEW**

1. How can you make more space on both sides of the text in a document?

2. **CRITICAL THINKING** When might you want the long edge of the paper to be at the top of a page?

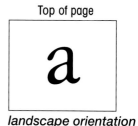

landscape orientation

8·5 Lab Practice

Open your *Technology Journal* file. Choose the entry for *Friday*.
To change the page margins, follow the steps. When you are
done, your screen may look something like the one below.

Friday, May 11

     Today, I used a tape recorder to record
my history class lecture. I can play the lecture
back to see if I missed any important facts when
I was taking notes.

STEP 1   Open the dialog box for setting up margins.

STEP 2   Click in the box for the **Left** margin. Enter 2.

STEP 3   Press the Tab key to move to the box for the **Right** margin.
Enter 3.

STEP 4   Click the OK button. Save and print your work.

STEP 5   Check Your Work: Measure the margins of your printed
page with a ruler. Is the left margin 2 inches wide? Is the
right margin 3 inches wide?

▶ **More Practice**

Use your *Technology Journal*. Make both the top and bottom
margins 2 inches larger. Make both the left and
right margins each $\frac{1}{2}$ inch smaller. Check your work.

PROBLEM SOLVING
Fitting Extra Lines

The text of the letter below is too long. The last two lines do not fit on the page.

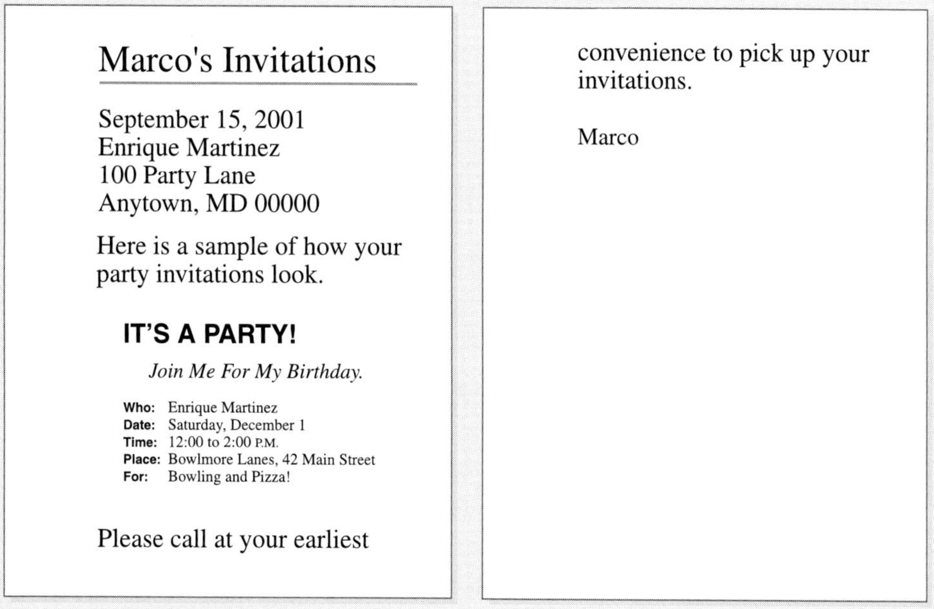

Marco's Invitations

September 15, 2001
Enrique Martinez
100 Party Lane
Anytown, MD 00000

Here is a sample of how your party invitations look.

IT'S A PARTY!

Join Me For My Birthday.

Who: Enrique Martinez
Date: Saturday, December 1
Time: 12:00 to 2:00 P.M.
Place: Bowlmore Lanes, 42 Main Street
For: Bowling and Pizza!

Please call at your earliest

---

convenience to pick up your invitations.

Marco

You can solve this problem by using commands for formats. For example, to fit the extra lines on the page you can:
- change some of the page margins
- change the point size of some of the text
- change the font of some of the text

Look at the diagram above.

1. Which margins would you change to correct the problem? How would you change them?

2. How would changing the point size solve the problem?

Critical Thinking
What could you do if the last line still does not fit on the page?

Applying: Presenting a Poster

Formats can be used to present information clearly.

Example

Mandy is making a poster to advertise a concert. The diagram below shows how Mandy's poster looks now.

Format the rest of Mandy's poster.

STEP 1 GET READY What do you need to do first?
Make a new document. Enter the text for the poster. Use Page Setup commands to change the orientation of the paper. Make each margin 1.25". Use Alignment and Style commands to match the screen above. Use 14-point text for the first line, 22-point text for the second line, 36-point text for the third line, and 12-point text for the last line.

STEP 2 THINK What do you know about the information?
Decide which line of text should draw the most attention. Decide what format to use for that part.

STEP 3 APPLY Format the information.
Select the title *Classical Concert*. Center the text. Make the point size 48 points. Choose an interesting font.

STEP 4 CHECK How does the information look?
Look at the poster's title. Make any format changes. Save and name the file **Music Poster**.

GET READY to present information in a poster. Answer the questions under THINK. APPLY what you know to format the information. CHECK your finished work.

Classical Concert

West Side Music Hall June 10, 6 P.M. - 9 P.M.

Come Hear the Music!

Tickets go on sale April 10

1. Jason thinks it is hard to read the second line of the poster above. He wants to move the date and time away from the words **West Side Music Hall**. He thinks he can use a tab to move the date and time. Set the tab and move the text.

   THINK

   How can I set a tab in the document?

   Where should the tab be to make the text easier to read?

2. Louisa thinks the last line is too small. She wants to make the last line stand out more.

   Change the format of the last line.

   THINK

   How can I make the text look different?

Making Connections

Create a poster about a topic you are learning about in math, science, social studies, or language arts. Format your poster to present the information clearly. Display your poster in class for other students to see.

Summary

Using Formats
Formats make text look a certain way. You can use formats to make a document more interesting.

- **Change text style** by using **bold**, *italic,* or <u>underline</u> styles.
- **Change size** of **text characters** by choosing different point sizes from the Size list.
- **Change the text fonts** from the Font list.
- **Set tabs** by clicking in the horizontal ruler where you want the tabs.
- **Align text** using buttons for left, centered, right, or justified alignment.
- **Use the Page Setup commands** to change page margins, choose the paper orientation, and paper size.
- **Present information** in a poster using different formats.

---

alignment
bold
font
format
italic
margin
point size
style

Vocabulary Review
Complete each sentence with a word from the list.

1. The design of the text characters is called the _____.
2. _____ is the way text lines up with the margins.
3. The measure of the height of the characters is _____.
4. When text has _____ style, it slants to the right.
5. The way text looks on a page is the _____ of the document.
6. Bold, italic, and underline are examples of the _____ of characters.
7. The space from the edge of the paper to the text area is the _____.
8. When characters look darker or thicker, they have _____ style.

Chapter Quiz

Answer the following questions.

LESSON 8·1

What Are Formats?

1. What are three things you can do using formats?

LESSONS 8·2 and 8·3

Computer Tip
The Style and alignment buttons are usually found on the toolbar.

Changing Styles, Sizes and Fonts

2. What are three ways to change the style of text?

3. Which size text has taller characters, 12-point text or 20-point text?

4. How can you change the font of text that is already typed?

LESSONS 8·4 and 8·5

Aligning Text and Setting Up the Page

5. How can you indent a paragraph 2 inches?

6. How is centered text lined up with the margins?

7. What are two things you use Page Setup commands for?

8. How could you fit more text in at the bottom of a document?

LESSON 8·6

Applying Formats

9. How can applying formats help you make a good poster?

Group Activity

With your group, create a text newsletter about your school. As a group, choose one of the following topics for your newsletter: favorite teacher, lunch food, favorite class, dress code, clubs, or school trips or dances. All group members should contribute ideas for the newsletter. Take turns typing the text for the newsletter. As a group, decide how to format the newsletter. Display the newsletter in your classroom.

Unit 2 **Review**

Choose the letter of the correct answer.

1. Which task is done to remove a sentence from a document?
   A. Copy and paste text
   B. Delete text
   C. Style text
   D. Enter text

2. Which task is done by using formats?
   A. Find a word in a document
   B. Check spelling and grammar
   C. Put text in italics
   D. Cut and paste text

3. Which task is done when you point, click, and drag the mouse pointer over text?
   A. Select text
   B. Style text
   C. Replace text
   D. Enter text

4. Which task is done when you move a sentence from the third to the fourth paragraph?
   A. Check and correct spelling
   B. Change the font
   C. Cut and paste
   D. Change text alignment

5. Which toolbar button will help you change the alignment of text?

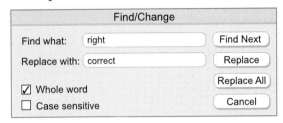

6. Look at the screen below. What will happen when the **Replace** button is pressed?

   A. The word *correct* will be changed to the word *right*.
   B. The word *right* will be changed to the word *correct*.
   C. The word *correct* will be found in the text.
   D. The word *right* will be found in the text.

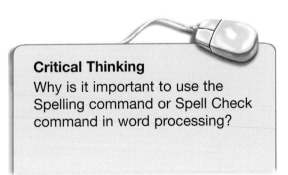

Critical Thinking
Why is it important to use the Spelling command or Spell Check command in word processing?

162

Unit 3 ▶ Databases and Spreadsheets

Chapter 9   **Using Databases**

Chapter 10 **Making Spreadsheets**

Chapter 11 **Working with Spreadsheet Data**

This is a map of Mars' surface. Higher areas are shown in red and white. Lower areas are shown in blue.

During 1998 and 1999, the *Mars Global Surveyor* mission helped scientists make maps of Mars. Read the story on the right to find out how much data was collected to make the maps.

1. How can the data from the *Surveyor* mission help scientists?

2. Why do scientists use computers to store and manage the information they receive from the *Surveyor* mission?

 The Red Planet in 3D

New data from the Mars Global Surveyor satellite are helping scientists make maps of Mars. Scientists have used 27 million measurements of elevation to map the planet s surface. During the Surveyor mission, about 900,000 measurements are collected every day. These data will help NASA choose future landing sites.

This car dealer is searching a database of vehicles at all dealers in the state. The database has information about when new cars will be delivered. Why is this information important to a car dealer?

What You Need to Know

How to use a mouse and a keyboard

How to use commands, menus, and toolbars

How to use a dialog box and scroll bars

How to save and name files

How to enter text

This chapter is about Using Databases.

What You Will Learn

Uses of databases; How to plan a database

How to make and change records

How to find and sort records

How to work with layouts

How to present data

Chapter 9 ▶ Using Databases

Words to Know

database	software that stores similar information in an organized way
field	a place in a database where specific groups of data are entered and stored
record	data about a single person, place, or thing
Browse mode	a view on the screen used to enter data, as well as to add, edit, delete, copy, and sort records
sort	to arrange data in a certain order, such as alphabetical, numerical, or by date
layout	the way fields and records in a database look on the screen

Address Book Project

Build your own database. Start by collecting the street addresses, phone numbers, e-mail addresses, and birth dates of your friends and relatives. Then organize all the information in a table in your notebook. As you go through this chapter, you will use the information in your table to create your own electronic address book.

Learning Objectives

- Identify uses of databases.
- Plan and make database fields.
- Make database records by entering and editing data.
- Move through, copy, and delete records.
- Find and sort records.
- Make a database layout.
- Apply database layout skills to communicating data.
- PROBLEM SOLVING: Solve a problem using Find in a database.
- COMPUTERS IN YOUR LIFE: Search an online database.

9·1 ▶ What Is a Database?

Whenever you need to organize and keep track of large amounts of information, you need a database. If you have an address book, then you already have a **database** on paper. A computer database is software that stores similar information in an organized way.

Look at the diagram below. It shows information about one book in a library. Together, all the information on all the books in a library would make up a library catalog. The catalog is an example of a database file.

Author:	Wharton, Edith, 1862–1937.
Title:	Ethan Frome
Publisher:	New York, C. Scribner's Sons, 1911.
Description:	3 p.l. 3-195 p.20 cm.
	Fiction Wharton

Together, the cards from a library catalog make up a database file.

Here are other examples of databases:
- the local telephone book.
- all the drivers licenses in your state.
- the report cards for all the students in your school.

With a database, you can
- enter and edit information.
- store and organize lots of information easily.
- search for specific information.
- arrange information by putting it in a certain order.
- present information to others using special layouts.
- print reports or forms with your data.

Here are some examples of how you can use a database.
- Print envelopes and labels for large mailings.
- Keep track of club members or team lists.
- Manage a video, music, or coin collection.
- Create a bibliography for a school paper.
- Search on the Internet.

▶ **LESSON REVIEW**

1. How can a database help you manage large amounts of information?

2. Name some examples of databases at your home.

3. **CRITICAL THINKING** What is an advantage of using a database rather than making a list or a table of information?

On the Cutting Edge

WEATHER DATA

Forecasting the weather is faster and better now, thanks to the databases kept by the National Weather Service. Data on temperature, wind speed, air pressure, rain, and snow are put into supercomputers. Database software organizes, stores, and analyzes the data. New data are added each day. This helps weather scientists understand dangerous storms. The database lets them quickly compare old weather data with new data. Then they can make better weather forecasts and warn people when storms are coming. Forecasters also use software to make pictures of storms, such as the hurricane shown in the picture.

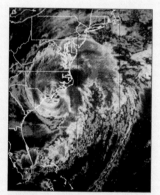

This picture shows a 1996 hurricane on the East Coast of the United States. Red, orange, and yellow show the storm.

CRITICAL THINKING Why do you think weather forecasting has improved with the use of computer databases?

In a database, the same kinds of data are grouped together. For example, in a database for a book collection, all the authors' names make one group. The book titles make another group.

Thinking About the Data

When you create a database, you enter different kinds of data by grouping them. A **field** is a place where each specific group of data is entered and stored.

Before you start a database, do some planning. Start by thinking about the groups of data you want to store. This will help you choose fields for your data. The number of fields you use depends on how many different groups of data you have. The first step in making a database is to identify the groups of data.

Look at the example below. It shows four groups of data used for a book database. They are Author, Book Title, Publisher, and Copyright.

Four field names:

Author	John Steinbeck
Book Title	The Grapes of Wrath
Publisher	The Modern Library
Copyright	1938

Data in four fields

Naming New Fields

Once you have a plan, you can define your fields. When you define fields, you give each one a name and a type. The field name describes the group of data. In the example above, the field names are *Author*, *Book Title*, *Publisher*, and *Copyright*. Choose useful names for fields, so you will remember what data to put in them.

The example below shows six field names used in an address book. It also shows sample data in each field.

Field names		Sample data in each field
Last Name	*Harrison*	
First Name	*George*	
Street	*100 Abbey Road*	
City	*San Francisco*	
State	*California*	
Zip code	*00020*	

Types of Fields

Once you name a field, you decide what type of data will be stored there. The table below shows three types of fields and the kinds of data you would store in them. When you make a new database, you name fields and choose the field type in the Define Fields (or New Field) dialog box.

Type of Field	Kind of Data
Text	Use for letters, numbers, and words. Examples: name, zip code, phone number.
Number	Use for numbers that will be added, subtracted, multiplied, or divided. Example: money
Date	Use for all dates. Example: birthday

▶ **LESSON REVIEW**

1. What two things do you do to define a field?

2. What type of field would you use for a street address?

3. **CRITICAL THINKING** Look at the information about a library book shown on page 166. Suppose you wanted to make a computer database for a library. What fields would you use?

9·2 Lab Practice

Open a new database file. Use the command for naming or defining new fields. To define fields, follow the steps below.

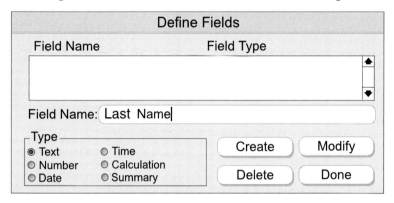

STEP 1 Look at the dialog box above. Click in the Field Name part of the dialog box. Type **Last Name**.

STEP 2 Choose Text as the Field Type. Click the Create (or OK) button to add the field to your database.

STEP 3 Repeat Steps 1 and 2 to make the following field names and field types:

First Name	Text
Street	Text
City	Text
State	Text
Zip Code	Text

STEP 4 Save the database file as *(your name) Address Book*.

STEP 5 Check Your Work: Did you choose Text or Number as the type for the zip code field? Explain your answer.

▶ **More Practice**

Repeat Steps 1 and 2 to define fields for phone number, e-mail address, and birthday. When you have finished, click Done to close the dialog box. Check your work, then Save.

Once you make a database, you need to enter your data. A book collector enters authors, titles, publishers, and copyright dates.

Look at the diagram below. It shows the data for one book in a book collection. All the data for a single person, place, or thing is called a **record**. Each record has all the fields defined for that database. The record below has four fields named *Author*, *Book Title*, *Publisher*, and *Copyright*. Together, all the records make up the database.

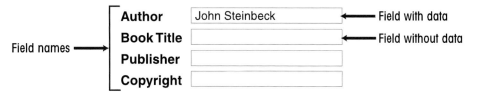

This is one record with four fields.

Most database programs have different ways, or *modes*, to view and work with records. The record above is shown in **Browse mode**. This mode is used to enter data. It is also used to add, edit, delete, copy, and sort records. Each mode lets you work with records in different ways. The table below describes these modes.

Database Modes		
Browse	**Find**	**Layout**
Use *Browse mode* to enter data, as well as add, edit, delete, copy, and sort records. You can view and work with a single record at a time. You can also view all records in a list that looks like a table. *Browse mode* is called *Form view* in some database programs.	Use *Find mode* to search for a record or group of records. See Lesson 9.5.	Use *Layout mode* to change how a record is shown on the screen or printed. You cannot edit or enter data in this mode. *Layout mode* is called *Form Design view* in some database programs. See Lesson 9.7.

Making a New Record

When you make a new record, you make a set of blank fields. Then you can enter new data. You can add a new record anytime you work in a database. The screens below show menu commands from two database programs for making a new record. The commands you use depend on the program you are working with.

Remember
Use the mouse pointer to select commands on a menu. See Lesson 3.1.

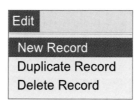

Look at the diagram below. It shows part of a database. The first record has data in all four fields. Below the first record is a new record. The new record has no data. The four fields are blank.

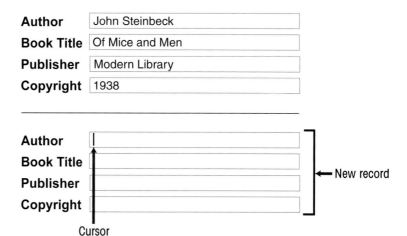

Remember
The cursor is a blinking vertical line that shows where text is being entered. See Lesson 6.2.

Look at the new record above. There is a cursor in the *Author* field. The cursor shows where you can enter data.

Entering and Editing Data

You can enter data into the blank fields in each record. You select a field by clicking in it with the mouse. Then you type in information. Look at the field below.

Author John Steinbeck| ◄——————— Cursor
Book Title

If you cannot see a field on the screen, you can use the scroll bars to bring it into view.

You can move from one field to the next in two ways:
- Click in it with the mouse.
- Press the Tab key.

Author John Steinbeck
Book Title | ◄——————— Cursor

Sometimes, after entering data, you need to edit it. You can edit data the same way you edit text in a word processing program. Just put the cursor in the field where you want to edit or replace data. Then select, delete, or type new information. Look at the example below.

Remember
Use the Delete (Backspace) key to remove text to the left of the cursor.

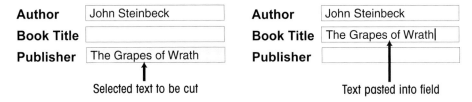

Author John Steinbeck   **Author** John Steinbeck
Book Title   **Book Title** The Grapes of Wrath|
Publisher The Grapes of Wrath   **Publisher**

Selected text to be cut   Text pasted into field

▶ **LESSON REVIEW**

1. How is Browse mode different from Layout mode?

2. How do you make a new record?

3. How do you edit data in a database?

4. **CRITICAL THINKING** Why might you want to add a new record between two other records in an address book database?

9·3 Lab Practice

Open the database file called *[your name] Address Book*. To enter the data shown in the diagram, follow the steps below.

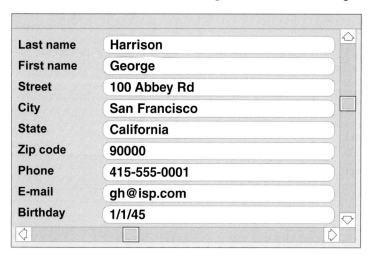

Last name	Harrison
First name	George
Street	100 Abbey Rd
City	San Francisco
State	California
Zip code	90000
Phone	415-555-0001
E-mail	gh@isp.com
Birthday	1/1/45

STEP 1 Click in the *Last Name* field. Type the last name **Harrison.**

STEP 2 Click in the *First Name* field, or press the Tab key. Type the first name **George**.

STEP 3 Press the Tab key to move to the next field, or click the cursor in the next field. Enter the data for that field.

STEP 4 Repeat Step 3 to fill in the rest of the fields.

STEP 5 Check Your Work: How many fields are in the new record you have just made?

▶ **More Practice**

Use the information you collected for the Address Book Project. Make a new record for the first person on your address book list. Then fill in the fields. Make new records and fill in fields for five more people on your list.

Changing Records

Sometimes you may want to look through your records so you can read or change data. You may also want to delete or make a copy of a record.

Moving Through Records

Different database programs let you move through records in different ways. The screen below shows one way. The database book is an icon that stands for the database file. It shows the active record—the record you are looking at. It also shows the total number of records you have.

Remember
An icon is a picture that stands for something.

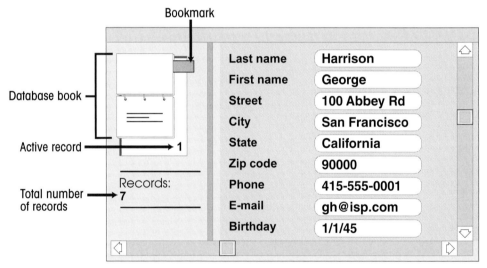

Bookmark

Database book

Active record → 1

Records:
Total number → 7
of records

Last name — Harrison
First name — George
Street — 100 Abbey Rd
City — San Francisco
State — California
Zip code — 90000
Phone — 415-555-0001
E-mail — gh@isp.com
Birthday — 1/1/45

The table below explains how to use the database book.

How to use the Database Book	
To move through records	**Do this**
To move back one record	Click on the top half of the book.
To move forward one record	Click on the bottom half of the book.
To move quickly through the database	Click and drag the bookmark up or down.

Deleting Records

Sometimes you may want to get rid of, or delete, a record. To delete a record, move through the records to find the one you want to delete. Select the record by clicking on it. Depending on the program you are using, choose a command from the Edit (or Record) menu. The command may be Cut or Delete Record. Look at the menu below.

Copying Records

You may also want to copy a record if you need most of its data in a new record. In the copy, you have to enter only new data. To copy a record, select the record by clicking on it. Depending on the program you are using, choose Duplicate Record or Copy from the Edit menu. *Duplicate* means copy. Look at the menu below.

▶ LESSON REVIEW

1. How do you move through records using the database book?

2. **CRITICAL THINKING** How does copying a record save you time?

9·4 Lab Practice

Open the database file called *[your name] Address Book*. To copy, change, and delete a record, follow the steps.

STEP 1 Go to the first record in your database—the *George Harrison* record. Select the record by clicking anywhere in it.

STEP 2 Use menu commands to copy the record.

STEP 3 Use the database book (or scroll bars) to go to the copy.

STEP 4 Edit the record. Change the zip code and phone number as shown in the screen below.

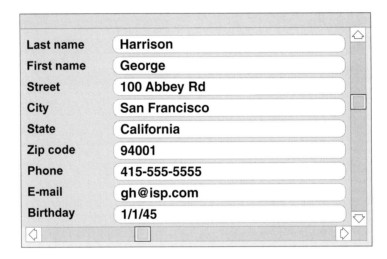

Last name	Harrison
First name	George
Street	100 Abbey Rd
City	San Francisco
State	California
Zip code	94001
Phone	415-555-5555
E-mail	gh@isp.com
Birthday	1/1/45

STEP 5 Use menu commands to delete the edited record.

STEP 6 Check Your Work: Did you delete the right record? How do you know.

▶ More Practice

Select a record from your address book. Copy the record. Then change the address and phone number. If you do not want to keep the new record, you can delete it.

9-5 ▶ Finding Records

Suppose you want to look at one set of records. For example, one set of records is all the books by John Steinbeck in the library. All people in your address book that have the same zip code is another set of records. The quickest way to get a certain set of records is to use Find mode.

Using Find Mode

When you want to find a set of records, you must tell the software what to look for. In some database programs, you use a form that looks like an empty record. You type the information you are looking for in its field. Suppose you have an address database. You want to find people who live in Kansas. You would enter **Kansas** in the *State* field. Then you would click the **Find** button.

The database will show all the records that have *Kansas* in the State field. When you find a set of records, the first record in the set appears on the screen. You can view the other records in the set by using the database book. Look at the screen below. It shows the third record in the set of three records found.

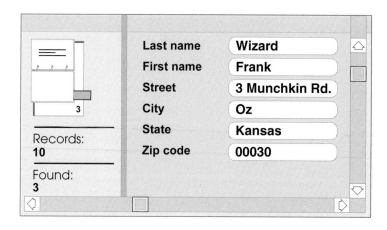

Last name	Wizard
First name	Frank
Street	3 Munchkin Rd.
City	Oz
State	Kansas
Zip code	00030

Records: 10

Found: 3

Using The Database Book

The database book shows you how many records were found out of the total number of records. Look at the diagram. It shows that 3 records out of 10 records in the database have Kansas in the State field.

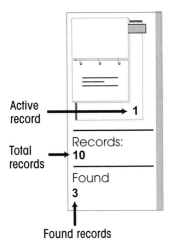

Active record → **1**

Total records → Records: **10**

Found **3**

Found records

The other 7 records—the ones that do not have Kansas in the State field—are still there. However, they are hidden from view. To see all the records again, look for the Show All Records or similar command in the program you are using.

You can type information in more than one field in the Find form. Only those records containing *all* the information you typed will be found.

▶ **LESSON REVIEW**

1. How would you find records that contain a particular piece of information in a date field?

2. If you type an area code in the phone field of a Find form, what records will be found?

3. **CRITICAL THINKING** How can using Find mode help save time when you are looking for certain records?

9·5 Lab Practice

Open the database file called *[your name] Address Book.*
Then follow the steps to find all the people in your
database whose last names start with the letter C.

STEP 1 Use menu commands to display the Find form.

STEP 2 Click in the Last Name field. Type the letter **C**.

STEP 3 Click the Find (or OK) button.

STEP 4 Look at the set of records found. The last names should start
with the letter C.

STEP 5 If no records were found, go back to STEPS 1 and 2. Use a
different letter for your search of last names.

STEP 6 Use menu commands to show all records again.

STEP 7 Check Your Work: In what field did you type the data you
wanted to find? What data did you enter in that field? How
many records did you find?

▶ **More Practice**

1. Search *[your name] Address Book* for all friends and
   relatives that have a zip code starting with the same
   three numbers as yours. Check your work. How many
   records are there?

2. Search *[your name] Address Book* for records that have
   the same state as your state. Check your work. How
   many records are there?

You search a database and you receive the error message shown below.

No records found.

OK

You can solve this problem by brainstorming. Think about why there might be no records containing a certain piece of data. Start by looking at the data entered in the Find form. Then think about what kinds of mistakes could have been made. For example, look at the screen below. Notice that Kansas was entered in the City field. Kansas is a state, not a city.

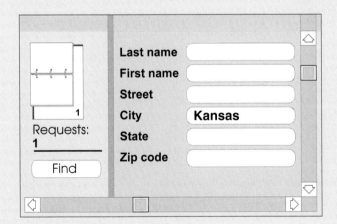

Requests:
1

Find

Last name

First name

Street

City   **Kansas**

State

Zip code

Look at the screen above.

What are two ways to correct the problem?

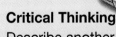

Critical Thinking
Describe another kind of mistake that would give you the same error message.

A database lists your records in the order in which you enter them. You can use Sort commands to change the order of the records. When you **sort** records, you arrange them in a certain order. For example, you can arrange records in alphabetical order by last name. Or you can arrange prices in numerical order.

Quick Sorting

One way to quickly sort records is to use the Sort buttons on the toolbar. Look for the buttons shown below.

This button sorts records in *ascending* order. Ascending means going up.
- It sorts alphabetically, from A to Z.
- It sorts numerically, from smallest number to largest.
- It sorts by date, from earliest to most recent.

This button sorts records in *descending* order. Descending means going down.
- It sorts alphabetically, from Z to A.
- It sorts numerically, from largest number to smallest.
- It sorts by date, from most recent to earliest.

These buttons let you arrange records based on the information in a field. Decide which field to use to sort your records. Then select the field by clicking in it.

After you select the field, click the button for the order in which you want the records. Look at the table at the left. If the field contains letters, the records are sorted in alphabetical order. If the field contains numbers, the records are sorted in numerical order. If the field contains a date, the records are sorted in date order.

Ascending Order	
Letters	**Numbers**
Carter	00030
Harrison	11210
Jones	92000

Descending Order	
Letters	**Numbers**
Jones	92000
Harrison	11210
Carter	00030

Using Sort Commands

Sometimes you may want to sort records using information in more than one field. For example, you can sort records alphabetically first by last name and second by first name. Look at the lists on the right. List 1 is sorted alphabetically by last name only. List 2 is sorted alphabetically by last name, then first name. Both lists are in A to Z, or ascending, order.

The Sort Records command lets you choose one or more fields to use for sorting. You can choose which field to use first, second, and so on. You can use the Sort Order box to choose how you want each field arranged. The screen below shows a Sort Records dialog box. It shows the sort order you can use to produce List 2.

List 1

Jones, Dorothy
Jones, Aunt Em
Wizard, Frank

List 2

Jones, Aunt Em
Jones, Dorothy
Wizard, Frank

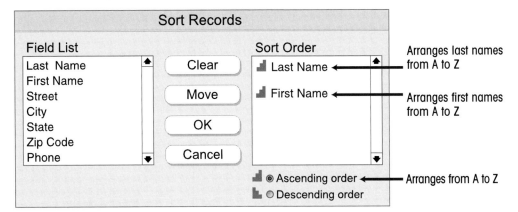

▶ **LESSON REVIEW**

1. What are two ways you can change the order of records?

2. How is doing a quick sort different from using Sort commands?

3. **CRITICAL THINKING** Suppose that address book data is sorted in ascending order using the State field. Which state would appear first, Texas or Virginia?

9·6 Lab Practice

Open your address book database. Look at the screen below. To sort your records alphabetically by first name, follow the steps below.

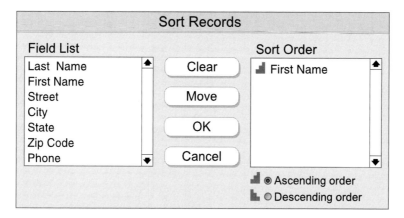

Sort Records

Field List		Sort Order
Last Name First Name Street City State Zip Code Phone	Clear Move OK Cancel	First Name

● Ascending order
○ Descending order

STEP 1 Use a command to display the Sort Records dialog box.

STEP 2 Select the First Name field from the field list. Click the Move button.

STEP 3 Click the button for Ascending order.

STEP 4 Click the OK button.

STEP 5 Check Your Work: After sorting alphabetically, what is the last name of the person in the first record on your screen? What is the last name of the person in the last record?

▶ **More Practice**

Use the Sort Records command. Use the Clear button to clear out the Sort Order box. First sort your records alphabetically by last name. Then sort your records by birthday to put them in order from youngest to oldest. Check your work.

One way to find a book in the library is to use the card catalog. Today, most libraries enter data about each book into a computer database. You use a computer at the library to look up the information you need. The library catalog may also be on the Internet.

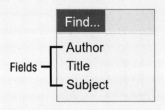

Find...

Fields — Author
Title
Subject

You choose the field from a Find menu.

Using an online catalog is like searching for information in a database program. You use commands from a menu. You type the data you want to find. The computer shows the set of records that match the data. The diagram below shows a set of records from a search for books by John Steinbeck.

You searched AUTHOR for: Steinbeck, John

SEARCH RESULTS   Titles found: 149

1 Steinbeck, John. 1902–1968. The moon is down: a novel. New York: Viking Press, 1942

2 Steinbeck, John. 1902–1968. The moon is down: a novel. New York: Bantam Books, 1966.

3 Steinbeck, John. 1902–1968. Of mice and men. New York: Covici-Friede, 1937.

This is a set of found records.

Use the diagram above to answer the questions.

1. What field was used for the search?

2. How many records were found?

3. What are the titles of two books by John Steinbeck that were found?

Critical Thinking
How can using an online library catalog save you time?

Working with Layouts

Databases can have different **layouts**. A layout is the way fields and records in a database look on the screen. You can use all or some of the fields in the layout. You can use different layouts to view and work with data.

Kinds of Layouts

Depending on the program you are using, you may have a choice of several types of layouts.

Standard Layout

Look at the screen below. In a *standard* layout, each field is on a separate line. This is the layout you see when you are in Find and Browse (or Form) modes.

Author	John Steinbeck
Book Title	Of Mice and Men
Publisher	Modern Library
Copyright	1938

Column Layout

Look at the screen below. A *column* layout looks like a table. Records are shown in rows. Fields are shown in columns. Field names are the column headings. You have to choose the fields you want to appear in a column layout.

Last name	First name	Street	City	State	
Jones	Dorothy	1 Cyclone Ln.	Anytown	Kansas	← Record
Jones	Aunt Em	1 Cyclone Ln.	Anytown	Kansas	
Wizard	Frank	1 Cyclone Ln.	Anytown	Kansas	

Field

Labels Layout

Look at the screen on the right. You use a *labels* layout when you want to print mailing labels. A mailing label usually contains fields for a person's name and complete address.

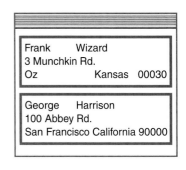

Making a New Layout

You use the Layout menu when you want to make or change a layout. When you choose New Layout, the dialog box shown below appears.

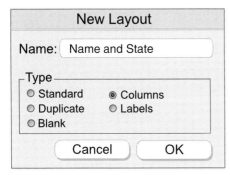

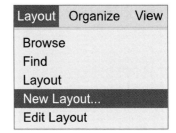

In this dialog box, Column is chosen as the Type for the layout called Name and State.

You type a name for the layout in the Name box. Use a name that describes the layout. Next choose the Type of layout you want. Then choose the fields for the layout and the order in which they will appear.

Look at the screen below. When you choose Column or Labels layout, the Set Field Order dialog box appears.

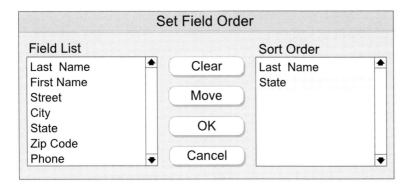

Layout   Organize   View

Browse
Find
Layout
New Layout...
Edit Layout
Delete Layout
Insert Field...
Layout Info
Name and State
Labels

Remember
You drag items by clicking on them and holding down the mouse button as you move the mouse.

To choose a field, you click on its name in the Field List. Then click the Move button. The screen on page 187 shows that the Last Name field and the State field have been selected. The Last Name field will appear first.

Look at the menu at the left. To see your records using a new layout, choose the layout's name from the bottom of the Layout menu. Then choose Browse. The screen below shows how the *Name and State* layout would look.

Last Name	**State**
Jones	Kansas
Wizard	Kansas
Harrison	California

Once fields are in place, you can move them where you want them. First choose the Layout command. Click on the field you want to move, then drag it where you want it.

You can also delete a field from a layout. Choose the Layout command. Click on the field and press the Delete key.

▶ **LESSON REVIEW**

1. What are layouts used for?

2. Name two types of layouts. How do they differ from each other?

3. How does the Set Field Order dialog box help you make a layout?

4. **CRITICAL THINKING** Which type of layout would you use for a library catalog? Why? P

9·7 Lab Practice

Open your address book database. To make a layout to list your friends' birthdays, follow the steps below.

STEP 1 Use menu commands to choose New Layout.

STEP 2 Type **Birthday** in the Name box. Click Column for the Type. Then click the OK button. The Set Field Order dialog box will appear.

STEP 3 Select *Last Name* from the field list. Click the Move button.

STEP 4 Select *First Name* from the field list. Click the Move button.

STEP 5 Select *Birthday* from the field list. Click the Move button. Click OK. Your layout should look this this:

Last Name	First Name	Birthday
Wizard	Frank	11/11/80

STEP 6 Check Your Work: How many fields are in the new layout you made?

▶ More Practice

Choose New Layout from the Layout menu. Use Column layout for the type. Name the new layout *E-mail Addresses*. Select the fields *Last Name, First Name,* and *E-mail* from the field list.

Applying: Communicate Your Data

You can use a database to communicate your data in different ways. You can make mailing labels to communicate to the Post Office. You can display a list of names and phone numbers for your friends.

Example

You want to use your address book database to make a set of mailing labels.

STEP 1 GET READY What do you need to do first?
Open your address book database. Decide what type of layout you want to use.

STEP 2 THINK What do you know about the information?
Think about how the mailing labels should look. Decide what fields to include in the layout.

STEP 3 APPLY Make a new layout.
Use the New Layout command. Name the layout and choose Labels as the type. Click OK. A Label Layout dialog box, like the one shown at the right, will appear. Fill in the information about the labels. Click OK. Choose the fields and field order for the labels. Change to Browse (or Form view) to see the labels. Here is how one of the labels might look.

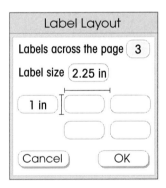

My Address Book

Dorothy Jones
1 Cyclone Ln
Anytown KS, 00031

STEP 4 CHECK How does the information look?
Look at the labels. Choose Edit Layout from the menus. Fix any errors. Print the labels.

9·8 Lab Practice

GET READY to display information from a database. Answer the questions under THINK. APPLY what you know to display the information. CHECK your finished work.

1. You want to create an alphabetical phone list of all the people in your address book database. Make a layout for the phone list.

   THINK
   What is the best layout to use?

   What fields should be included in the phone list?

2. You want to create a birthday list of all the people in your address book database. Make a layout for the birthday list.

   THINK
   What layout should you use?

   What fields should be included?

Making Connections

Think about how databases could help you with your school work. Create a database for vocabulary words you learn in math, science, social studies, or language arts. Enter new words, and their definitions as you learn them. Use your database to help you study. An example database is shown below.

New Word	paragraph
Definition	three or more sentences that are placed together and that cover the same idea
Subject	English
Use in sentence	All of the sentences in a paragraph must relate to the main idea.

Summary

Using Databases
Databases are used to organize and keep track of information. They allow you to find, sort, and display information in different ways.

- **Plan a database and define fields** by thinking about the data it will contain.
- **Make new records** by entering information into blank fields.
- **Delete or duplicate records** by selecting commands from the menus.
- **Find a record** using Find mode.
- **Sort records** in order by choosing the Sort Records command.
- **Work with layouts** by displaying records in different ways.
- **Present information** using a database to display information in different ways.

Browse mode

database

field

layout

record

sort

Vocabulary Review
Complete each sentence with a word from the list.

1. Data about a single person, place, or thing is a _____.

2. The way fields and records in a database look on the screen is a _____.

3. Software that stores information in an organized way is a _____.

4. A specific kind of data or a place to enter one piece of data in a database is a _____.

5. When you arrange data in a certain order, either numerical or alphabetical, you _____ it.

6. You enter, edit, delete, copy, and sort records in _____.

Chapter Quiz

Answer the following questions.

LESSONS 9.1 and 9.2

Computer Tip
Choosing the right type for a field makes it easier to work with and manage the data.

LESSONS 9.3 and 9.4

LESSONS 9.5 and 9.6

LESSONS 9.7 and 9.8

Computer Tip
When you make a layout, you can choose the fields you want to display.

Using and Planning Databases

1. What are three things you can do with a database?
2. Why do you have to name fields in a database?
3. Name three types of fields.

Making and Changing Records

4. Why might you want to edit or delete a record?
5. Why might you want to duplicate a record?

Finding and Sorting Records

6. How can you find records in a database?
7. What information do you enter in the Sort Records dialog box?

Working with Layouts

8. What do you do in the New Layout dialog box?
9. Which fields should be in a report that communicates all the e-mail addresses in your address book database?

Group Activity

With your group, create a new database file. Gather data on a topic that interests everyone in the group, or on a topic that will help you with your school work. For example, you might make a database for facts about the 50 states. Or you might make a database for favorite movies. Have each group member do part of the research. Then plan and create your database. Define at least four fields. Enter data for at least five records. Make two different layouts for the records.

This supermarket has 80 workers. They record the hours they work on time sheets. How might the store manager use computer software to keep track of everyone's hours?

What You Need to Know

How to use a mouse

How to use a keyboard

How to use a dialog box

How to enter text

How to use formats

This chapter is about Making Spreadsheets.

What You Will Learn

The purposes of spreadsheets

How to enter data into a spreadsheet

How to set up a spreadsheet

How to edit data in a spreadsheet

How to format data

How to analyze information

Chapter 10 ▶ Making Spreadsheets

Words to Know

spreadsheet	a table that displays data
cell	a place where a row and a column meet in a spreadsheet
formula bar	a box to enter or view information that goes in a cell
submenu	a menu that appears on the monitor when a command from a main menu is selected.

Research Project

Contact a business nearby, such as a store or local corporation, that uses computer spreadsheets. Find out how they are used, and how the same tasks were done before computer spreadsheets were available. Get a copy of a spreadsheet used by the company, if possible. Present your findings to the class.

Learning Objectives

- Explain the parts and uses of a spreadsheet.
- Enter and edit spreadsheet data.
- Set up a spreadsheet.
- Format data in a spreadsheet.
- Apply an understanding of spreadsheets to make a budget.
- **PROBLEM SOLVING:** Find the best format for a cell.
- **COMPUTERS ON THE JOB:** Explain how to use a spreadsheet to make estimates.

A **spreadsheet** is a table that displays data. The data might be numbers, text, dates, or a mixture of all three. A computer spreadsheet is software in which you can enter, display, and store data.

Use of Spreadsheets

Here are some things you can do with a computer spreadsheet.

- You can make your data look special by using formats.
- You can do math to analyze data made of numbers.
- You can make graphs and charts to present data in a colorful way.

Spreadsheets can do many things. Here are a few ways you can use them.

- Use them to add up money you spend or earn.
- Use them to keep track of payments and dates.
- Use them to keep lists of supplies and amounts.

Many people use a computer spreadsheet to make a budget, like the one shown below.

	A	B	C	D
1	**My Budget**	**January**	**February**	**March**
2	**Rent**	$900.00	$900.00	$900.00
3	**Groceries**	$250.00	$300.00	$280.00
4	**Phone**	$75.00	$70.00	$65.00
5	**Car**	$80.00	$90.00	$80.00
6	**Savings**	$100.00	$50.00	$100.00
7	**Totals**	**$1,405.00**	**$1,410.00**	**$1,425.00**

In the example above, money used in January was listed under the letter **B**. The spreadsheet was also used to add up the dollar amounts.

Parts of a Spreadsheet

A spreadsheet is made up of rows and columns. Look at the spreadsheet example below. It shows three rows and three columns in a spreadsheet. The rows go *across* and are labeled 1, 2, and 3. The columns go *down* and are labeled A, B, and C.

This is Column C

	A	B	C
1	This is one cell. It is in column A and row 1.	This is cell B1.	
2		Z	
3			

This is Row 3

Each little box is called a **cell**. A cell is a place in a spreadsheet where a row and a column meet. Each cell is a place to enter data. Each cell also has a name. The cell name is its column letter and its row number. For example, A1 and B1 are cell names.

There are nine cells in the example above. The boxes with A, B, C and 1, 2, and 3 are not cells.

▶ **LESSON REVIEW**

1. What are two ways spreadsheets are used?

2. Find the letter *Z* in the spreadsheet shown above. What is the name of the cell with the *Z*?

3. Look at the spreadsheet on page 196. How many cells are shown?

4. **CRITICAL THINKING** Why do you think a cell is named according to the letter of its column and the row number of its row?

Entering data into a spreadsheet is similar to entering text into a word processing document.

Typing in a Spreadsheet

Look at the diagram below. It is about players on a baseball team. Each row contains information about one team member. To enter data, first point and click in a cell. When you point and click in a cell, it is active. Cell D2 is active in the example below. This cell name is shown in the upper left.

Look at the **formula bar** shown in the diagram below. A formula bar is a place to enter or view information that goes in a cell. Sometimes it is called the *entry bar*.

Cell name   Resize arrow   Formula bar

D2	✕	✓	

	A	↔ B	C	D
1	Player Name	Position	Age	Height
2	Kanisha Allen	Shortstop	15	

↑ Active cell

Computer Fact

You can make columns in a spreadsheet wider. Point your mouse at the top of Column A. Move the mouse to the right. When your mouse pointer gets to the line between Column A and Column B, it changes from a ✛ to a ↔. Click and drag the ↔ resize arrow to the right. Column A will get wider. Look at the diagram. You can also make spreadsheet rows taller.

After making a cell active, you can enter the information for that cell. What you type appears in the formula bar as shown below. To make the entry appear in the cell, click on the ✓ next to the formula bar. You can also press the Return or Enter key. To delete the entry, click on the ✕ next to the formula bar. Look at the diagram below.

Deletes data   Makes data appear

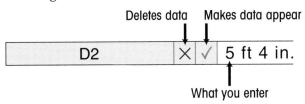

D2	✕	✓	5 ft 4 in.

↑ What you enter

Moving From Cell to Cell

To move from cell to cell, you can use the keyboard or the mouse. Press the Tab key once to move one cell to the right. Press the Enter (or Return) key to move one cell down. Use the arrow keys to move up, down, or across. You can also use the mouse to point and click in any cell.

Remember
The arrow keys are to the lower right of the character keys. They are used to move the cursor up, down, left, and right. See Lesson 2.2.

 LESSON REVIEW

1. How can you enter into a cell text you have typed in the formula bar?

2. How can you cancel text you have typed in the formula bar?

3. **CRITICAL THINKING** Do you think that the formula bar is a useful part of spreadsheet software? Why or why not?

On the Cutting Edge

NUMBER CRUNCHING BY SUPERCOMPUTERS

Supercomputers can solve complicated calculations with huge numbers in the blink of an eye. The most powerful supercomputer can do more than one trillion calculations in a minute. As a result, supercomputers have become important in science and math. They can create weather forecasts from thousands of pieces of data. They can design supersonic aircraft and plot the path of rockets. They have even been used to find the world's largest prime number. It has 378,682 digits. Try that on a handheld calculator!

A supercomputer

CRITICAL THINKING How have supercomputers made handling large numbers easier?

10·2 Lab Practice

Make a new spreadsheet document. Look at the diagram.
To enter the data, follow the steps below.

	A	B	C	D
1	Player Name	Position	Age	Height
2	Kanisha Allen	Shortstop	15	5 ft 4 in.
3				
4				

STEP 1   Point and click in Cell A1. Enter the words **Player Name**.

STEP 2   To make Player Name appear in Cell A1, click on the ✓
next to the formula bar. If you made a typing error, click on
the ✕ to delete the text. Then re-enter it correctly.

STEP 3   Move to Cell B1. Enter the word **Position**. Click on the ✓.

STEP 4   Enter the word **Age** in Cell C1. Enter the word **Height** in
Cell D1.

STEP 5   Move to the second row. Enter the data shown in the
diagram for Cells A2, B2, C2, and D2.

STEP 6   Save your work. Name the spreadsheet **Baseball Team**.

STEP 7   Check Your Work: What data is in cell C2?

▶ **More Practice**

Use the spreadsheet named *Baseball Team*. Enter the
following data in Row 3.

　　The player's name is **Drew Benton**.
　　The position is **catcher**
　　The age is **15**.
　　The height is **5 ft 9 in**.

Before setting up a spreadsheet, you need to organize your information. You need to make a list of the kinds of information you have. The list can include numbers, money, dates, names of items, or names of people. Then you should decide which information will go into the columns and which information will go into the rows.

Here is an example of how to organize information for a spreadsheet. Suppose you want to keep track of how you spend your money each month. You would need to know what you buy with your money. You would also need to know how much you spend. To organize the information, you could make a list that looks like the one below.

> ROWS
> Food
> Clothing
> Movies
> Music
> Savings
> COLUMNS
> Week 1 spending
> Week 2 spending
> Week 3 spending
> Week 4 spending

The list above contains two kinds of information. One kind of information is made up of the things you do with money. The second kind of information tells you how much you spend in each of the four weeks of the month.

You then decide to set up your spreadsheet like the example shown below. Notice that the names of rows and columns tell you how the information will be organized. The names of rows go in Column A. Each row shows how you spend money. Row 2, for example, shows how much money you spend on food.

The names of columns go in Row 1. Each column shows how much you spend each week of the month. Column B, for example, shows how much you spend in Week 1.

Look at the active cell, B2. In that cell you would enter how much money you spent on food in Week 1. In Cell B3, you would record how much money you spent on clothing in Week 1.

B2	✕ ✓			
	A	**B**	**C**	**D**	**E**
1		Week 1 spending	Week 2 spending	Week 3 spending	Week 4 spending
2	Food				
3	Clothing				
4	Movies				
5	Music				
6	Savings				

The data in this spreadsheet will be dollars. Look at Rows 2 through 6. Each cell in Columns B through E will have dollar amounts. What makes this spreadsheet useful is how the data are organized. This organization helps you see how you use your money.

 LESSON REVIEW

1. What do you need to decide when you set up a spreadsheet?

2. What information will be recorded in Cell B6?

3. **CRITICAL THINKING** How might you have set up this spreadsheet differently?

10·3 Lab Practice

Here are six different items of information. You can set up the information in a spreadsheet.

Food   *Movies*   *Week 1 spending*
Savings   *Week 2 spending*   *Clothing*

Make a new document. To set up and enter the text, follow the steps below.

STEP 1 Decide which information will go in rows and which information will go in columns.

STEP 2 To name a row, use a cell in Column A. To name a column, use a cell in Row 1.

STEP 3 Point and click to make a cell active. Enter text to name a row or column. Click on ✓ or press Return or Enter to make the entry appear in the active cell.

STEP 4 Continue to name rows or columns until you have entered all six items of information.

STEP 5 Save your spreadsheet. Name it **Monthly Budget**.

STEP 6 Check Your Work: How many cells do you have in which to put data?

▶ More Practice

1. Add two more weeks to your spreadsheet. Name two more columns or rows for these weeks.

2. Add two more ways to spend money to your spreadsheet. Name two more columns or rows for these expenses. Here are some suggestions: music, magazines, books, sneakers, or boots.

3. Enter numbers in Cells B2 and C2. Save your work.

COMPUTERS ON THE JOB
Building Contractor

Michela is a building contractor. She is in charge of large construction projects, such as the building of housing developments. It is important that she knows everything about building houses. But Michela must also be a good manager. She needs to think about the tasks that must be completed. She needs to think about how many people are needed to complete each task on time. She also has to estimate the cost of completing each task and the entire job.

Michela plans tasks with a worker.

Here is part of the spreadsheet that Michela uses.

	A	B	C	D
1	**Building task**	**Days needed**	**People needed**	**Cost**
2	Dig foundation	4	5	$5,000.00
3	Pour foundation	3	7	$6,000.00
4	Build frame	10	8	$26,000.00
5	Complete exterior	20	7	$60,000.00
6	Complete interior	20	8	$40,000.00
7	Landscape	4	5	$3,000.00

Use the information in the spreadsheet to answer the questions.

1. Which part of the spreadsheet shows how long will it take to complete this entire project?

2. Which spreadsheet cell shows how many people will work on the frame?

3. What information is found in cell D6?

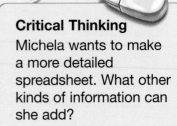

Critical Thinking

Michela wants to make a more detailed spreadsheet. What other kinds of information can she add?

Editing Data

Editing data in a spreadsheet is similar to editing text in word processing. You can edit, delete, copy, cut, and paste information.

Deleting the Contents of a Cell

To delete the contents of a cell, point and click to select the cell. Then press the Delete (or Backspace) key on the keyboard. In some programs, the data is deleted immediately. In other programs, you may press Return (or enter). Then the data in the cell is deleted.

Copying, Cutting, and Pasting

To copy or cut the contents of a cell, first click in the cell. Then choose Copy or Cut from the Edit menu. Now you can paste the data into another cell. To do that, click in the cell where you want the data to appear. Then select Paste from the Edit menu. The data that you copied or cut will appear in the second cell.

Most programs have a toolbar. You can use toolbar buttons instead of menus to give the commands Copy, Cut, and Paste.

Remember
To select information with the mouse, click and hold the mouse button while you drag the mouse with your hand.

You can also copy, cut, and paste data from several cells at the same time. Point and click on the first cell. Then drag the pointer over the cells to be selected. A border appears around the group of cells, as shown in Screen 1.

Screen 1

	A	B	C	D
1		Column B	Column C	Column D
2	Row 2	10	20	30
3	Row 3			
4	Row 4			

←—— Selected cells

Copy or cut the data using the toolbar or Edit menu. Then click in the first cell where you want to paste the data. Select Paste from the Edit Menu or toolbar. The data appears in a new group of cells. Screen 2 shows data pasted in Row 4. This is the same data cut from Row 2 in Screen 1.

Screen 2

	A	B	C	D
1		Column B	Column C	Column D
2	Row 2			
3	Row 3			
4	Row 4	10	20	30

← Data pasted into new cells

Correcting a Mistake

Sometimes you need to correct a mistake in a cell. To do this, you can click in the cell that has a mistake, then type new data. The new data will appear in the formula bar. You can click on ✓ or press Return (or Enter). The new data will replace the mistake in the cell.

Here is an example of a cell with a spelling mistake.

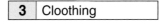

3	Cloothing

To correct the mistake, you can make the cell active, then type a correction. Your correction will appear in the formula bar, as shown below. You can click on ✓ or press Enter (or Return) to correct the mistake.

✕	✓	Clothing

▶ **LESSON REVIEW**

1. How do you delete data from a cell?

2. How do you cut data and paste it somewhere else?

3. **CRITICAL THINKING** In this lesson you learned how to cut and delete data from a cell. How are these actions similar to each other?

10·4 Lab Practice

Open the spreadsheet named *Monthly Budget*. To edit data in the cells, follow the steps below.

STEP 1 To select Cells B2 and C2, click on Cell B2, hold the mouse button, then drag to the right. Release the mouse button when Cell C2 is also highlighted.

STEP 2 Choose the Copy command from the Edit menu or click on the Copy toolbar button.

STEP 3 Select Cell B3. Choose the Paste command. The data will appear in Cells B3 and C3.

STEP 4 Select Cell B2 again. Type a new number that you want to appear in that cell. Your typing will replace the data that was there before.

STEP 5 Repeat Step 3 for Cell C2. Use a different number.

STEP 6 Check Your Work: How many cells have data?

 More Practice

1. Enter new numbers into Cells B4 and C4 in the spreadsheet. Then use Cut and Paste commands to put these numbers in two different cells.

2. Rename one of your rows or columns. Think of a new name for one of the ways you spend money. Use your new name to replace one of the old names.

You can change format of characters in spreadsheets in the same way you did in word processing. There are also special formats for numbers, dates, and *currency*. Currency is the money that a country uses.

Changing Font, Size, and Style

To change the format, first select the cell or cells you want to change. In some programs, you can use the toolbar to change the font, size and style. In other programs, you will use a submenu. A submenu is a menu that appears when you select a command from a main menu.

Look at the diagram below. It shows a Format menu with commands for font, size, and style. Notice the arrows next to these commands. The arrows mean that there is a submenu for each command. If you select the Font command, a submenu will appear. It will show a list of fonts. Screen 1 shows the Font command and the Font submenu. Screen 2 shows the Size command and Size submenu.

Screen 1

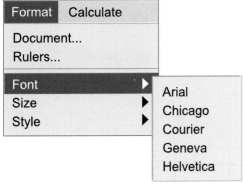

Screen 2

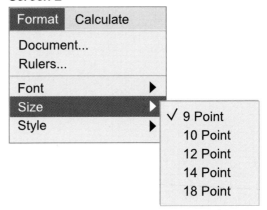

In some programs, you can use a Format Cells dialog box. This dialog box will appear when you select the Cells command from the Format menu.

Changing Number Formats

Most programs use a dialog box to make changes in currency, dates, and other number formats. Look at the screen below. To make a change, first select the cell or cells you want to format. Then, depending on the program, select the Cells or Number command from the Format menu. Choose the category of format you want to change, such as Number, Date, or Time. Choose the format from the options available. Then click on OK. When you format numbers, you can choose the number of decimal places.

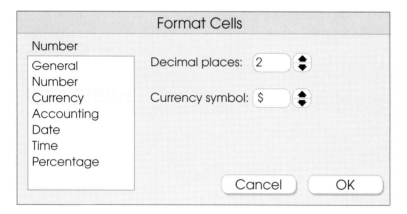

Format Cells

Number

| General |
| Number |
| Currency |
| Accounting |
| Date |
| Time |
| Percentage |

Decimal places: 2

Currency symbol: $

Cancel   OK

▶ **LESSON REVIEW**

1. What are some different ways to make changes to font, size, and style?

2. In the screen shown above, what selection would you make if you wanted to show amounts with one decimal place?

3. **CRITICAL THINKING** Why would you want to select the Currency option in the Numbers dialog box to show how much money you spend each week in your budget spreadsheet?

10·5 Lab Practice

Open the spreadsheet named *Monthly Budget*. To make format changes, follow the steps below.

STEP 1   Select cell A2.

STEP 2   Select the Font or Cells command from the Format menu. Use the submenu or dialog box to change the font.

STEP 3   Select Cell A3.

STEP 4   Select the Font or Cells command. Change the point size to 12.

STEP 5   Select Cell B1.

STEP 6   Select the Font or Cells command. Change the style to Bold.

STEP 7   Select Cell C2.

STEP 8   Select the Number or Cells command from the Format Menu. Use the dialog box to change the numbers to appear as currency.

STEP 9   Check Your Work: How did the text in Cell B1 change?

▶ **More Practice**

1. Use the spreadsheet named *Monthly Budget*. Change the font of Cell B2.
2. Use the spreadsheet named *Monthly Budget*. Change the point size of Cell A4 to 14.
3. Use the spreadsheet named *Monthly Budget*. Change the style of the text in Cell C1 to bold.
4. Use the spreadsheet named *Monthly Budget*. Change the data in Cell C3 to appear as currency.

In this spreadsheet, the currency amounts do not show a dollar sign and have only one decimal place.

JUNE BUDGET					
	A	**B**	**C**	**D**	**E**
1		Week 1	Week 2	Week 3	Week 4
2	Food	45.0			
3	Bus fare	10.0			
4	Clothing	25.0			
5	Music/entertainment	7.0			
6	Savings	30.0			
7	Other	20.0			

When you enter currency, the amounts should have two decimal places and a dollar sign. You can solve this problem by using the Format menu.

Select the Cells or Number command from the Format menu. Look at the choices in the dialog box. Perhaps a wrong choice is made. Make sure that Currency is chosen. Some programs even offer different choices for showing currency. Select the choice you want.

In some programs you can preview the option you chose. Click OK when you see the currency displayed correctly.

Answer the following questions.

1. What is troubleshooting?

2. How would the dialog box help you troubleshoot when numbers do not seem to have the right format?

Critical Thinking

Why would checking Style format not help you solve the problem of showing dollars correctly?

Applying: Organizing Budget

A spreadsheet can help you organize a budget for the costs of equipment and supplies for a baseball team.

Example

Create a spreadsheet to organize the following data. Show the items, the amount of each item, and the costs.

BASEBALL TEAM EQUIPMENT AND SUPPLIES

3 bags of sand: $25 each   *4 bases: $25 each*

6 bats: $20 each   *2 bags of grass seed: $8 each*

9 caps: $6 each   *5 balls: $10 each*

9 pairs of socks: $4 each   *1 bag of chalk: $15*

3 mitts: $40 each   *6 new uniforms: $50 each*

5 water bottles: $2 each

STEP 1   GET READY What do you need to do first?
Read the list above. Look for different kinds of data in the list.

STEP 2   THINK What do you know about the information?
Think about how you will organize the spreadsheet to display the data. Think about what will go in the rows and columns.

STEP 3   APPLY Organize the information.
Create a new spreadsheet. Enter the names for each row and column. Enter the data. Edit data if necessary. Format the font, size, and style. Change the number formats where you show money. Save the spreadsheet.

STEP 4   CHECK Does the information look correct?
Check to make sure the information is clearly presented and looks correct.

10·6 Lab Practice

GET READY to create a spreadsheet. Answer the questions under THINK. APPLY what you know to organize the data. CHECK your finished work.

1. The School Dance Committee needs to create a spreadsheet. The spreadsheet should include all the costs of the dance. Make a list of the kinds of information to put in the spreadsheet. Decide what information should go in rows and what information should go in columns.

   THINK

   What should be included in the costs?

   What data should go in each row?

   What data should go in each column?

2. Make a new spreadsheet. Use your list from number 1, above, to enter names for rows and columns. Then, enter some sample data into the spreadsheet. Use number formats so that the costs appear with a dollar sign. Show dollars and cents.

   THINK

   What menu would you select?

   What command would you select?

Making Connections

Think of a way that you might use a spreadsheet for a math, science, history, or English assignment in school, or for a personal project at home. Set up the spreadsheet and enter your data. Share what you have done with your classmates.

Summary

Making a Spreadsheet
Spreadsheets are used to organize and display data.

- **To type in a spreadsheet,** select a cell, type, and then click ✓ or press the Enter key.

- **To move from cell to cell,** use the mouse or keyboard.

- **To delete the contents of a cell,** select a cell and press the Delete (or Backspace) key.

- **To Copy, Cut and Paste,** edit data using the copy, cut and paste commands.

- **To correct an error or replace data,** select a cell, type in the formula bar, and then click ✓ or press the Enter key.

- **To change Font, Size, and Style,** use the Format menu to select and change the text.

- **To change number formats,** use the Format menu to select and change numbers.

- **To organize information,** use a spreadsheet to put data into rows and columns.

cell
formula bar
spreadsheet
submenu

Vocabulary Review
Complete each sentence with a term from the list.

1. A table that displays data is a _____.

2. The place used to enter or view information that goes in a cell is the _____.

3. A menu that appears on the monitor after selecting a command from a main menu is called a _____.

4. The place where a row and column meet in a spreadsheet is a _____.

Chapter Quiz

Answer the following questions.

LESSON 10·1

What Is a Spreadsheet?

1. What useful things can you do with a spreadsheet?
2. How is a cell named?

LESSON 10·2

Computer Tip
Think about how to organize the data by first making a list of the kinds of data you have.

Entering Data

3. What does clicking on the ✓ next to the formula bar do?
4. What does clicking on the ✕ next to the formula bar do?

LESSONS 10·3 and 10·4

Setting Up a Spreadsheet and Editing Data

5. How is data organized in a spreadsheet?
6. How do you cut and paste data in a spreadsheet?

LESSON 10·5

Using Formats

7. In which menu do you find format commands?
8. To change number format, what do you do after you get the dialog box?

LESSON 10·6

Organizing a Budget

9. What are the different kinds of data shown in the list on page 212?

Group Activity

Find out how to use one of the toolbar buttons, menu commands, or dialog boxes you have never used. Experiment to find out how to use it with your spreadsheet. Practice and then write directions that others can follow. Share what you find with other members of your class.

Bank workers must keep track of money in many different bank accounts. The amount of money in each account can change every day. A spreadsheet program can help them. How is this possible?

What You Need to Know

- How to do basic word processing
- How to set up a spreadsheet
- How to enter data in a spreadsheet
- How to edit data in a spreadsheet

This chapter is about Working with Spreadsheet Data.

What You Will Learn

- What a formula does
- How to make & edit formulas
- How to use functions
- How to make charts
- How to analyze data

Chapter 11

Working with Spreadsheet Data

Words to Know

spreadsheet formula	a math expression that shows a calculation. A spreadsheet formula is written using numbers, cell names, and math symbols.
function	a built-in shortcut formula that does calculations in a spreadsheet

Spreadsheet Project

Keep a record of how many hours you spend doing homework, watching TV, and talking on the phone each school day for a week. At the end of this chapter, use this record to make a spreadsheet with a chart. This will help you analyze your data.

Learning Objectives

- Make formulas in a spreadsheet.
- Use cell names in formulas.
- Edit formulas.
- Use a function.
- Make a chart in a spreadsheet.
- Apply spreadsheets to analyze information about time spent.
- **PROBLEM SOLVING:** Fixing error messages in formulas.
- **COMPUTERS IN YOUR LIFE:** Use a spreadsheet to set up a budget.

11·1 Making Formulas

A spreadsheet is useful for working with lots of numbers. It can help you understand, or *analyze,* what your numbers mean. When you analyze data, you may need to add, subtract, multiply, or divide some numbers. Spreadsheet software can help you do the math.

What is a Spreadsheet Formula?

A spreadsheet can do math quickly and easily. But first you must tell it what to do by writing a **spreadsheet formula**. This is a math expression that shows a calculation.

You write a formula using numbers, cell names, and math symbols. Look at the math symbols in the table on the left.

Remember
A spreadsheet is a table that displays data. Spreadsheets are arranged in columns and rows. A cell is where a column and a row meet.

Formula Symbols	
Symbol	Operation
+	addition
−	subtraction
*	multiplication
/	division
=	Is equal to

With a formula, you can use a spreadsheet like a calculator. Every spreadsheet formula begins with an equal sign (=). Look at the examples below.

=1+4–3   Add 1 and 4; then subtract 3.
=9*5   Multiply 9 times 5.
=50/2   Divide 50 by 2.
=C3*2   Multiply the data in Cell C3 by 2.
=A3+A8   Add the data in Cells A3 and A8.
=B6–B5   Subtract the data in Cell B5 from Cell B6.

Suppose you wanted to plan how to spend your money. You could make a budget spreadsheet that shows what you spend. Then you could use formulas to find sums for your data. You could use formulas to find the average amount you spend for a month. These are ways to analyze data using a spreadsheet.

Math in a Spreadsheet

To use a spreadsheet like a calculator, you enter a formula in the formula bar. Click in a cell to make it active. Then you type an equal sign. You also type the numbers and operations you want to use. You do not need to type any spaces in a formula. Look at Screen 1 below.

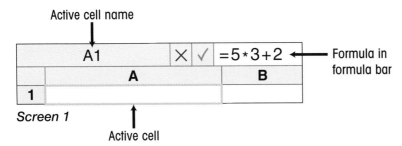

Active cell name

A1 $\times$ $\checkmark$ =5*3+2 — Formula in formula bar

Screen 1

Active cell

When you press the $\checkmark$ button, or the **Enter** (or **Return**) key, the formula will calculate an answer. The answer will be shown in the active cell. If you click in the cell with the answer in it, the formula will be shown in the formula bar. Look at Screen 2.

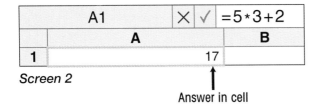

A1 $\times$ $\checkmark$ =5*3+2

	A	B
1	17	

Screen 2

Answer in cell

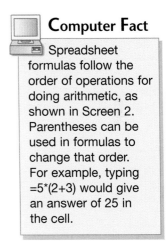

Computer Fact

Spreadsheet formulas follow the order of operations for doing arithmetic, as shown in Screen 2. Parentheses can be used in formulas to change that order. For example, typing =5*(2+3) would give an answer of 25 in the cell.

LESSON REVIEW

1. What is an advantage of using a spreadsheet to analyze data?

2. What do you type to start a spreadsheet formula?

3. What symbols do you use in a formula?

4. **CRITICAL THINKING** What would be the formula to divide 6 by 3?

11·1 Lab Practice

1. Make a new spreadsheet. Look at the screen below. Then follow the steps to find the sum of 3 + 4 + 67 + 203 using a formula.

A1	$\times$ $\checkmark$ =3+4+67+203		
	A	**B**	**C**
1	277		

STEP 1 Click in Cell A1.

STEP 2 Enter the formula. Type an equal sign (=). Type **3+4+67+203** after the equal sign. If you make a typing mistake, press the $\times$ button and type the formula again.

STEP 3 Press the $\checkmark$ button or the Enter (or Return) key. The sum will be in Cell A1.

STEP 4 Save your spreadsheet. Name it **Formulas**.

STEP 5 Check Your Work: Click on Cell A1. What appears in the formula bar?

If your formula has a typing error in it, go to Step 6.

If your formula is correct, go to the top of the next page.

STEP 6 Put the cursor in the formula bar next to the mistake. Delete the mistake. Then enter the correct number or math symbol. Press the $\checkmark$ button or the Enter (or Return) key. Check your work.

2. Work with the same spreadsheet you made in number 1. Follow the steps to write a formula for multiplying and dividing.

A2		$\times$ $\checkmark$	=6*2/3	
	A	**B**		**C**
1	277			
2				

STEP 7   Click in Cell A2. Enter the formula **=6*2/3**.

STEP 8   Press the Enter (or Return) key. The answer will be in Cell A2. Save your work.

STEP 9   Check Your Work: Click on Cell A2. What appears in the formula bar?

▶ **More Practice**

Use the spreadsheet named *Formulas*. Use formulas and the cells in Column A to do the math below. Start in Cell A3.

3. Click in Cell A3. Calculate 463×7.

4. Click in Cell A4. Calculate $799 - 35$.

5. Click in Cell A5. Calculate $9738 \div 9$.

6. Click in Cell A6. Calculate $14 + 10 - 2$.

7. Click in Cell A7. Calculate $514.23 + 90.8 + 82.045 + 0.77$.

8. Click in Cell A8. Calculate 246.09×11.4.

9. Click in Cell A9. Calculate $8 \times 65 - 24 \times 7$.

10. Click in Cell A10. Calculate $365 \div 5 + 31.6$.

11·2 Making Formulas with Cell Names

You can use formulas to add, subtract, multiply, and divide data that you have already entered in a spreadsheet. You write these formulas by using the names of the cells that contain the data.

Look at the screen below. Column B has data that show the amount of each kind of drink sold. You can write a formula to find the total number. You click in the cell where you want the total to appear. You type an equal sign. Then you write a formula using cell names. To find the total you need the cell names B3, B4, and B5. Look at the formula in the formula bar.

Remember
A cell name is made of a column letter and a row number.

Formula in formula bar

B6	× ✓	=B3+B4+B5	
	A	**B**	**C**
1	Drinks Sold in Cafeteria		
2	Kinds of Drinks	Amount Sold	
3	Bottled water	5	
4	Juice	6	
5	Milk	2	
6	Totals	13	
7			

Total appears here

B
Amount Sold
5
6
2
13 ← Cell B6

In the example above, Cell B6 is active. The formula in the formula bar will be entered in Cell B6 when you press the Enter (or Return) key. The total number of drinks sold, 13, appears in Cell B6. The number 13 comes from adding the data in Cells B3, B4, and B5. Here is the formula:

=B3+B4+B5
↓ ↓ ↓
5 + 6 + 2

There is a good reason to use cell names in formulas instead of numbers. You may need to change the data in a cell. Suppose that 3 milks, not 2, were sold. You would change the data in Cell B5 from 2 to 3. Then you would find the new total.

If you use numbers in the formula, you have to type the formula again. By using cell names, you can change a number in a cell without changing the formula. The spreadsheet calculates the new answer for you. Look at the screen below. Look at Cell B5 and Cell B6.

Same formula

B6	× ✓	=B3+B4+B5
	A	**B**	**C**
1	Drinks Sold in Cafeteria		
2	Kinds of Drinks	Amount Sold	
3	Bottled water	5	
4	Juice	6	
5	Milk	3	← New number
6	Totals	14	← New total

Notice that the data in Cell B5 is 3. The new total, 14, is shown in Cell B6. The data changed, but the formula is the same. Here is the formula:

=B3+B4+B5
↓ ↓ ↓
5 + 6 + 3

▶ **LESSON REVIEW**

1. What are two ways to write a formula to find the total of data in a column?

2. **CRITICAL THINKING** What is an advantage of using cell names in a formula instead of numbers?

Open the spreadsheet named *Drinks Sold*. It will have the information shown in the screen below. Follow the steps to make a formula and use it.

D3	X √		
	A	**B**	**C**	**D**
1	Drinks Sold in Cafeteria			
2	Kinds of Drinks	Amount Sold	Unit Price	Total Received
3	Bottled water	5	$1.25	
4	Juice	6	$1.50	
5	Milk	3	$1.00	
6	Totals	14		

STEP 1 Click in Cell D3.

STEP 2 Decide which cells to use in the formula. To find the total received for bottled water, use Cells B3 and C3.

STEP 3 Enter the formula =**B3∗C3**.

STEP 4 Press the √ button. $6.25 will appear in Cell D3.

STEP 5 Save your spreadsheet.

STEP 6 Check Your Work: What is the amount in Cell D3?

▶ **More Practice**

1. Use the spreadsheet named *Drinks Sold*. Use a formula with cell names to find the total received for juice. Place this total in Cell D4.

2. Use a formula with cell names to find the total received for milk. Place this total in Cell D5. Save your work.

Sometimes you may want to change a formula. There are two ways you can change a formula. One way is to edit part of it. Another way is to replace the whole formula.

Click in the cell with the formula you want to change. Then click in the formula that is displayed in the formula bar. Place the cursor where you want to edit the formula.

Cursor

$$\boxed{\times}\ \boxed{\checkmark}\ \boxed{=B3|+B5}$$

Look at the screen below. B6, the active cell, has the formula =B3+B5. The formula in Cell B6 should add the Amount Sold for bottled water, juice, and milk. These numbers are in cells B3, B4, and B5. The formula in Cell B6 is missing the cell name B4.

B6		✕ ✓ =B3+B5	
	A	**B**	**C**
1	Drinks Sold in Cafeteria		
2	Kinds of Drinks	Amount Sold	Unit Price
3	Bottled water	5	$1.25
4	Juice	6	$1.50
5	Milk	3	$1.00
6	Totals	8	

You can edit the formula by clicking in the formula bar. You can put the cursor where you want to type new text. After you have edited the formula, press ✓ button or the Enter (or Return) key. The edited formula will appear in the formula bar. The edited formula also changes the calculation in the active cell. The screen below shows the edited formula in Cell B6.

Cursor

B6		✕ ✓ =B3+B4|+B5	
	A	**B**	**C**

The second way to change a formula works best when you want to replace a whole formula. Click in the cell with the formula you want to change. Then type the new formula. Press the Enter (or Return) key. The new formula will be in the active cell.

If you want to remove the whole formula, delete all the text. Then press Enter (or Return). The cell will then be empty.

▶ **LESSON REVIEW**

1. What is one way you can edit a formula?

2. **CRITICAL THINKING** Suppose you want to completely change a formula in a cell. How would you do it?

On the Cutting Edge

THE FIRST COMPUTER SPREADSHEET

The inventors of the first spreadsheet program wanted to use computers to make math easier to do. They called the program VisiCalc. It was introduced in 1979 by Software Arts, Inc. With this program, math operations that used to take hours could be done in minutes.

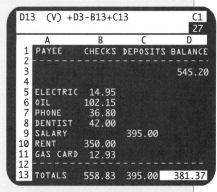

VisiCalc users could use formulas to do math.

VisiCalc had only 254 rows and 63 columns. Today's programs have thousands of rows and hundreds of columns. Even so, VisiCalc was a very important invention. It helped make personal computers more popular. Before VisiCalc, most computer programs could only do tasks that were not very useful to many people. VisiCalc was a program that almost anyone could use.

CRITICAL THINKING What made VisiCalc different from earlier computer programs?

11·3 Lab Practice

Open the spreadsheet named *Drinks Sold*. Click in Cell D6.
Next, enter the formula shown in the screen below. Then,
to edit the formula, follow the steps below.

D6	✕ ✓ =D3+C4+D5		
	A	**B**	**C**	**D**
1	Drinks Sold in Cafeteria			
2	Kinds of Drinks	Amount Sold	Unit Price	Total Received
3	Bottled water	5	$1.25	$6.25
4	Juice	6	$1.50	$9.00
5	Milk	3	$1.00	$3.00
6	Totals	14		

STEP 1   Click in the formula bar. Place the cursor after the **C**.

STEP 2   Delete the letter **C**. Use the Backspace (or Delete) key.
Then type the letter **D**.

STEP 3   Press Enter (or Return), or click the ✓ button. The edited
formula and the new total will appear in your spreadsheet.

STEP 4   Save your edited *Drinks Sold* file.

STEP 5   Check Your Work: What is the new amount in Cell D6?

▶ More Practice

Use the *Drinks Sold* spreadsheet. Click in Cell D6. Enter the
formula shown below. Then edit the formula so it finds the
correct total. Save your edited *Drinks Sold* file to use in the
next lesson.

| ✕ | ✓ | =C3+D4+D5 |

11·4 Using a Function

You may want to do more than simple arithmetic with the numbers in your spreadsheet. For example, you might want to find the average of a row of numbers. Or you might want to count how many numbers are in a particular column.

You can use a **function** for these tasks instead of writing a long formula. A function is a built-in shortcut formula that does calculations in a spreadsheet. It is a small program that does one special thing. You write a function with words and numbers or cell names. The table below lists some common functions and what they do.

Common Functions	
Function	**What It Does**
SUM	adds a list of numbers
MAX	finds the greatest number in a list of numbers
COUNT	counts how many numbers are in a list
AVERAGE	finds the average of a list of numbers

Look at the screen below. It shows the function for calculating an average. The data for the calculation are in four cells: A1, B1, C1, and D1.

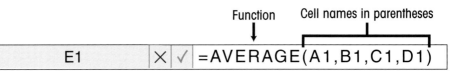

The steps that follow tell you how to enter a function.
- Click in the cell where you want to use the function.
- Begin by typing an equal sign.
- Type the function name in capital letters.

- Enter the numbers or cell names you want to use in parentheses.
- Use commas to separate the numbers or cell names. Do not add spaces after the commas.

Once you press Enter (or return), the function will calculate a number. This number will appear in the active cell. The screen below shows an example. The average, 11.5, appears in Cell E1.

E1	× ✓	=AVERAGE(A1,B1,C1,D1)		
A	**B**	**C**	**D**	**E**
1 10	13	8	15	11.5

When you use a list of cells all in one row or all in one column, you can use a shortcut. You can enter the name of the first cell and last cell. Depending on the program you are using, you separate the cell names with a colon (:) or two periods (..). For example, the function shown on page 228 would be entered as =AVERAGE(A1:D1) or =AVERAGE(A1..D1). The screen below shows an example.

E1	× ✓	=AVERAGE(A1..D1)

After you enter a function, you can edit it. Just follow the steps you used in Lesson 11.3.

▶ **LESSON REVIEW**

1. What is placed inside the parentheses in a function?

2. How does using a function help you do math in a spreadsheet?

3. **CRITICAL THINKING** Suppose you type the function MAX(4,17,9,12) in a cell. What would appear in the cell when you press the Enter key?

11·4 Lab Practice

Open the spreadsheet named *Drinks Sold.* Enter the text
Function Totals in Cell A7, as shown in the screen below.
Then follow the steps to find the total number of drinks
sold, using a function.

B7	✕ ✓	=sum(B3,B4,B5)	
A	**B**	**C**	**D**
1 Drinks Sold in Cafeteria			
2 Kinds of Drinks	Amount Sold	Unit Price	Total Received
3 Bottled water	5	$1.25	$6.25
4 Juice	6	$1.50	$9.00
5 Milk	3	$1.00	$3.00
6 Totals	14		$18.25
7 Function totals			

STEP 1   Click in Cell B7.

STEP 2   Type =**SUM**.

STEP 3   Enter the names of the cells you want to add. Use
parentheses and commas. Type **(B3,B4,B5).**

STEP 4   Press the Enter (or Return) key, or the ✓ button.

STEP 5   Save the spreadsheet file.

STEP 6   Check Your Work: What total appears in Cell B7?

▶ More Practice

1. Use your *Drinks Sold* spreadsheet. Use a function to find
the sum for the *Total Received* column. Show the sum in
Cell D7.

2. Use a function to find the average of the *Unit Price*
column. Show the average in Cell C7. Save your *Drinks
Sold* file to use in the next lesson.

Sometimes you can make a mistake when you enter data or a formula in a spreadsheet. Then the program cannot use the formula or data to do the math correctly. The spreadsheet helps you by showing you an error message. It tells you what kind of mistake you have made.

The error message **#VALUE!** means that the spreadsheet cannot use or find a number needed in a formula. This message is displayed in Cell D4 in the screen below. You can solve this problem by checking that all parts of the formula have been entered correctly.

D4			✕ ✓ =C1/C4
	A	**B**	**C**	**D**
1		Miles	Hours	Speed (Miles/Hours)
2	Driver 1	315	5.0	63
3	Driver 2	330	5.5	60
4	Driver 3	290	5.0	#VALUE!

Error message

Suppose that you are not sure how to correct the formula. Try looking at other formulas in the spreadsheet. In the example above, Cell D3 has the formula =B3/C3. This gives you a hint about what to put in Cell D4.

Look at the screen above.

1. What problem do you see with the formula =C1/C4?

2. How would you fix this problem?

Critical Thinking
How are error messages helpful?

You can use a spreadsheet program to make a graph of your data. In a spreadsheet program, graphs are also called *charts*.

To make a chart, you first select all the cells that have data you want to use. You can select cells with text as well as cells with numbers. Look at the screen below. It shows selected cells in a spreadsheet. In this example, Rows 2 through 6 in Columns A through D are selected.

	A	B	C	D
1	Drinks Sold in Cafeteria			
2	Kinds of Drinks	Amount Sold	Unit Price	Total Received
3	Bottled water	5	$1.25	$6.25
4	Juice	6	$1.50	$9.00
5	Milk	3	$1.00	$3.00
6	Totals	14		$18.25
7	Function totals	14		$18.25

Remember
Click and drag the mouse to select, or highlight, a group of cells.

After you select cells, you can choose the Insert Chart or Make Chart command. Or , you can click the Chart button on the toolbar. This button may look like this . Then click OK or Finish in the dialog box that appears. The chart will be displayed in front of your spreadsheet. Look at the example shown on the next page.

You can use this process to make several types of charts, including

- vertical bar graphs or column charts
- horizontal bar graphs
- line graphs
- circle graphs or pie charts
- area charts
- scatter plots

	A	B	C	D
1	Drinks Sold in Cafeteria			
2	Kinds of Drinks	Amount Sold	Unit Price	Total Received
3	Bottled water	5	$1.25	$6.25
4	Juice	6	$1.50	$9.00
5	Milk	3	$1.00	$3.00
6	Totals	14		$18.25
7	Function totals	14		$18.25
8				
9				
10				
11				
12				
13				
14				
15				
16				

Putting your spreadsheet data in a chart helps you show the data more clearly. This is important when you need to show other people what your data mean. A chart makes data easier to understand. A chart can also help you compare data. For example, you could use the chart on page 232 to see how much bottled water was sold compared to milk or juice.

A chart is linked to its spreadsheet. That means if you change the data in the spreadsheet, the chart will change too. Suppose you changed the number of juices sold from 6 to 7. The bar graph for juices sold will change to 7. The height of the bar will be greater.

▶ **LESSON REVIEW**

1. What are four kinds of charts you can make?

2. What happens to a chart if you change the data in the spreadsheet?

3. **CRITICAL THINKING** Why would you show someone a chart of your data instead of the numbers?

11·5 Lab Practice

Open the spreadsheet named *Drinks Sold*. Look at the screen below. Then follow the steps below to make a bar graph based on the data.

	A	B	C	D
1	Drinks Sold in Cafeteria			
2	Kinds of Drinks	Amount Sold	Unit Price	Total Received
3	Bottled water	5	$1.25	$6.25
4	Juice	6	$1.50	$9.00
5	Milk	3	$1.00	$3.00
6	Totals	14		$18.25
7	Function totals	14		$18.25

STEP 1   Click and drag the mouse to select all the cells in Rows 2 through 7, and Columns A through D.

STEP 2   Click the Chart button or choose the Make Chart command.

STEP 3   Click OK. A bar graph will appear on your spreadsheet.

STEP 4   Save the spreadsheet file.

STEP 5   Check Your Work: How is the chart different from the one on page 232?

▶ **More Practice**

Use the *Drinks Sold* spreadsheet. Select all the cells in Rows 2 through 5. Make a new chart using this data. You will have two charts in your spreadsheet. Click on one chart to select it. Then drag it so you can see both charts at the same time. Compare the charts to each other.

COMPUTERS IN YOUR LIFE
Setting Up a Budget

Every family has bills that have to get paid each month. A spreadsheet can be useful for keeping track of bills. By analyzing the data, a family can set up a budget. That way they will know how much of the money they earn to put aside for bills. They will also know how much spending money will be left.

The screen below shows a spreadsheet for a family that earns a total of $2,200 each month.

Phone bills and rent bills are part of a family's monthly expenses.

	A	B	C	D	E	F
1		January	February	March	April	Totals
2	Rent	$900.00	$900.00	$900.00	$900.00	$3,600.00
3	Telephone	$65.00	$52.00	$74.00	$68.00	$259.00
4	Gas and Electricity	$185.00	$193.00	$187.00	$172.00	$737.00
5	Groceries	$455.00	$485.00	$500.00	$461.00	$1,901.00
6	Transportation	$250.00	$240.00	$250.00	$275.00	
7	Totals	$1,855.00	$1,870.00	$1,911.00	$1,876.00	

Use the screen above to answer the questions.

1. What function was used to find the number in cell B7?

2. What formula would you use to fill in Cell F6?

3. Write a formula the family could use to find out how much money is left at the end of January.

Critical Thinking
How could the family find the average amount they pay for each expense?

Applying: Analyzing Time Spent

Spreadsheet formulas and functions help you analyze information. You can also make charts to present data.

Example

Angie kept the record shown below. Use a spreadsheet to compare the amounts of time she spent on these activities.

> **MY JOURNAL**
> Monday: Homework 3 hours, TV 2 hours, Phone 0.5 hours
> Tuesday: Homework 2 hours, TV 2 hours, Phone 1 hour
> Wednesday: Homework 4 hours, TV 1 hour, Phone 0.25 hours
> Thursday: Homework 3 hours, TV 2 hours, Phone 0.75 hours
> Friday: Homework 1 hour, TV 3 hours, Phone 1.5 hours

STEP 1 GET READY What do you need to do first?
Make a new spreadsheet. Label the columns and rows. Enter Angie's data.

STEP 2 THINK What do you know about the information in the spreadsheet?
Think about what you need to do with the data. Decide what math should be done. For example, decide if Angie should add numbers. If so, think about what formulas or functions she needs to use.

STEP 3 APPLY Analyze the information.
Set up and name a row or column for the numbers to calculate. For example, name a row or column *Total Hours* if the spreadsheet should calculate the hours spent on the phone. Then use a formula or function to add the data for phone time.

STEP 4 CHECK Does the information look correct?
View the formulas used to find each total. Correct any formulas that give you an error message. Compare the totals for each day.

11·6 Lab Practice

GET READY to analyze information using a spreadsheet. Answer the questions under THINK. APPLY what you know to analyze the information. CHECK your finished work.

1. For the chapter project, you kept a record for five days of the hours spent doing homework, watching TV, and talking on the phone. Now, use a spreadsheet to compare the amounts of time spent on these activities.

   THINK How will you organize your data?

   What math calculation will you do?

2. You want to find out which activity, on average, takes the most time per day. Add a function to your spreadsheet to show this information.
   THINK Which rows or columns are needed?

   What function could you use?

   What formula would you write to find the daily average for TV? Sample answer:
   =AVERAGE(C2,C3,C4,C5,C6)

3. Make a bar graph of the data to show which days you spent the least amount of time doing each activity. Put a chart in your spreadsheet.

   THINK What cells should you select?

   How can the chart help show the data?

Making Connections
Use a spreadsheet to keep track of your test and quiz scores for all your classes: math, science, social studies, language arts, and so on. Use your spreadsheet to find your average scores for each subject. Make a bar graph based on your spreadsheet data.

Summary

Working with Spreadsheet Data
*Spreadsheet formulas, functions, and charts help you
analyze your data.*

- **Use formulas to do math.** Type an equal sign (=) followed by numbers and operations (Add, +; subtract, –; multiply, *; divide, /).

- **Make formulas with cell names** by typing = followed by cell names and operations.

- **Edit formulas** by clicking in a cell and then clicking in the formula bar.

- **Use functions** by typing = and the function name. List the cell names or numbers in parentheses.

- **Make a chart to show data.** Select the cells with the data. Then click the Chart button.

- **Analyze information** by using a spreadsheet.

---

function

spreadsheet formula

Vocabulary Review
Complete each sentence with a word from the list.

1. A _____ is a built-in shortcut that does calculations.

2. A math expression that shows a calculation is a _____.

Chapter Quiz

Answer the following questions.

LESSON 11·1

Computer Tip
Always start a formula with an equal sign.

LESSONS 11·2 and 11·3

Computer Tip
Use * for multiplication and / for division in formulas.

LESSON 11·4

LESSON 11·5

LESSON 11·6

What Is a Formula?

1. What does a formula do?

2. How can you do math in a spreadsheet?

Making and Editing Formulas

3. Explain what this formula does: $=(B4*B5)-2$

4. How do you display a formula so you can edit it?

5. Where do you edit a formula?

Using a Function

6. What function would you use to add the numbers in a row of cells?

7. What does the function MAX do?

Making a Chart

8. How can a bar chart help you analyze your data?

Applying: Analyzing Information

9. How do formulas and charts in spreadsheets help you analyze information?

Group Activity

With your group, create a new spreadsheet file. Measure the height of each group member. Enter the data in a spreadsheet. Find the average height for your group. Then make a chart of your data. Use the chart to find who is taller than the average and who is shorter than the average for your group.

Unit 3 **Review**

Choose the letter of the correct answer.

1. For which task would you use a database?
   A. Write a letter to a club member
   B. Make a record for each member in a club
   C. Find the total amount of dues collected from club members
   D. Make a chart showing how club dues are spent

2. For which task would you use a spreadsheet?
   A. Print mailing labels
   B. Search for an address
   C. Make a chart showing monthly costs
   D. Make a list of birth dates

3. Which task is done when you order numbers from smallest to largest using a database?
   A. Make records
   B. Sort records
   C. Edit a formula
   D. Make a layout

4. Which task is done when you find the average amount spent each month using a spreadsheet?
   A. Use a function
   B. Make a cell active
   C. Define fields
   D. Format data

Look at the list of information below. Then answer Question 5 and the Critical Thinking question.

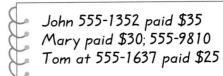

John 555-1352 paid $35
Mary paid $30; 555-9810
Tom at 555-1637 paid $25

5. If you wanted to store this information in a database, what field types would you define?
   A. A text field for *Name* and number fields for *Phone* and *Paid*
   B. Text fields for *Name, Phone,* and *Paid*
   C. Text fields for *Name* and *Phone* and a number field for *Paid*
   D. Text fields for *Name* and *Paid* and a number field for *Phone*

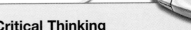

Critical Thinking
Set up a spreadsheet for the data in the list above. Enter information and data in rows and columns. Write a formula to find the total amount of money paid.

Chapter 12 **Desktop Publishing**

Chapter 13 **Presentations**

The Lincoln Memorial, in Washington, D.C., is a popular tourist site.

Washington, D.C. is our nation's capital. It is a great place to visit. You can learn about the places to visit by seeing a tour presentation or by reading a tour guide. A good guide or presentation will have both pictures and text. Computer software can be used to make tour guides and presentations. Look at the guide shown on the right to answer the questions.

1. Why is it helpful to put pictures together with text when showing information?

2. How do you think computers make this job easier?

These students are putting together a school newspaper. Desktop publishing lets them arrange the way that pictures and text look on the page. How do you think this task was done without computers?

What You Need to Know

How to use a mouse and a keyboard

How to use commands, menus, and toolbars

How to use a dialog box and scroll bars

How to enter text

How to format text

This chapter is about Desktop Publishing.

What You Will Learn

What desktop publishing is used for

How to lay out a page

How to use clip art and make your own art

Presenting page layouts

Words to Know

publishing	the printing of many copies of a book, magazine, newspaper, or other document
desktop publishing	using a personal computer to combine text and art on a page
clip art	a piece of art that is already drawn
border	a frame around text or art on a page
page layout	the way text and art are arranged together on a page
column	a section of text that runs from top to bottom on a page
head	a title that is used to separate parts of text on a page
freeform	a way to draw your own objects without using shapes made by the computer

Portfolio Project

Look through magazines and newspapers to find three examples of page layouts. Cut out the pages. Paste each on a sheet of construction paper to make three posters. For each page, write a title for the poster. Then write one sentence that explains what the page is about. Label the different features used in each layout, such as text, art, photos, heads, or columns.

Learning Objectives

- Identify uses of desktop publishing.
- Plan and make a page layout.
- Use clip art in a page layout.
- Make your own art.
- Apply page layouts to making a newsletter.
- PROBLEM SOLVING: Solve the problem of overlapping art.
- COMPUTERS ON THE JOB: Analyze the parts of a magazine page.

What Is Desktop Publishing?

Publishing is the printing of many copies of a book, newspaper, magazine, or other types of documents. In these materials, text and art often appear on the same page. Text includes sentences, paragraphs, captions, and titles. Art includes photographs, drawings, tables, diagrams, and other illustrations.

Today, many publishing jobs are done on personal computers. For example, you can create a small magazine, newspaper, or poster using a personal computer. When you use a computer to combine text and art on a page, it is called **desktop publishing**.

Arranging a Page

Most word processing software includes tools for desktop publishing. These tools allow you to change the way a page in your document looks. Look at the diagrams about the space shuttle below. They show two ways to arrange text and art on a page.

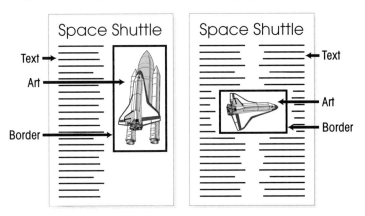

Remember
Text formats include styles, point sizes, and fonts used with text on a page.

You can use software to give text special formats. You can also use software to make a special **border** in your document. A border is a frame around text or art on a page. Look at the diagrams above. The thick black lines around the pictures are borders.

Adding Art

Your software also has commands that let you add art into a document. **Clip art** is a piece of art that is already drawn. You can insert clip art into a document. Your computer also has commands and tools that let you draw your own art.

▶ **LESSON REVIEW**

1. Look at the pictures of the two space shuttle pages on page 244. What differences do you see?

2. Name two different types of art.

3. **CRITICAL THINKING** Why is clip art a useful tool for desktop publishing?

On the Cutting Edge

DIGITAL CAMERAS

Desktop publishers often use photographs. However, many of the photographs they use are now taken with digital cameras. You can take photos with a digital camera in the same way as with any other type of camera. But a digital camera does not have film. It has a small computer that stores images on a small disk. You can look at your photos right away on a tiny screen.

Digital camera

The photos can easily be moved from the camera to a computer. From there, you can use software to view, change, or print the photos. Then you can add them to a document and print it. You can also take the disk to a photo developer. The developer will print the photos for you.

CRITICAL THINKING Why might someone want a digital camera instead of a film camera?

12·2 Making Up a Page

When you want to make a newsletter, flyer, or magazine page, you have to plan the **page layout**. The page layout is the way the text and art are arranged together on the page.

Planning a Page Layout

Start by thinking about the size of the page and what must fit on it. Make a rough drawing of your page. This kind of drawing is called a *thumbnail sketch*. A thumbnail sketch helps you plan and design your page layout. It does not show many details.

Look at the thumbnail sketch below. It shows pages for a newsletter layout. There are two pieces of art on the pages. The horizontal lines show where the text will go.

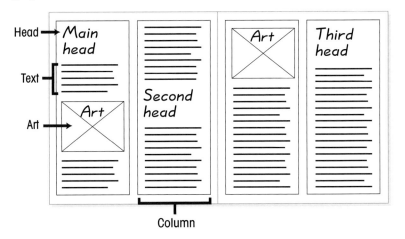

A **column** is a section of text that runs from top to bottom on a page. For a flyer, a letter, or a report, you usually use only one column of text. For a newsletter, like the one above, you often use two or more columns.

A **head** is a title. It is used to separate different parts of text on a page. You can use formats to make heads stand out more than other text. The most important or main head should stand out the most. The newsletter layout on page 246 has three heads.

Making Columns

Once you have a thumbnail sketch of your layout, it is time to make up the page. To add columns to a document that contains text, first select the text with the mouse. Then choose Columns from the Format menu. A dialog box will appear. Look at the example below:

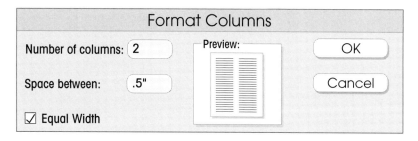

You can type in the number of columns you want in the Number of Columns box. Choose Equal Width to make all the columns the same size. Then click OK.

Look at the diagram below. When you make columns, the software automatically puts some space between them. The text you selected goes from the top to the bottom of the first column. Then it continues at the top of the next column. If you add more text, the lengths of the columns change to fit it. When both columns are full, a new page with two columns forms.

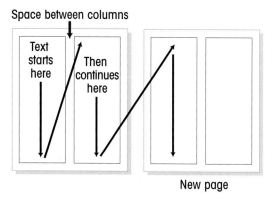

Formats for Text and Heads

You can now change the formats of your text and heads. Decide which fonts, styles, and point sizes will look best.

For text, choose a font that is simple and easy to read. For heads use a larger point size than for the rest of your text. Make the most important head larger than the others. You can use bold, italic, or underline to make your heads stand out. Here are some examples of head formats.

You can use this for a Large Head.

This font is called Helvetica. The point size is 16. The style is bold.

You can use this for a Medium Head.

This font is called Arial. The point size is 14. The style is underlined.

You can use this for a Small Head.
This font is called Avante Garde. The point size is 11. The style is italics.

You can use different combinations of fonts, sizes, and styles to make your heads look different.

▶ LESSON REVIEW

1. Why is a thumbnail sketch useful?

2. What are three important steps in planning a page layout?

3. How can you add columns to a page of text?

4. **CRITICAL THINKING** Why is it important to change the font and point size when making a head?

12·2 Lab Practice

Open the document called *Using Technology*. To make a page layout, look at the thumbnail sketch shown on the right. Then follow the steps.

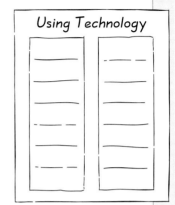

STEP 1   Use the Save As command to name your document **Layout 1**.

STEP 2   Enter a title at the beginning of the document. Add two lines of blank space under the title. Press the Enter (or Return) key twice.

STEP 3   Select the text portion of your document. Find and click on the Columns command. Enter **2** for the number of columns. Then click OK.

STEP 4   Select the text in the columns. Format it to make the size 10 points.

STEP 5   Select the title to make it a head. Format it to make the size 24 points. Make the head bold. Then align it in the center.

STEP 6   Check Your Work: Did you make the point size of the head larger or smaller than the text? Why?

▶ **More Practice**

Make a thumbnail sketch of a different page layout for the same document. Include another head somewhere in your layout. Open *Layout 1* and use the Save As command to name it *Layout 2*. Make the page layout match your sketch. Choose a different point size for your text. Choose a different point size and font for the heads.

COMPUTERS ON THE JOB
Desktop Publisher

Matt is a desktop publisher. He works for a magazine. As part of his job, Matt meets with the magazine editors. They give him the text and tell him how many pages each magazine article must be. The editors also give him photos and art for each page. It is Matt's job to make the page layouts for the magazine.

For each page, Matt thinks about how many columns of text there will be. He thinks about how many pieces of art must fit on the page and what size they should be. He also thinks about how many heads will be on the page and which is the most important one. After he sketches the layout, he makes the pages on the computer. Here are thumbnail sketches for two pages.

Matt makes thumbnail sketches to plan the page layout.

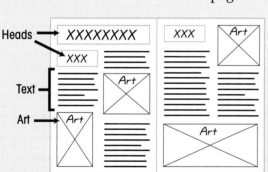

Use the thumbnail sketches to answer the questions.

1. How many columns of text are on each page?

2. How many pieces of art are in this two-page layout?

3. How many heads are in this two-page layout?

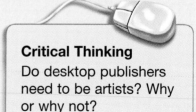

Critical Thinking
Do desktop publishers need to be artists? Why or why not?

Word processing programs usually have commands to add clip art to the text on your page. Many programs also come with a gallery, or library, of clip art. You can choose art from a clip art gallery.

Inserting Clip Art

To insert clip art, click in the document where you want the art to appear. What you do next depends on the program you are using.

In some programs, an Insert menu appears in the main menu bar. Then look for the command for inserting a Picture and/or Clip Art. In other programs, you may need to choose Insert or Library from the File menu.

A dialog box or window like the one below will appear.

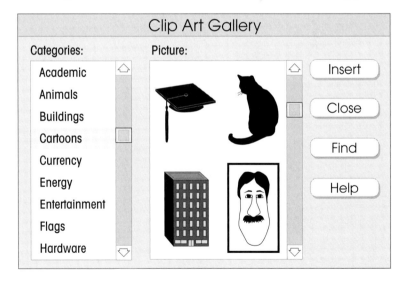

Look through the subjects and pictures to find the one you want. You can click on the picture. Then click Insert (or Use) to put the art in your document. Click the Close button when you are done.

Computer Fact

You have a right to use the Clip Art that comes with your software. You do not have a right to use art owned by someone else in your document. You must first get persmission before using art owned by someone else. This is part of the Copyright Law.

Changing Clip Art

Clip art in your document will be inside a box. The box has one or more dots called handles. If you do not see the box or handles, click on the art.

The handles let you change the size and shape of the art. Click and drag a corner handle. A dotted box will appear around the art. Drag out to make the art larger. Drag in to make the art smaller. Look at the art below.

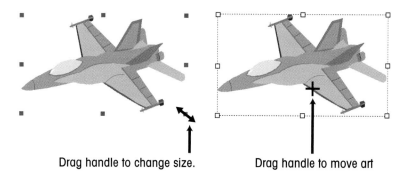

Drag handle to change size.   Drag handle to move art

You also can move art in a document from place to place. Click on the edge or middle of the art and then drag it to a new place. A dotted box shows you where the art will go. When you stop dragging, the art moves to the new spot.

▶ **LESSON REVIEW**

1. How would you insert a piece of clip art into your document?

2. What should you click on to change the size of art?

3. What should you click on to move art?

4. **CRITICAL THINKING** Why might you want to make a piece of art smaller? larger?

12·3 Lab Practice

Open the document *Layout 1* you created in Lesson 12.2. Look at the thumbnail sketch below. Then follow the steps to insert a piece of clip art into your layout.

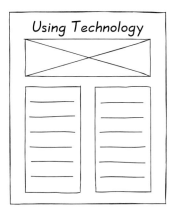

STEP 1 Put the cursor in the first blank line under the title.

STEP 2 Use menu commands to open a Clip Art dialog box.

STEP 3 Select the art you want to use. Click Insert (or Use). Close the Clip Art dialog box.

STEP 4 Resize the art to fit across the columns. If necessary, move the art in place under the title.

STEP 5 Save the document *Layout 1*.

STEP 6 Check Your Work: How wide is the art in your document?

▶ **More Practice**

Open the document *Layout 2* that you created in Lesson 12.2. Insert a piece of clip art in the second column. Change the size and move the art if needed. Save the document *Layout 2*. Check your work.

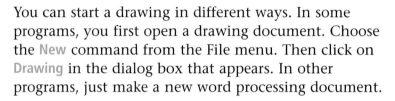

12·4 Making Your Own Art

Sometimes clip art does not have a picture you want. In that case, you can use your software's drawing tools to create your own pictures. Most word processing programs have drawing tools that allow you to draw lines, shapes, and patterns to make your own art.

Starting a Drawing

You can start a drawing in different ways. In some programs, you first open a drawing document. Choose the New command from the File menu. Then click on Drawing in the dialog box that appears. In other programs, just make a new word processing document.

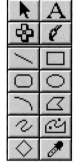

Drawing tools

Once you have a document, use the Drawing menus or toolbars to create your art. Look at the drawing tools at the left. Notice that there are tools for drawing lines and shapes. There is also a pointing tool for selecting, moving, and sizing objects.

Using Drawing Tools

To draw a rectangle, click on the rectangle tool. Then move the mouse pointer to the document window. The pointer changes. As you click and drag the pointer, a dotted outline of a rectangle appears. When you let go of the mouse button, the rectangle is done. To make a square, hold down the Shift key as you use the rectangle tool. Look at the screen at the top of the next page.

You can draw lines, curves, ovals, and circles in the same way. First click on the tool for the object you want to draw. Then click and drag the mouse pointer in the drawing area. To make a circle, hold down the Shift key as you draw an oval.

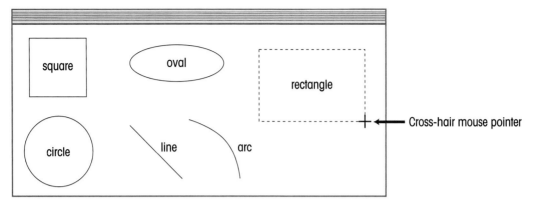

You can draw lines and shapes to add to a document.

You can also draw **freeform**. Drawing freeform means drawing objects without using shapes made by the computer. Just click on the freeform tool. When you draw freeform, the mouse pointer is the pen point. As you move the mouse, the freeform tool draws.

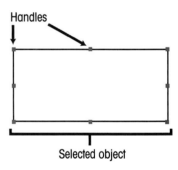

Use the pointing tool to select an object. Look at the diagram on the right. When an object is selected, you can see its handles. You can move the object or change its size, just as with clip art. You can remove the object by pressing the Delete key. You can also use the Copy and Paste commands to make a copy of an object.

▶ **LESSON REVIEW**

1. Which icon can you use to draw a straight line?

2. How do you move an object after drawing it?

3. **CRITICAL THINKING** What is the difference between using the rectangle tool and using the freeform tool?

12·4 Lab Practice

Look at the screen below. Then follow the steps to make a drawing like the one shown.

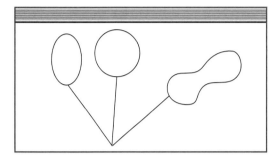

STEP 1   Use menu commands to open a new drawing document.

STEP 2   Click on the oval tool. Then click in the drawing area. Drag the pointer to draw an oval. Let go of the mouse button.

STEP 3   Click on the oval tool. Draw a circle. Hold down the Shift key while you drag the pointer in the drawing area. Let go of the mouse button and the Shift key.

STEP 4   Click on the freeform tool. Draw your own shape.

STEP 5   Click on the line tool. Draw three lines. Attach one line to the bottom of each shape; as shown in the diagram above.

STEP 6   Check Your Work: What does your drawing look like?

 More Practice

Open a new drawing document. Use the drawing tools to make a rectangle, a square, and two circles. Move the shapes to make the drawing at the right. Use the freeform tool to draw headlights and a bumper.

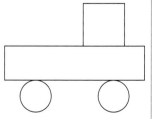

There is a problem with the art of an ice-cream cone shown in Picture A. The circle covers up part of the cone. The ice cream does not look like it is in the cone.

You can solve this problem by using commands for moving objects to the front or back. The commands will be in a menu called Arrange or Order. You can use the commands to move art in front of or behind other art.

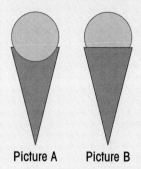

Picture A   Picture B

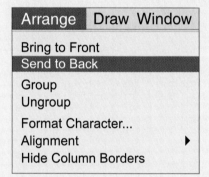

Select the piece of art you want to move. If you use Send to Back (or Move to Back), the art will go behind any other object. Use Send to Front (or Move to Front) to put the art in front of another object and overlap it.

Look at the art above.

1. If you select the cone in Picture A, what command should you use to make it look like Picture B?

2. In Picture B, which shape is in the front?

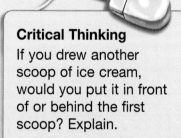

Critical Thinking

If you drew another scoop of ice cream, would you put it in front of or behind the first scoop? Explain.

Applying: Presenting Page Layouts

Desktop publishing can be used to present information. You can combine text and art to create a page layout for a newsletter or yearbook.

Example

You want to put together a newsletter for your club. The newsletter needs one page with two stories. Each story needs one head and one piece of art. Plan, write, and make a page layout for your newsletter.

STEP 1 GET READY What do you need to do first?
Make a list of what will appear on the page.

STEP 2 THINK What do you know about making a page layout?
Decide how many heads and text columns to use. Decide where to place the art. Draw a thumbnail sketch of your layout like the one shown at right.

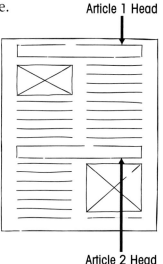

Article 1 Head

Article 2 Head

STEP 3 APPLY Make a page layout.
Make a new word processing document. Enter the heads and the text. Make two columns for the text in each story. Format the style and point size of the heads. Insert clip art or make your own art for each story. Change the size of the art and move the art if necessary.

STEP 4 CHECK How does the information look?
Look at the page layout. Make sure it includes all the features. You should see all the text and art clearly. Fix any errors. Save and print.

12·5 Lab Practice

GET READY to plan a page layout. Answer the questions under THINK. APPLY what you know to arrange the text and art on the page. CHECK your finished work.

1. Nathan works on the high school yearbook. He helps arrange the pages that show clubs and sports. On one page, he has to fit two club photos, some text, and a head. Make a page layout that Nathan could use.

   THINK

   How many text columns should there be?

   Which is more important, the photos or the text?

2. Miriam also works on the yearbook. She helps arrange pages with the photos of the senior class. Each page has the same layout. She needs to fit 11 photos on each page, with the name of the student under each photo. Make a page layout that Miriam could use.

   THINK

   What is the most important feature of the layout?

   What should you decide about the size and placement of the photos?

Making Connections

Use a report from your science, social studies, or language arts class. Make a thumbnail sketch for a page layout to arrange your work in a new way. Add a head and make two columns. Insert clip art or draw your own for the report. Present the "Before" and "After" reports to the class. Explain the changes you made.

Summary

Desktop Publishing
When you use desktop publishing, you use a computer to combine text and art on a page.
• **To plan a page layout,** make a thumbnail sketch.
• **To format text in a page layout,** use different fonts, styles, and point sizes for heads.
• **To insert art in a page layout,** use clip art.
• **To make your own art,** use drawing tools to make lines and shapes.
• **Present information clearly,** by applying desktop publishing to making different page layouts.

border

clip art

column

desktop publishing

freeform

head

page layout

publishing

Vocabulary Review

Complete each sentence with a term from the list.

1. The printing of many copies of a book, magazine, newspaper, or other document is _____.

2. A piece of art that is already made and can be inserted into a document is _____.

3. The way text and art are arranged together on a page is a _____.

4. A title used to separate parts of text on a page is a _____.

5. Using a personal computer to combine text and art on a page is _____.

6. When you draw art without using shapes created by the computer, you draw it _____.

7. A section of text that runs from top to bottom on a page is a _____.

8. A frame around text or art on a page is a _____.

Chapter Quiz

Answer the following questions.

LESSON 12·1

What Is Desktop Publishing?

1. What does desktop publishing allow you to do?

2. What does art include in desktop publishing?

LESSON 12·2

Planning and Making Page Layouts

3. What are the steps for planning a page layout?

4. When might you use more than one column for text?

LESSON 12·3

Inserting Art

5. How can you insert art into a document?

6. How can you change the size of a piece of art?

LESSON 12·4

Making Your Own Art

7. How can you make a square in a drawing?

8. Which tool lets you draw your own shapes and lines?

LESSON 12·5

Computer Tip
Making a thumbnail sketch helps you plan a page layout.

Applying: Presenting Page Layouts

9. Why does making a page layout help you present information better?

Group Activity

With your group, make up a list of features that must be included on a page. Include at least one head and at least one piece of art, along with text. Exchange lists with another group. Make at least two different thumbnail sketches of page layouts using the features on the list. Enter text and create at least two page layouts based on your sketches.

This man is giving a presentation about sales in different parts of the United States. How do you think the colors on the map help him communicate information?

What You Need to Know

How to enter and edit text

How to format text

How to make a page layout

How to insert art on a page

How to make art with drawing tools

This chapter is about Presentations.

What You Will Learn

What presentation software does

How to plan a presentation and choose slide layouts

How to add text and art to a slide

How to show a presentation

How to present information to an audience

Chapter 13 ▷ Presentations

Words to Know

presentation	a way to use text and art to communicate information or ideas to other people
slide	a page in a presentation document
handouts	documents with information printed from a presentation
storyboard	a series of sketches that shows the order in which slides will appear

Events Log Project

Keep a log of ten different events that take place in your life during one week. Events may include activities you do, places you go, things you see, or special occasions you are part of. In your log, include the date of the event and a short description of what happened. Then make a poster highlighting the five most important events of your week. Use pictures and text in your poster.

Learning Objectives

- Explain what presentation software does.
- Plan a presentation.
- Choose slide layouts.
- Add text and art to slides.
- Show a presentation.
- Apply presentation software to communicate about events.
- PROBLEM SOLVING: Solve problems in slide order by rearranging slides.
- COMPUTERS IN YOUR LIFE: Make a presentation about yourself.

One way to share information with others is to make a **presentation**. A presentation uses text and art to communicate information or ideas to other people. Art can mean clip art, drawings, photographs, diagrams, charts, or graphs.

Remember
Clip art is a piece of art that is already made and can be inserted in a document.

Presentation software helps you put text and art together using a computer. Each page of a presentation document is called a **slide**. A slide may have only text, only art, or both text and art. Some software also lets you use sounds and short movies on slides.

Look at the picture below. It shows a slide made with presentation software. Sometimes a presentation is called a *slide show*. You can use a projector to view presentation slides. A projector makes the slides look larger. This allows more people to see the slides.

What is Presentation Software?

☑ **It can put text and art together in a slide.**

☑ **It is used to make slide shows.**

☑ **It can make handouts for talks.**

☑ **It can use drawings, charts, and photographs.**

This is a slide made with presentation software.

Presentation software also helps you make **handouts**. A handout is a printed document with information from a presentation. For example, you can print an outline of your presentation to give to an audience. Or you can print your slides with notes about important ideas.

Slides and handouts help an audience understand your presentation. You can use slides with art to get the audience's attention. You can use text to highlight the important points as you speak.

Microsoft® PowerPoint® is one example of presentation software. ClarisWorks® also can be used to make a presentation on a computer.

 LESSON REVIEW

1. What does presentation software help you do?

2. **CRITICAL THINKING** Why might you want to use presentation software?

On the Cutting Edge

COMPUTER-CONTROLLED PROJECTORS

When making a presentation, the presenter can connect a projector to a computer. The presenter can use the computer to control the projector. This type of projector is called a multimedia projector.

Newer projectors have built-in computer parts that read computer files. Presentation files can be stored on a disk the size of a credit card. The disk can be inserted into the projector. There is no need to bring a computer. The presenter can use the remote control with a built-in mouse to run the show.

This projector and remote control use software to show a presentation.

CRITICAL THINKING What is an advantage of a projector with built-in computer parts? What is a disadvantage?

Suppose you have chosen a topic you want to present. Before you make a presentation, you must plan it. The first step in planning is to choose information about your topic. The second step is to organize the information.

Choosing Information

To choose what to put in your presentation, start by reading the information that you have about your topic. Make a checklist using a few main ideas. The checklist below shows some ideas for a presentation about popular music.

Ideas for Popular Music Presentation
- ✓   *Most popular recording artists*
- ✓   *Best-selling popular music CD*
- ☆☆✓ *Favorite popular music concert*
- X   *Popular instrumental music*
- X   *Country music*
- ☆☆✓ *Rock music*

Put check marks next to the ideas you want to keep. Put stars next to the most important ideas. These are the ideas you will put in your presentation. Put Xs next to ideas you decide not to use.

Organizing Information

Now you are ready to decide the order in which you will present your ideas. Make a **storyboard** to help you. A storyboard is a series of sketches. It shows the order in which each slide appears. It also shows how much text and art will go on each slide.

Use a storyboard to decide how many slides you will need to show each main idea. Some ideas may need more than one slide. Include a slide for the title of your presentation. Your storyboard will also help you decide where you will put text and art.

Look at the storyboard below. It shows sketches for five slides in a presentation. Each slide has a different page layout. Slide 1 has only a title. Slide 2 has a title, art, and one column of text. The X in a box shows where art will go in a slide. The box with little lines across it shows where text will be. Slide 3 has a title and art. Slide 4 has a title and two columns of text. Slide 5 has a title and four pieces of art.

Remember
A page layout is the way items are arranged together on a page or screen.

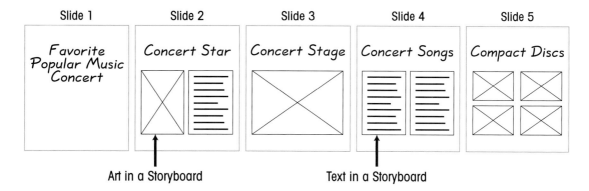

The storyboard above shows a plan for a presentation.

▶ **LESSON REVIEW**

1. What are the main steps for planning a presentation?

2. How does a storyboard help in planning a presentation?

3. **CRITICAL THINKING** How are slide layouts similar to page layouts used in desktop publishing? How are they different?

13·2 Lab Practice

Read the information below. To organize the information for a presentation, follow the steps below.

> Cheetahs run faster than all other four-footed animals. An adult cheetah can run as fast as 70 miles per hour. It weighs from 110 to 130 pounds. Its body is about four feet long. It has very long legs, and a small head. A cheetah's coat is yellowish-brown with many round, black spots.

STEP 1 Make a checklist of the ideas about cheetahs: speed, weight, coat, and length. Decide which ideas are the most important.

STEP 2 Put the ideas in order, starting with the most important. For example, the order of your ideas might be as follows: Speed, Size, Appearance.

STEP 3 Use the checklist to draw a storyboard. You will need a slide for each idea in the checklist. Decide how many slides you will need. Sketch the layout for each slide. Sketch the slides in order.

STEP 4 Check Your Work: How many slides have you sketched?

▶ More Practice

Read the information in the screen below. Add any new ideas to your checklist. Reorder your list. Make changes to your storyboard. Save and check your work.

> Cheetahs hunt by chasing their prey. They eat gazelles and small antelope. A cheetah's face has black stripes from its eyes to the sides of its nose.

When you make a Blank Presentation in Microsoft® PowerPoint®, you must choose slide layouts. A blank presentation is a new document with no slide layouts already chosen. You start with the New Slide dialog box. Look at the screen below. You can choose the layout you want to use by clicking on it. Then click OK.

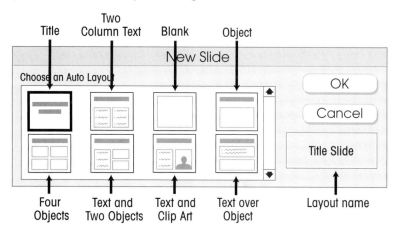

To add another slide, choose New Slide from the Insert menu. Use your storyboard to help you choose a layout.

To change a slide layout, you would do the following.
1. Click on the slide to select it.
2. Choose Slide Layout from the Format menu. The Slide Layout dialog box will appear.
3. Click on the layout you want to use.
4. Click the Apply button.

Computer Fact

In Clarisworks®, the Slide feature on the View menu lets you make presentations. Each page of a document becomes a slide.

▶ **LESSON REVIEW**

1. How do you select a slide layout from the dialog box?

2. **CRITICAL THINKING** Look at the storyboard on page 267. What layouts would you choose for Slides 4 and 5?

Look at the storyboard below. It shows sketches for a presentation about favorite activities.

Make a new blank presentation document. To choose layouts for the first two slides in the storyboard, follow the steps below.

STEP 1 You should be in the New Slide dialog box. Click on the Title Slide layout. Click OK. This will make Slide 1.

STEP 2 To add Slide 2, click on Slide 1 in the document window.

STEP 3 Choose New Slide from the Insert menu. Choose the layout named *2 Objects & Text*. You may need the scroll bar to find it. Click OK.

STEP 4 Check Your Work: Look at Slide 2. How many places can hold art? How many places can hold text?

▶ More Practice

Look at the storyboard above. Use menu commands to add Slides 3 and Slide 4 to the presentation. Choose layouts for the slides that match the sketches in the storyboard. Save your presentation as *My Activities*. Check your work.

You can enter your own text to slides. This works just like word processing. Look at the screen below. It shows the presentation window for a Title Slide layout.

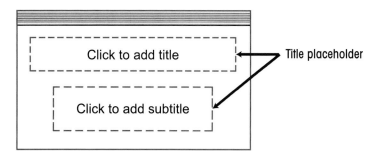

The boxes with gray or dashed lines around them are *placeholders*. The placeholders will appear when you make a new slide. They show you where text or art will go on a slide. To enter text, click in the placeholder. You will see a blinking cursor. Enter text using the keyboard.

Remember
A cursor is a blinking vertical line. It shows where the text is being entered.

You can edit or replace text in a slide just as in word processing. You can also use formats for style, size, font, and alignment of text in a slide.

Remember
You learned about inserting, moving, and resizing clip art in Lesson 12.3.

You can resize a placeholder with or without text in it. Resizing a placeholder is like resizing art. Look at the diagram below. Click on the border to select it. Then drag one of the corner handles. You can also move a placeholder the same way you move art. To delete a placeholder, first select it. Then press the Delete key.

Click to add title

Click and drag here

Look at the screen below. It shows a new slide for the cheetah presentation from Lab Practice 13.2 on page 268.

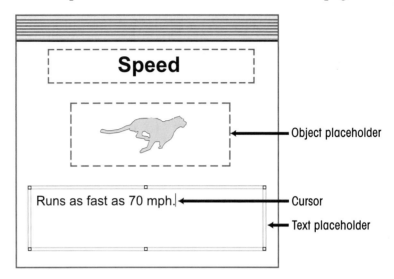

The text for the title, *Speed*, has already been typed in the placeholder at the top. The title text is bold and centered. The slide also has a placeholder for an object, such as a picture.

At the bottom of the slide is a text placeholder. Text about a cheetah's speed has already been entered in the text placeholder. Notice the cursor at the end of the line of text. You can add another line by pressing the Enter (or Return) key. You can use the same formats with this text as you can in word processing. You can use different styles, point sizes, and fonts. You can also change the alignment of text.

▶ **LESSON REVIEW**

1. How do you enter text for a title in a slide?

2. How do you add another line to a text placeholder?

3. **CRITICAL THINKING** How is a text placeholder similar to a title placeholder?

13·4 Lab Practice

Open the *My Activities* presentation. To add text to slides 1 and 2 in your presentation, follow the steps below. Look at the slides to the right to help you.

STEP 1 In Slide 1, click in the *Click to add title* placeholder. Enter the title **My Favorite Activities**.

STEP 2 Remove the subtitle placeholder. Click on its border, then press the Delete key.

STEP 3 Use the scroll bar to go to Slide 2. Enter the title **My Favorite Sports**.

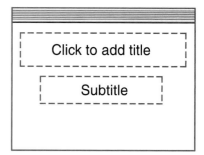

Slide 1

STEP 4 Click in the *Click to add text* placeholder. Enter one of your favorite sports.

STEP 5 Press the Enter (or Return) key to add another line. Enter another of your favorite sports.

STEP 6 Check Your Work: How many lines of text are in Slide 2?

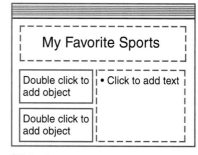

Slide 2

 More Practice

Use your *My Activities* presentation. Enter the title **My Favorite Hobbies** in Slide 3. Enter two hobbies in the text placeholder. In Slide 4, enter the title **Other Activities**. Save your presentation. Check your work.

COMPUTERS IN YOUR LIFE
Making a Presentation About Yourself

When you apply for a job, you may need to go to an interview. During an interview, you answer questions about yourself. You can use a presentation to tell things about yourself and any work experience you have had. Then the interviewer will remember a lot about you.

Do a little planning before you make a presentation. Start by making a list of ten things about yourself. These are things you would want people to know. You should include your grades at school, activities you do, groups you belong to, and other skills you have. The example below shows one student's list. You could make a storyboard from this list.

Ideas For Interview Presentation

1. I have high grades in English, Math, and Science.
2. I can type 60 words per minute.
3. I do volunteer work at a local hospital.
4. I won an award for good citizenship.
5. I like to build things out of wood.
6. I belong to an honor society.

Use the list above to answer the questions.

1. How would you group the items on the list to use them in a presentation?

2. What text would you enter under the title *My Skills?*

Critical Thinking
In what other ways would using a presentation be helpful?

13-5 ▶ Adding Art to Slides

Adding art, such as clip art and pictures, helps make a presentation more interesting. To make a slide with art, choose a slide layout with one of the placeholders shown at the left.

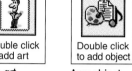

Clip art placeholder

Any object placeholder

You can add clip art to an object placeholder in a slide. Click in the placeholder. Then choose Clip Art from the Insert menu. This will open the Clip Art Gallery or Library. Select a subject from the Categories list. Then click on the art you want to use. Click OK to add the art to your slide.

Remember
You learned how to select and resize art in Lesson 12.4.

You can also insert art or photos from a file. Look at the screens below. They show before and after art has been added to a slide. Click in the placeholder. Choose Picture from the Insert menu. Choose the file you want from the Insert Picture dialog box. Then click the Insert button. You can move and resize art the same way you do in desktop publishing.

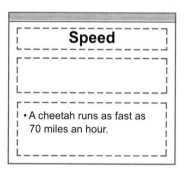

Before inserting art

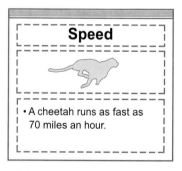

After inserting art

 LESSON REVIEW

1. How can you add clip art to a slide?

2. **CRITICAL THINKING** Why might you add a photo or your own drawing to a slide instead of using clip art?

Open the *My Activities* presentation. To add art to your presentation, follow the steps.

STEP 1   Go to Slide 2. Click in the first object placeholder.

STEP 2   Choose Clip Art from the Insert menu. Look for a category about sports. Choose a picture to go with the first sport on your list. Click OK.

STEP 3   If you cannot find clip art to use, try to insert art from a file instead.

STEP 4   Repeat Steps 1 to 3 to choose a picture to go with the second sport on your list. Resize or move your art, if necessary.

STEP 5   Check Your Work: On which side of Slide 2 does your art appear?

When you are done, your slide should look something like the one below.

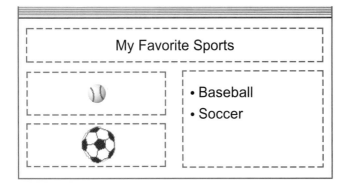

▶ **More Practice**

Use your *My Activities* presentation. Go to Slide 3. Add two pieces of art to go with the hobbies you listed. Go to Slide 4. Add up to four pieces of art that show your other favorite activities. Save your presentation. Check your work.

The simplest way to show your slides is on a computer screen. You can use a mouse or the keyboard to move through the presentation one slide at a time.

To show Microsoft® PowerPoint® slides, there are two commands that you can use. To start a slide show, you can use the Slide Show command in the View menu. You can also use the View Show command in the Slide Show menu. When you use either command, the first slide in the presentation will fill the screen.

To move forward one slide, press the Page Down key. To move back one slide, press the Page Up key. You can also use the arrow keys to move forward or backward in your presentation. Use the right arrow key to move forward. Use the left arrow key to move backward. You can also move forward one slide with a single mouse click on the slide.

After the last slide in a presentation, the software will leave the Slide Show view. It will return to the first slide in Slide view. Slide view is the view you use to enter text and insert art in slides. You can also leave the slide show before you get to the last slide. Press the Escape key to leave the Slide Show and return to Slide view.

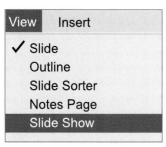

Microsoft® PowerPoint®

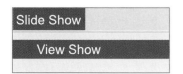

ClarisWorks®

▶ **LESSON REVIEW**

1. In Slide Show, what happens when you click on a slide with the mouse?

2. How can you use the keyboard to move back to a slide?

3. **CRITICAL THINKING** Why might you want to go back to a slide when giving a presentation?

13·6 Lab Practice

Open the presentation called *My Activities*. Follow the steps to show your presentation.

STEP 1   Choose Slide Show from the View menu. Or, choose the View Show command from the Slide Show menu.

STEP 2   Press the → key or the Page Down key once to move to Slide 2.

STEP 3   Press the → key twice to move to Slide 4.

STEP 4   Press the Page Up key or the ← key three times to go back to Slide 1.

STEP 5   Check Your Work: How many times did you press a key to move from Slide 3 to Slide 1? What key did you press?

▶ **More Practice**

Use your *My Activities* presentation document. Start a slide show.
Move to Slide 4.
Move to Slide 2.
Move to Slide 3.
Move to Slide 1.
Leave the slide show.

Sometimes you may need to change the order of the slides in a presentation. In Microsoft® PowerPoint® you can solve this problem by changing to Slide Sorter view. Choose Slide Sorter from the View menu.

In Slide Sorter view, you can see all your slides at once. You can also move slides from one place to another. Look at the screen below. Notice that the title slide is out of order. So is the *Concert Songs* slide.

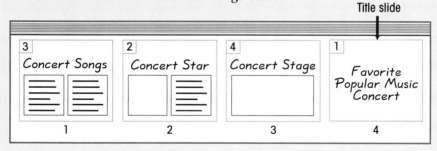

To move the title slide, click on it and drag it in front of Slide 1. Then let go of the mouse button. The order of the slides changes, as shown below.

Look at the screen above.

1. Which slides are still out of order?

2. How would you fix this problem?

Critical Thinking
What other task might be easier to do in Slide Sorter view?

13·7 ▶ Applying: Presenting an Event Log

You want to use your Events Log from the Chapter Project on page 263 to give a presentation about the events of your week.

Example

Plan and make a presentation using the information from your Events Log.

STEP 1 GET READY What do you need to do first?
Make a checklist to help you choose what information to use. Put the information in order.

STEP 2 THINK What do you know about planning a presentation?
Make a storyboard to show the order and layout of your slides. Think about how many slides you will need. Think about where you will put titles, text, and art. Here is how a storyboard might look.

STEP 3 APPLY Make a presentation document.
Add slides, and choose a layout for each one. Add titles, text, and art to the slides. Each slide can present one event.

STEP 4 CHECK How does the information look?
View your slide show. You should see all the text and art clearly. Fix any errors. Edit text and move or resize art. Rearrange the slide order, if needed.

13·7 Lab Practice

GET READY to plan a new presentation. Answer the questions under THINK. APPLY what you know to make a presentation document. CHECK your finished work.

Millie has to give a book report in class about *The Hobbit*. Use the information below to make a presentation she could use.

Summary
Bilbo joins Gandolf and 13 dwarfs to get back treasure stolen by a dragon. Bilbo helps an archer kill the dragon. Everybody fights over the treasure. They unite to defeat the goblins and wolves. They decide to share the treasure. Bilbo goes home.

Main Characters
1. Bilbo Baggins, the Hobbit
2. Gandolf, the wizard
3. Thorin, son of the king of dwarfs
4. Smaug, a dragon

Main Ideas
1. You can be a hero if you care enough about others.
2. You can do good deeds by working together.
3. It is wise to listen to those with experience.

THINK How many slides would you use?

What information would you put on each slide?

Where would you use titles, text, and art?

What layouts would you choose for each slide?

Making Connections

Make a presentation about something you learned in science, social studies, or language arts class in the last month. For example, you could discuss data collected in a science lab, an event in history from social studies, or a book you read for language arts. Give your presentation in class.

Summary

Presentations
A presentation uses text and art to communicate information. Presentation software helps you put text and art together using a computer.

- **Plan a presentation** by making a checklist to choose and organize information. Make a storyboard to show slide order and layouts.

- **Choose slide layouts** from the New Slide dialog box.

- **Add text** by clicking in a title or text placeholder. Enter the new text.

- **Add art** such as clip art, other art, or photos from a file.

- **Show a presentation** by choosing Slide Show from the View menu. Move through slides using the arrow or Page Up and Page Down keys.

handout

presentation

slide

storyboard

Vocabulary Review

Complete each sentence with a term from the list.

1. A page in a presentation document is a _____.

2. A series of sketches showing the order in which each slide appears is a _____.

3. A _____ is a way to use text and art to communicate information.

4. A printed document with information from a presentation is a _____.

Chapter Quiz

Answer the following questions.

LESSON 13·1

Test Tip
Making a storyboard helps you organize and plan your presentation.

What Is Presentation Software?

1. What are two ways to view presentation slides?
2. How does presentation software make it easier for an audience to understand your presentation?

LESSON 13·2

Planning a Presentation

3. What are the steps for planning a presentation?

LESSON 13·3

Choosing Slide Layouts

4. How can you choose a layout for a new slide?

LESSONS 13·4 and 13·5

Adding Text and Art

5. How do you enter text in a slide?
6. How can you insert clip art in a slide?

LESSON 13·6

Showing a Presentation

7. What are three ways to move forward through a presentation?

LESSON 13·7

Presenting an Event Log

8. How many events can you present on one slide?

Group Activity

With your group, choose a subject for a presentation. Divide the information so that each group member has something to research. Put all the research together. Make a checklist to organize the information you want to use. Finish the planning by drawing a storyboard. Then make a presentation document. Have each group member make at least one slide. View your slide show. Show your presentation to the class.

Unit 4 **Review**

Choose the letter of the correct answer.

1. For which task would you use presentation software?
   A. Write a report about new computers
   B. Prepare a school newsletter
   C. Show slides about new computers to your class
   D. Make a list of museum exhibits you saw

2. Which of the following is considered text?
   A. Charts
   B. Photographs
   C. Clip art
   D. Heads

3. Which task is part of desktop publishing?
   A. Make a thumbnail sketch
   B. Choose a slide layout
   C. Arrange slides in order
   D. Make a storyboard

4. How would you change the size of a piece of clip art?
   A. Press the Enter or Return key
   B. Click in the middle and drag it
   C. Click on a corner handle and drag it
   D. Press the Page Down key

5. What must you do before you add text to a slide?
   A. Choose the Columns command
   B. Press the Enter or Return key
   C. Make a new document
   D. Click in a text placeholder

6. Which command would you need to use to make a page layout like the one shown below?

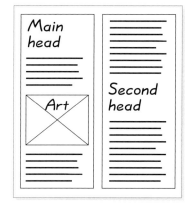

   A. Columns command
   B. Cut button on the toolbar
   C. Paste command
   D. Spelling command

Critical Thinking
You are using desktop publishing to make up a page with text and art. What is one reason to use clip art on the page? What is one reason to draw your own art on the page?

Unit 5 ▶ The Internet

Chapter 14 Internet Communication
Chapter 15 The World Wide Web

You can use the Internet to see and learn about places such as the pyramids of Egypt.

When you connect with the Internet and the World Wide Web, all kinds of things can happen. You can send mail across the world, visit foreign countries and museums, find a job, play games, go shopping, and even see pictures sent to Earth from space. Look at the Internet Facts at the right to answer the questions.

1. According to the Internet Facts, about how many Americans use e-mail?

2. **CRITICAL THINKING** Why do you think the Internet and e-mail have become so popular?

1998–1999 INTERNET FACTS (U.S. data)
- over 63 million active Internet users
- over 6.5 million web sites visited
- e-mail was used by 84% of all Internet users
- over 200 million e-mail messages per day were sent

These friends live thousands of miles apart. But they keep in touch by using e-mail. How would e-mail be more useful than regular mail in helping them communicate?

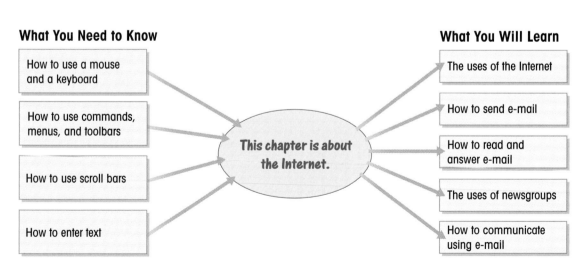

What You Need to Know

How to use a mouse and a keyboard

How to use commands, menus, and toolbars

How to use scroll bars

How to enter text

This chapter is about the Internet.

What You Will Learn

The uses of the Internet

How to send e-mail

How to read and answer e-mail

The uses of newsgroups

How to communicate using e-mail

Chapter 14

Internet Communication

Words to Know

Internet	millions of connected computers that share information
network	a group of computers that are connected
server	a computer that provides information and manages it for a network
client	a personal computer connected to a server in a network
ISP	Internet Service Provider; a company that connects personal computers to the Internet
e-mail	electronic mail; a way to send written messages and files between computers

Flowchart Project

Make a flowchart on posterboard that shows how information flows through the Internet. For example, your flowchart might show how e-mail goes through the Internet from your computer to a friend's computer. You can review how to make a flowchart in Lessons 1.3 and 1.4.

Learning Objectives

- Describe the Internet, networks and servers.
- Send e-mail and attachments.
- Read and answer e-mail.
- Explain how newsgroups work.
- Apply using e-mail to communicating in school.
- PROBLEM SOLVING: Solve the problem of undelivered e-mail.
- COMPUTERS ON THE JOB: Describe how e-mail helps with contacting customers.

What Is the Internet?

The **Internet** is millions of connected computers that share information. The Internet is used all over the world.

Using Networks

The Internet is made up of many **networks**. A network is a group of computers that are connected. Telephone lines, cables, and satellites can connect the computers. They make it possible for computers in a network to share files and information.

A network usually has a **server**. A server is a computer that provides information and manages it for the network. The server allows several computers to use the same information at the same time. The personal computers that are connected to a server in a network are called **clients**.

A network can be a *local area network*, or LAN. An example is a network in one classroom or one school building. A network can be a *wide area network*, or WAN. For example, an airline's computers are connected on a WAN.

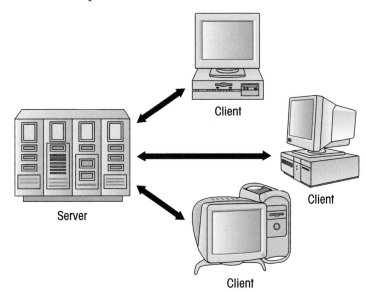

Client

Client

Server

Client

The server has special hardware and software. It allows clients to share the same information.

Using the Internet

Different networks use different computer languages. The Internet helps millions of computer networks worldwide to "speak" the same computer language.

To use the Internet, you need to connect your computer with an **ISP**, or Internet Service Provider. An ISP is a company that connects personal computers to servers connected to the Internet. A client uses a telephone line or a data line to connect to the ISP's server. The ISP's server connects to networks in the Internet.

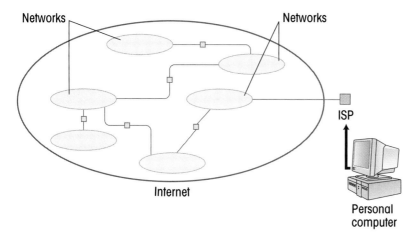

The Internet lets you do many things. You can

- send and receive e-mail.
- research information.
- join discussion groups.
- shop for goods and services.
- use the World Wide Web.

▶ **LESSON REVIEW**

1. Name two or more ways that computers can be connected in a network.

2. What does a network server do?

3. **CRITICAL THINKING** Why do you need an ISP?

You can use electronic mail, or **e-mail**, to send written messages and files between computers.

E-Mail Letters

When you send a letter, you write a message and an address. The same is true for e-mail. An e-mail message window has an address line, a subject line, and a text area. Look at the screen below.

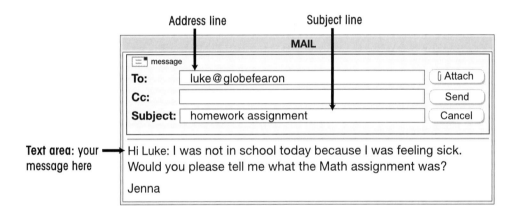

Address line   Subject line

MAIL

message

To: luke @ globefearon   ⌷ Attach

Cc: Send

Subject: homework assignment   Cancel

Text area: your message here →

Hi Luke: I was not in school today because I was feeling sick. Would you please tell me what the Math assignment was?

Jenna

friend1@friendsaddress.net

E-mail name   Where to send e-mail

Computer Fact

E-mail is not private. Anyone can read it, so be polite when writing messages. Do not write or send anything you would not want someone else to see.

To enter an e-mail address, use the address line. An e-mail address gives the person's e-mail name and tells where to send the message. Look at the address at the left as an example. You can enter more than one e-mail address in the address line.

To tell the person receiving the message what your letter is about, use the subject line. Briefly describe your message in the subject line.

If you want someone else to have a copy of the message, put their address in the Cc: or Copy to: line.

To write your message, use the text area. When you are ready to "mail" your message, click the Send button.

E-Mail Attachments

Sometimes you may want to send a file, such as a picture or a spreadsheet document, along with an e-mail message. You need to attach the file. Some examples of buttons for attaching files are shown at the right.

Attachments:

When you click an attachment button, a dialog box like the one below appears.

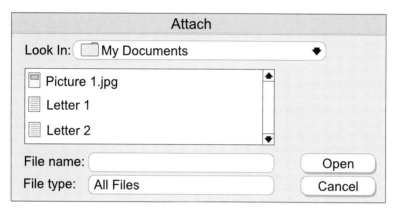

Attach	
Look In: 📁 My Documents ▼	
🖼 Picture 1.jpg	
📄 Letter 1	
📄 Letter 2	
File name: _____	Open
File type: All Files	Cancel

To attach a file, find the folder with the file you want to send. Select the file, then click Open, or Add, or Attach. Click OK (or Done) to return to the message window. Look for an icon or a list that shows the file is attached.

Once an e-mail message has been sent, it is stored in a folder often called *Sent Mail* or *Sent Items*. When you open the folder, you see a window like the one at the right. An icon shows if there was a file attached.

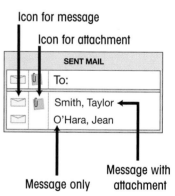

Icon for message
Icon for attachment

SENT MAIL

		To:
		Smith, Taylor
		O'Hara, Jean

Message only
Message with attachment

▶ **LESSON REVIEW**

1. What are the three main parts of an e-mail message?

2. Why should you fill in a subject line?

3. **CRITICAL THINKING** Why might you want to attach a word processing document to an e-mail message?

14·2 Lab Practice

Open a new e-mail message window. To send an e-mail message with an attachment to your teacher, follow the steps.

STEP 1 Click on the address line. Type your teacher's e-mail address.

STEP 2 Click on the subject line. Enter the text **Term Paper**.

STEP 3 Click on the text area. Type the message shown below.

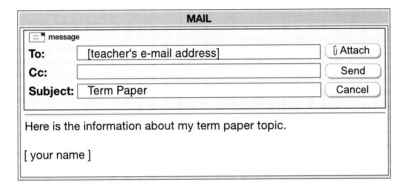

STEP 4 Click the attachment button. Select a file to attach. Click Open (or Add). If needed, click OK (or Done).

STEP 5 Click the Send button to send your e-mail message.

STEP 6 Check Your Work: Look in the folder containing the e-mail you sent. Is the "To" address correct? Is there an attachment icon?

▶ **More Practice**

Open a new message window. Send an e-mail message to someone in your class. Fill in the address line, subject line, and text area. Attach a file to the message. Then click Send. See Steps 1 to 6. Check your work.

Once you receive an e-mail message, you can read it and answer it.

Reading E-Mail

E-mail you receive is stored in a folder often called *New Mail* or *Inbox*. The window below shows who sent the message, the subject, and if a file is attached.

E-mail address of sender   Message subject

INBOX			
✉ 📎	From:	Subject:	Date:
✉	gil@globefearon	Assignment	4/3/01

Remember

A folder is a place where you can save and organize files. See Lesson 4.1.

To read a message, you can click (or double-click) on it. The message appears in a window like the one below. Notice that the message window starts with

- the e-mail address of the sender.
- the date the e-mail was sent.
- the e-mail address of the receiver.
- the subject of the e-mail.

If there is a file attached, the name of the file may also be listed. The message text appears below this information.

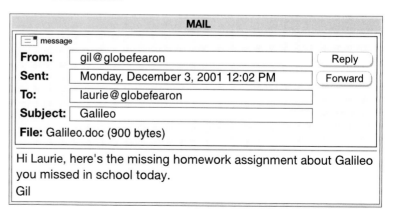

MAIL	
📧 message	
From: gil@globefearon	Reply
Sent: Monday, December 3, 2001 12:02 PM	Forward
To: laurie@globefearon	
Subject: Galileo	
File: Galileo.doc (900 bytes)	
Hi Laurie, here's the missing homework assignment about Galileo you missed in school today. Gil	

Answering E-Mail

After you have read a message, you can answer the sender, or you can send the message to someone else. You can also delete the message. The diagram below shows examples of buttons in two e-mail programs.

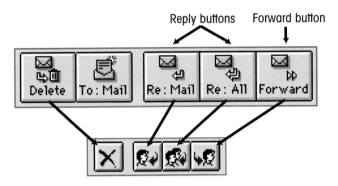

Reply buttons   Forward button

Delete   To: Mail   Re: Mail   Re: All   Forward

To answer the sender, you can click the Reply button. When you answer, or reply, a new message window appears with the person's e-mail address and the subject already filled in. The word *Re:* that appears before the subject means "in reference to" or "concerning."

You can click on the Forward button to send a copy of an e-mail message to someone else. The term *Fwd:* followed by the subject appears in the subject line. The entire message is sent to the new e-mail address.

To delete an e-mail message, click on the Delete button in the message window. Or select the message from the list in the *Inbox* folder, and click Delete.

▶ **LESSON REVIEW**

1. What four pieces of information are found at the beginning of any e-mail message you receive?

2. **CRITICAL THINKING** Why might you want to forward a message to another person?

14·3 Lab Practice

Open an e-mail message that was sent to you by a classmate in Lab Practice 14.2. To reply to the sender, follow the steps below.

STEP 1 Open the message you received. Click the Reply button. The address will already be filled in. The subject will start with **Re**:.

STEP 2 Enter an answer to the message in the text area.

STEP 3 Click the Send button.

STEP 4 Check Your Work: Is the e-mail message listed in the *Sent Files* window?

Now forward the same message to another classmate.

STEP 5 Open the same message again. Click the Forward button. The address will be blank. The subject will start with **Fwd**:.

STEP 6 Type in the e-mail address of a different student in your class.

STEP 7 Click the Send button.

STEP 8 Check Your Work: Is the e-mail message listed in the *Sent Files* window?

 More Practice

Open the message you received from your teacher about the information for the term paper. Forward the message to another student in your class. Open the message again and send a reply to your teacher thanking him or her. See Steps 1 to 4. Check your work.

Sometimes you may send an e-mail message that gets returned as "Undelivered Mail." You may get a message like the one shown below.

MAIL		
From: MAILER-DAEMON@jihjk.com (mail deliver sub-sysem)	Reply	
Sent: Monday, December 3, 2001 3:32 PM	Forward	
To: [your address]		
Subject: **Returned mail: Host unknown (Name server: globefaeron: host not found)**		

The original message was received at Mon, 3 December 2001 15:32:17 from root@localhost

* * * ATTENTION * * *

An e-mail you sent to an internet destination could not be delivered.

You can solve this problem by reading the subject line above. It says that the *host*, or user's computer, is unknown. The address *globefaeron.com* could not be found.

The problem is that part of the address has been typed incorrectly. The address *globefaeron.com* should be *globefearon.com*. When an e-mail address is incorrect, the mail program does not know where to send it. The message is returned.

To fix the problem, find and open the message in the *Sent Mail* folder. Resend the e-mail message using the correct address.

Look at the e-mail message above.

1. What is the problem?

2. How would you fix this problem?

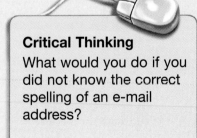

Critical Thinking
What would you do if you did not know the correct spelling of an e-mail address?

E-mail is used to communicate with the people you know. However, you can communicate with thousands of people by using Internet newsgroups.

A *newsgroup* is a place where people with the same interests can send and read messages. Newsgroup members share information, ask questions, and exchange opinions and ideas. They do this by posting, or sending, messages to the newsgroup. It is like putting a note up on a bulletin board for everyone to read.

There are thousands of newsgroups on almost any subject. Each one is about a topic, such as politics, sports, music, or TV. The name of a newsgroup tells you the topic discussed by the group.

Look at the newsgroup name below. The first part of the name tells you the main topic area. The letters *rec* are an abbreviation for *recreation*.

rec.arts.movies.reviews

Main topic area

The rest of the words tell more about the topic and interests of the newsgroup. The newsgroup above discusses and gives reviews about movies.

To use a newsgroup, you need to use software with a newsreader. Some Internet software has a built-in newsreader. Microsoft® Internet Explorer® and Netscape Communicator® are two examples of such software. The Help feature of the software will explain how to set up the newsreader.

Some Internet Service Providers subscribe to lists of newsgroups. This means that they make the newsgroups available to their customers.

The table below lists some newsgroup topic areas.

Newsgroup Topic Areas		
Topic Area	**Subjects**	**Example**
alt (alternative)	unusual subjects	alt.music.alternative
biz (business)	jobs, advertising, business issues	biz.jobs.offered
comp (computers)	hardware, software, computer science	comp.sys.laptops
rec (recreation)	recreation activities and hobbies	rec.food.recipes
sci (science)	scientific research and social sciences	sci.space.shuttle
soc (social)	social issues, politics, world culture	soc.history

 LESSON REVIEW

1. What is a newsgroup?

2. **CRITICAL THINKING** Which main topic area might include discussions on Native American culture?

On the Cutting Edge

INTERNET SAFETY

The Internet lets you visit with people all over the world by using newsgroups and e-mail. You may not know that there can be danger on the Internet. Since anyone can use the Internet, you may come in contact with people that can cause you harm. To use the Internet safely, you should follow the "Rules for Online Safety" shown on the right.

CRITICAL THINKING Why is it important to follow Online Safety Rules?

Rules for Online Safety

1. Never send any personal information over the Internet to places you don't know. Do not send your name, age, address, or parents' information.
2. Do not meet strangers that you have contacted online.
3. Talk to parents and teachers if anything you get or read online makes you uncomfortable.
4. Never send a picture of yourself over the Internet.

COMPUTERS ON THE JOB
Sales Assistant

Lars is a sales assistant for a large company. He has many customers in several states. As part of his job, Lars must let his customers know about new products and take their orders. When Lars receives orders from his customers, he must send those orders to the home office. Lars does all of this using e-mail.

Look at the screens below. Lars has a list of his customers' e-mail addresses stored on his computer. He selects the *Customers list* and clicks the Send To button. All the addresses of his customers appear in the address line of the e-mail message window. When he clicks Send, the message goes to all his customers at once.

Lars uses e-mail to communicate with his customers.

ADDRESS BOOK	
Name/Address	
Associates	Send To
Customers	Cancel
Employees	

MAIL	
◻ message	
From: Lars@globefearon	⬗ Attach
Sent: Friday, November 17, 2000 8:32 AM	Reply
To: customers	Forward
Subject: New Products	Send

Use the screens above to answer the questions.

1. How does an address list help Lars save time when contacting his customers?

2. Why might communicating by e-mail not work for all customers?

Critical Thinking
How would Lars' job be harder if he did not use e-mail?

Applying: E-Mail Communication

You can communicate with other people using e-mail. You can send messages, attach files, reply to messages, and forward mail to other people.

Example

Your teacher sends you the e-mail message below. You have to reply to the message and send your term paper file to your teacher.

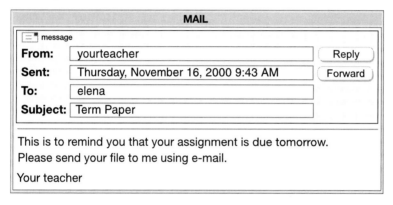

	MAIL	
	message	
From:	yourteacher	Reply
Sent:	Thursday, November 16, 2000 9:43 AM	Forward
To:	elena	
Subject:	Term Paper	

This is to remind you that your assignment is due tomorrow.
Please send your file to me using e-mail.

Your teacher

STEP 1 GET READY What do you need to do first?
Open the message from your teacher and read it.

STEP 2 THINK What do you know about sending e-mail?
Decide what to say in your reply message. Decide which file to attach.

STEP 3 APPLY Reply to the message and send the file.
Click the Reply button. Write a message telling your teacher the title of your term paper and the name of the file you are sending. Attach the file to your reply.

STEP 4 CHECK How does the message look?
Look at the message. Make sure the message shows that a file is attached. Fix any errors. Then click Send.

14·5 Lab Practice

GET READY to send e-mail. Answer the questions under THINK. APPLY what you know to send messages and attach files. CHECK your finished work.

1. Send two e-mail messages to your partner. In one, ask for a story or poem for the school magazine. In the second message, ask that your partner share a spreadsheet with a third student.

2. You receive an e-mail message asking for a story or poem for the school magazine. Send a reply with a file containing a poem or story.

   THINK
   What will you say in the e-mail message?

   Which file will you attach?

3. You receive an e-mail asking you to share your spreadsheet work with another student. Forward the message to another student, adding additional text to the message. Attach a spreadsheet file.

   THINK
   What will you say in the e-mail message?

   Which file will you attach?

Making Connections

Send an e-mail message to a friend in your math, science, social studies, or language arts class. Ask the friend to send you that day's homework assignment. When you receive the assignment, send a reply thanking your friend. You might also ask if your friend would like to share class notes with you using e-mail.

Summary

Internet Communication
The Internet lets you communicate with people around the world.
• **The Internet** is a large network connected by ISP servers.
• **To send an e-mail and attachments,** fill in the address line, subject line, and text area. Use the Attach button to include files.
• **Read and answer e-mail** by clicking on an incoming message. Click Reply to answer e-mail. Click Forward to send it to another person.
• **You can use newsgroups** to discuss subjects that interest you.
• **Communicate with e-mail** by sending and receiving messages with or without attached files.

e-mail
client
Internet
ISP
network
server

Vocabulary Review

Complete each sentence with a word from the list.

1. A group of connected computers form a _____.

2. A computer that provides information and manages it for a network is a _____.

3. A way to send written messages and files between computers is _____.

4. The network of millions of connected computers that share information is called the _____.

5. A company that connects personal computers to the Internet is an _____.

6. The _____ is the personal computer connected to a server in a network.

Chapter Quiz

Answer the following questions.

LESSON 14·1

What Is the Internet?

1. How does an ISP help you use the Internet?
2. What are two things you can do with the Internet?

LESSONS 14·2 and 14·3

Sending, Reading, and Answering E-Mail

3. How is sending e-mail like sending a letter?
4. Why might you want to attach a file to an e-mail message?
5. How can you tell if a file is attached to an e-mail message you receive?
6. How is replying to a message different from forwarding a message?

LESSON 14·4

Newsgroups

7. How can you tell the main topics of a newsgroup?

LESSON 14·5

E-Mail Communication

8. How can e-mail help you communicate at school?

Computer Tip
To use e-mail and news groups, you must be connected to a network or to the Internet.

Group Activity

With your group, brainstorm a list of topics that interest you. Then decide on a newsgroup you would like to join. Read some of the messages already posted to the newsgroup to learn what the members have been discussing. Write a summary of the information and come up with at least three ways you could contribute to the newsgroup. Post your messages and share any responses with the rest of the class.

You can get on the World Wide Web anywhere there is a computer connected to the Internet. These people are on the web at a café! Why do you think they like to eat at this café?

What You Need to Know

- How to use a mouse
- How to use a keyboard
- How to use menus, commands, and toolbars
- How to use scroll bars
- What the basics of the Internet are

This chapter is about the World Wide Web.

What You Will Learn

- What the World Wide Web is
- How to use Web browsers
- How to follow links
- How to use search engines
- How to use keywords to search
- How to search for information on the Web

Chapter 15 ▶ The World Wide Web

Words to Know

World Wide Web	a collection of documents or files connected together on the Internet; the Web; (www)
Web browser	a software program used to view documents and move from site to site on the World Wide Web
Web site	a collection of documents on a World Wide Web server
home page	the Web page that a Web browser automatically opens first; the starting Web page for any Web site
URL	an address of a particular page or document on the Web; it means **U**niform **R**esource **L**ocator
link	a button, text, or image that connects to a Web page
search engine	a program for finding information on the Web
keyword	a word that describes information being searched for

Journal Project

For one week, keep a journal of the topics you are working on in different classes. For example, you might be studying Europe in world history and Mars in a science class. For each topic, write a description and a question in your journal. Search the Web for the topics you describe in your journal. Try to answer your questions.

Learning Objectives

- Describe what is found on the World Wide Web.
- View Web pages and follow links.
- Use search engines and keywords.
- Apply the use of search engines to find information.
- PROBLEM SOLVING: Solve why a URL cannot be found.
- COMPUTERS IN YOUR LIFE: Shop on the World Wide Web.

The **World Wide Web** is a collection of documents or files connected together on the Internet. It is also called the *Web* or *www* for short. The Web is made up of millions of documents or files that you can view. The Web is a part of the Internet, but it is not a network.

Each document or file that is part of the World Wide Web is called a Web page. Web pages about similar topics are usually connected. You can move forward from one Web page to another, then back again.

All kinds of information is available on the Web. You can view newspapers, magazines, pictures of people, and paintings. You can listen to music, sound effects, and speeches. You can also watch movies, cartoons, and video tours of museums and other places.

You can visit famous places on the Web. Look at the example of a Web page below. It is from the Rock and Roll Hall of Fame and Museum. Notice that you can view text and images on the same Web page.

This is a Web page published by the Rock and Roll Hall of Fame and Museum.

Many people all over the world publish information in Web pages. You can look for and find this information using special software. This makes the Web a useful tool for research.

You can use the Web to look for a job, hire help, and do your banking. You can also go shopping online for books, clothing, and many other things.

People publish Web pages using a special language called HTML. This stands for HyperText Markup Language. Documents written in HTML are special text files. Other kinds of files that contain art, sounds, and moving images can be added to HTML files. This makes many Web pages multimedia.

 LESSON REVIEW

1. What are three things that make the Web useful?

2. **CRITICAL THINKING** How is the World Wide Web different from the Internet?

On the Cutting Edge

THE FIRST WEB SOFTWARE

The first software for finding and viewing documents on the Internet was developed in 1990. Tim Berners-Lee wanted to make it easier for scientists to share and find information. He called the software *World Wide Web*.

The software made finding information on the Internet easier. Different documents were linked together. A person could use a mouse to click on text and view different documents. Each document appeared in a separate window. The documents had text that was formatted. They had images, sounds, and even movies.

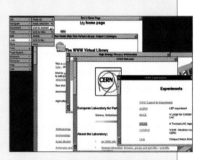

These are screens from the first software for finding and viewing documents on the Internet.

CRITICAL THINKING How do you think this software made the Internet better?

15·2 Using Web Browsers

To view documents on the Web, you need a **Web browser**. A Web browser is software. It is used to view documents and to move around on the World Wide Web.

A **Web site** is a collection of Web pages stored on an Internet server. Your computer can display Web sites using a Web browser.

Remember
A server is a computer that provides and manages information for other computers in a network.

A Web browser can help you find Web sites. It can view Web pages, and go from one Web page to another. Look at the browser window below.

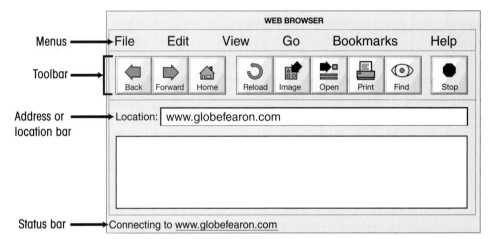

Menus

Toolbar

Address or location bar

Status bar

A Web browser has a toolbar and menus, an address bar, and a status bar.

Address Bar

The address or location bar shows the address of the Web page you are on. When you start your Web browser software, you see the address of your **home page**. A home page is the Web page that your Web browser displays when you start it.

You can get to any page or site on the Web if you know its address, or **URL**. URL stands for **U**niform **R**esource **L**ocator. Each Web site has its own URL. All Web sites have a URL that starts with http://.

Here is the URL for the Rock and Roll Hall of Fame and Museum.

http://www.rockhall.com

Tells the kind of file or document   Address of a web server

To go to a Web page or Web site, click in the address, or location, bar and type the URL. Then press the Enter (or Return) key. The Web browser will connect to the server at that Web site. Then the browser will display a Web page on your screen. This is called loading a web page.

Toolbar Buttons

The toolbar contains buttons for doing common tasks. You click the button you want to use with the mouse.

 Back returns you to the last Web page viewed.

 Forward moves you forward through Web pages already viewed.

 Stop stops a Web page from being loaded.

 Home returns you to the starting Web page. You can return directly to this page at any time by clicking the Home button on the toolbar.

Status Bar

The status bar shows you what happens as you connect to a Web site. Messages you might see include *Web site found, Opening picture,* and *Done.*

▶ **LESSON REVIEW**

1. How do you move backward and forward through Web pages that you have already viewed?

2. How is the Home button useful?

3. **CRITICAL THINKING** Why must each URL be different or unique?

15·2 Lab Practice

Open your Web browser. To view the Web site for CNN news, follow the steps below. Then return home.

STEP 1 Click in the address or location bar.
Type the following URL:

http://www.cnn.com

Press the Enter (or Return) key on the keyboard.

STEP 2 When the entire CNN Web page is displayed, click the Back button to go back to your home page.

STEP 3 Click the Forward button to return to the CNN Web page. Use the scroll bars to view all the text and images on the page.

STEP 4 Click the Home button to go back to your home page.

STEP 5 Check Your Work: What is the name of the Web site you are on now?

▶ More Practice

Open a new Web browser window.

Go to the White House's Web site by typing the URL **http://www.senate.gov** in the address bar.

Look at the text and images on the Web page.

Click the Back button. Note the Web page that you return to.

Click the Forward button. Note the Web page that you are on now.

Click the Home button. Check your work.

There are many sites on the Web where you can go shopping. Many of the same stores you would see at a mall or on the streets of your town have Web sites. Look at the screen below. It shows the directory for one Web store.

Shop Online

Departments

Mens
Womens
Kids
Sporting Gear & Apparel
Travel Apparel & Luggage
Sales Store

Shopping Guides

Book Packs
Family Sleeping Bags
Family Tents
Fleece
Holiday Gift Guide
Travel

Catalog Quickshop

Enter Item #

Shop Off-Line

Free Catalogs

Shop from a variety of seasonal catalogs

Phone

Call in your order to:
1-800-567-1234

Holiday Gift Guide

Everything you need to wrap holiday shopping, including ideas under $50.

Electronic Gift Certificate

Cooler than cash —and always well received.

You can click on the department you want to visit. You will be able to see pictures of the items the store sells. Items you select can be added to a *shopping cart*. A shopping cart lists the items you wish to buy. When you are finished, you can go to the *checkout* area. To check out, you enter your credit card information to pay for your purchases. The items you buy are sent to you by mail.

Use the screen above to answer the questions.

1. In which department would you probably find hiking boots?

2. What are some services this store provides?

Critical Thinking

How is a Web store directory like a walk-in store directory? How is it different?

Each Web site has its own home page. This is the starting page for the Web site. A Web site's home page has links that connect it to other Web pages. A **link** is a button, an image, or text that connects one Web page to another Web page. Links are one reason that the Web is so useful for doing research.

Look at the home page for the United States Environmental Protection Agency (EPA) below (www.epa.gov). There are button links to pages for Students, Teachers, and Concerned Citizens. There are underlined text links at the bottom of the page. You can find <u>What's New</u> or click on the link <u>Español</u> to see the Web site in Spanish. The photos on the page are links to more information about the EPA.

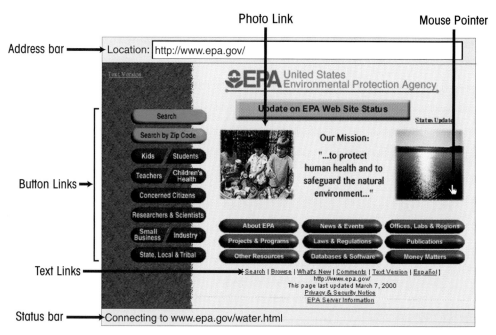

As you move the mouse pointer over a link, the mouse pointer changes from an arrow to a pointing hand. The URL of the linked Web page appears in the status bar.

You can move from one Web page to the linked Web page by clicking on the link. This is called *following a link*. You do not need to type a new URL.

You can compare a URL in the status bar to the one in the address, or location, bar. That way you can tell if the link connects to a page in the same Web site or a different one. Many of the links you follow will be on the same Web site. Look for a link that takes you back to the Web site's home page.

When you move among different Web pages, it may be hard to keep track of all the links you have followed. Most Web browsers keep track of the text links you have followed by changing their color. Notice the color of the underlined text links on a Web page before you click on them. Then return to that Web page and look at the links. Once you have used a link, the color should change. Look at the examples below. It shows a link before and after it has been clicked.

Remember
You can also use the Back and Forward buttons to go to Web pages you have already viewed.

Before

www.globefearon.com

After

www.globefearon.com

Another way to trace your links is to use the Web browser's History or Go command. When you use these commands, a list of the Web pages you have already viewed appears.

▶ **LESSON REVIEW**

1. How might a link appear on a Web page?

2. How do you know when you are on a link?

3. How do you use a link to get to another Web page?

4. **CRITICAL THINKING** How are links useful?

15·3 Lab Practice

Open your Web browser. To visit NASA's Web site, follow the steps below. Follow different links at the site.

STEP 1   Go to NASA's Web site using the following URL:

   http://www.nasa.gov

STEP 2   Click on one of the underlined text links on the Web page, such as *today@nasa.gov*.

STEP 3   Return to NASA's home page by using the Back button.

STEP 4   Scroll down the page. Click on a link from a photo or other image, such as *Nasa's Top 10*.

STEP 5   Check Your Work: Use the Go or History command to see if the links you followed are listed.

▶ More Practice

1. Open your Web browser. Go to the National Park Service's Web site by entering the URL **http://www.nps.gov**. Follow three different links. Return to the National Park Service's home page after visiting each link. Check the list of links you followed.

2. Open your Web browser. Go to The Weather Channel's Web site by entering the URL **http://www.weather.com**. Follow three different links. Return to The Weather Channel's home page after visiting each link. Check the list of links you followed.

Suppose you need to research information about astronauts going to the moon. You could follow all the links on NASA's Web site until you found the information. Or you could use a **search engine** to find the information you need. A search engine is a computer program for finding information on the Web.

Look at the screen below. It shows you a link to NASA's search engine. This link is from a NASA home page.

When you click on the link, the NASA search engine screen appears. This screen is shown below. You type the subject you want to look up in the search bar or space provided. Then click the Search button.

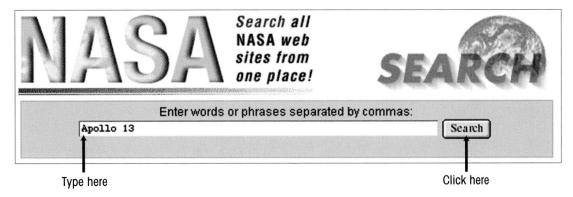

Type here   Click here

The search engine finds and shows you a *hit list* or an index of search results. The list consists of links with descriptions. The links that best match the subject are listed first. You can read the descriptions to see which ones you want to follow. If you do not see what you want, you can go to the next page of the list. You can also start a new search.

Look at the screen below. It shows a hit list of links that NASA's search engine found for the subject Apollo 13. The first line at the top of the Web page tells you how many links were found.

Your search matched 1,076 of 984,097 documents. ➡

Your search matched 1076 of 984097 documents.　　　　　　[New Search] [New Search With Options]
1 2 3 4 5 6 7 8 9 10 11 12 13 14 15 16 17 18 19 20 [Next]

Additional Information on Apollo-13
KSC mirror of JSC's Apollo-13 Image Directory Apollo-13 Press Kit (HTML) / (PDF 4Mb) / (TXT) Return to Apollo Missions Menu
_____ Last Updated
Wednesday June 21 18:49:05 EDT 1995 Jim Dumoulin (d
Size: 2K

Apollo 13 Mission
Apollo 13 was the thirteenth in a series of missions using Apollo-specification flight hardware and was to be the third lunar landing. Back-up crew for this mission were John W. Young (back-up mission commander), Ken Mattingly (back-up command module pil
Size: 12K

The screen below shows some information found by following the second link listed in the screen above.

Mission Plan

Apollo 13 was the thirteenth in a series of missions using Apollo-specification flight hardware and was to be the third lunar landing. The launch vehicle and spacecraft were similar to those of Apollo 12. There were some differences in the makeup of the ALSEP.

💻 Computer Fact

Not all information you find on the Web is accurate. Always find two to three sources about the same information to be sure of your research. Sites ending in .gov or .edu are usually good sources. Also, use sites of organizations you know over those you do not.

▶ **LESSON REVIEW**

1. What can a search engine help you do?

2. How do you use a search engine?

3. **CRITICAL THINKING** When you see a search results list, how do you decide which links to follow? Why?

15·4 Lab Practice

Open your Web browser. Then follow the steps to search
for information about a National Park.

STEP 1 Enter the URL **http://www.nps.gov** in the address or
location bar to go to the National Park Service's home page.

STEP 2 Scroll down until you see the Search link at the bottom right
of the page. Click on the Search link.

Search link

STEP 3 You will be at the National Park Service's search engine.
Enter **Yellowstone** in the search space provided. Click the
Seek button.

STEP 4 Read the hit list. Choose and follow one of the links to find
out the location of Yellowstone National Park.

STEP 5 Check Your Work: Where is Yellowstone National Park?

 More Practice

Go Back to the National Park Service's search engine.
Enter **Grand Canyon** into the search space provided.
Click the Seek button. Read the results. Choose and
follow a link. Find out the location of the Grand Canyon.
Check your work.

Sometimes searching on the Web results in a list of hundreds or thousands of links. You can use **keywords** to help your search so that it better meets your needs. A keyword is a word that describes the information you are searching for.

Entering Keywords

For example, suppose you want to find information about baseball teams that have won the World Series. If you use only the keyword *baseball*, the list may include thousands of links. Many of these links will have nothing to do with the World Series.

Look at the screen below. You can add a space and the keywords *World Series* to help narrow the search. You can also put quotation marks around a phrase. This will make the search engine look for those exact words in that order.

Search for: | baseball "World Series" | Search

This search returned some of the Web sites shown below. Notice that this search engine lists popular links under a special heading. Different search engines will organize their lists differently.

POPULAR

2 of the Web sites match your search:

1. Your **Baseball** News — Browse the Baseball pages for Major League standings, team records, and complete World Series stories.
http://www.yourbaseballnews.com

2. Look For **Baseball** — Breaking World Series news, plus stats, rosters, and stories from past Series.
http://www.lookforbaseball.com

Clicking on Popular Subjects

Another way to narrow a search is to use the list of popular subjects provided by a search engine. The list is usually located near the search bar. The choices will change depending on the search engine you use.

You click on the popular subject you want. Another list of more specific subjects will appear. Look at the screens below. The left one shows popular subjects. The right one shows specific subjects in baseball under the main subject *sports*.

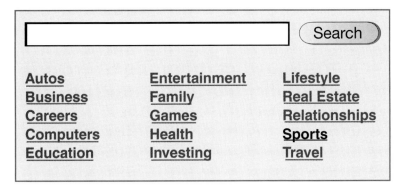

Autos	**Entertainment**	**Lifestyle**
Business	**Family**	**Real Estate**
Careers	**Games**	**Relationships**
Computers	**Health**	**Sports**
Education	**Investing**	**Travel**

Directory

Sports

- Baseball
- Basketball
- Football
- Golf
- Hockey
- Outdoors
- Soccer
- Sporting Goods
- Tennis
- Water Sports
- Winter Sports
- Wrestling

Keep clicking on subjects until you get a list of links that interest you. Sometimes, you may not find links that meet your needs. If so, click the Back button and choose another subject. Or you can try using keywords to search for topics about the subject you are currently in.

▶ LESSON REVIEW

1. What keywords would you use to find information about a recent space shuttle mission?

2. What popular subject might you click to find a job?

3. **CRITICAL THINKING** Why is it better to search using several keywords?

15·5 Lab Practice

Open your Web browser. Go to a search engine on the Web using the URL your teacher gives you. To perform a keywoard search for music videos featuring rock singers, follow the steps below.

STEP 1 Type **music videos** in the space in the search bar. Click the Search button.

STEP 2 Make a record of the first five Web sites in the hit list or index of search results.

STEP 3 Use the Back button to return to the search engine page. Add the word **rock** to your search. Click the Search button.

STEP 4 Record the first five Web sites in the hit list. Compare them with the items you saw in Step 2.

STEP 5 Check Your Work: Click on the first two links in the hit list. See if they have information about rock music videos.

▶ More Practice

Open your Web browser. Use the same search engine you used above.

Do a keyword search for information on gray wolves found in the United States or Canada. Some keywords you might use are: *wolf, gray, Canada, United States, North America.*

Decide which two keywords to start with. Then add more keywords to narrow your search further.

Check your work. Follow two links to see if the information you need is there.

PROBLEM SOLVING
A URL Cannot Be Found

You try to go to a Web site using a URL you typed in the address, or location, bar. You receive a message like the one shown below.

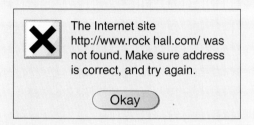

> ✖ The Internet site http://www.rock hall.com/ was not found. Make sure address is correct, and try again.
>
> (Okay)

You can usually solve this problem by checking that you typed the URL correctly. Notice that the URL in the screen has an extra space in it. You cannot enter any typing errors in a URL.

Other typing errors may include using a comma instead of a period, adding extra letters, leaving out letters or spaces, leaving out a forward slash (/), or misspelling a name or word.

To fix the problem, click OK to close the message window. Then edit or retype the URL in the address bar and try again.

Sometimes you may get this message for other reasons. The page may have been taken off the Web. Or a Web site's URL may have been changed.

Look at screen above.

1. What is the problem in the screen above?

2. How would you fix this problem?

3. What are two possible reasons you might receive a message like the one shown?

Critical Thinking

How could you locate a Web site if its URL has changed?

You can use a search engine to help you find information about almost any subject on the World Wide Web.

Example

You need to write a report about famous battles during the Civil War. You decide to search for the information you need on the Web.

STEP 1 GET READY What do you need to do first?
Make sure you know what kind of information you are looking for.

STEP 2 THINK What do you know about using a search engine?
Think about what keywords you can use to find the information.

STEP 3 APPLY Use a search engine.
Type the keywords in the space provided on the home page of the search engine. Some possible keywords are shown below. Click the Search button.

STEP 4 CHECK How does the information look?
Check the links in the search list. Change the keywords or add others to narrow the search more if needed. Choose two or three different links to research from.

15·6 Lab Practice

GET READY to search for information. Answer the
questions under THINK. APPLY what you know about
searching to find the information. CHECK your work.

1. Joanie likes comedy movies. She wants to find
   out about comedy movies with her favorite movie
   star. Search for Web pages that Joanie would like
   to read.

   THINK

   What keywords could you use for the search?

   How can you tell if Joanie should read one of the
   Web pages?

2. You want to search for information about a topic
   you listed in your Project journal. Search for Web
   pages on that topic.

   THINK

   What keywords would you use?

   What popular subjects might help you in your
   search?

Making Connections

Search for information on the Web about a topic you are
studying in science, social studies, or language arts
class. Write a short report summarizing the information
you found. Include the names and URLs of at least three
Web sites you used for reference.

Summary

The World Wide Web
The World Wide Web has millions of documents that you can view, read, and search through for information about almost any subject.

- **A Web browser** has an address bar for a URL. It has Back, Forward, and Home buttons to help you move around from page to page.

- **Follow links** by clicking on buttons, images, or underlined text.

- **Use a search engine** by typing a subject in the space provided.

- **Use keywords** to search for words or phrases about a subject.

- **Search for information** by using keywords and popular subjects.

home page
keyword
link
search engine
URL
Web browser
Web site
World Wide Web

Vocabulary Review

Complete each sentence with a term from the list.

1. A _____ is a program that helps you find information on the Web.

2. A _____ is an address of a particular page or document on the Web.

3. A _____ is a word that describes the information in a search.

4. The _____ is a collection of documents connected together on the Internet.

5. A _____ is a software program to view documents and move around the World Wide Web.

6. A _____ is a button, image, or text on a Web page that connects to another Web page.

7. A _____ is a collection of pages or documents on a World Wide Web server.

8. The _____ is the Web Page that your Web browser starts with.

Chapter Quiz

Answer the following questions.

LESSON 15·1

What Is the World Wide Web?

1. How do Web pages help you use the Internet?
2. What are two things you can do using the World Wide Web?

LESSONS 15·2 and 15·3

Computer Tip
Underlined text links often change color once you have used them.

Web Browsers and Links

3. What do you use a Web browser for?
4. What do you see in the address, or location, bar when you first open a Web browser?
5. What do links allow you to do?
6. How can you keep track of the links you have followed?

LESSONS 15·4 to 15·6

Search Engines and Keywords

7. How do keywords help you use a search engine?
8. How can you tell if a search found the information that meets your needs?

Group Activity

With your group, decide on a subject to search for information. Do the search using two to three different search engines. Compare the results. Report to the class about which search engine was best for your needs, and explain why. Combine your group's results with those of other groups. Make a list of tips about when to use different search engines, and why.

Unit 5 **Review**

Choose the letter of the correct answer.

1. Which task should be done to send a report to an e-mail address?
   A. Follow a Web link
   B. Attach a file to a message
   C. Forward a message
   D. Use a keyword search

2. Which task should you do to answer an e-mail message?
   A. Search the message
   B. Forward the message
   C. Attach the message
   D. Reply to the message

3. Which button would you use to give someone's message to another person?
   A. Home button
   B. Subject button
   C. Forward button
   D. Web browser button

4. Which newsgroup would have information about places to visit in Washington, D.C.?
   A. soc.history.Washington D.C.
   B. biz.companies.Washington
   C. comp.software.government
   D. rec.travel.Washington

5. What is your mouse pointing to when the pointer changes from a ⌖ to a ☝?
   A. Link on a page
   B. Status bar in a browser window
   C. Back button in toolbar
   D. Home button in toolbar

6. Which of the following would be found on an index of search results?
   A. Send button
   B. List of links
   C. Inbox
   D. Status bar

7. Which would be the best keywords to use to find information about the White House on the World Wide Web?
   A. Washington, D.C.
   B. "White House"
   C. White, house
   D. "George Washington"

Critical Thinking
Suppose you visit ten different Web pages about Washington, D.C. Then you want to return to the first page you visited. Describe two ways you can do that.

Reference: Keyboards

PC Keyboard

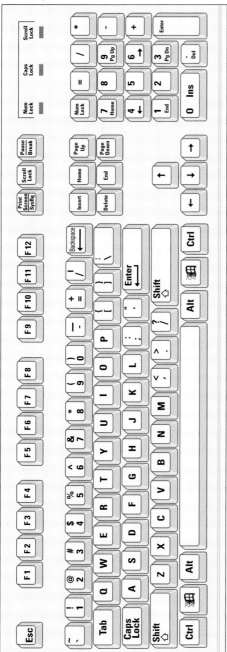

Mac Keyboard

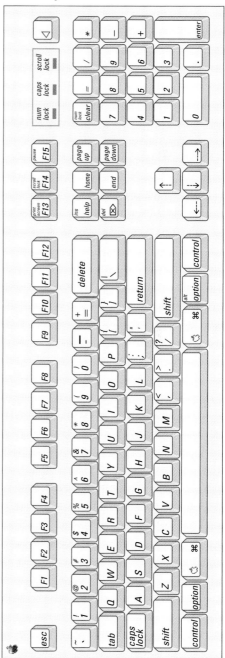

Glossary

address bar   in an internet browser, the place where the web address or URL is entered; also called a location bar (Lesson 15.2)

alignment   the way text lines up with the margins (Lesson 8.4)

Alt key   in Windows®, the key that helps open menus and gives commands when it is used together with other keys (Lesson 3.1)

application   a software program that helps you create documents with input and output; word processing, database, spreadsheet, and e-mail programs are all types of applications; also called applications software (Lesson 1.3)

applications software   a software program that helps you create documents with input and output; word processing, database, spreadsheet, and e-mail programs are all types of applications software; also called application (Lesson 1.3)

ascending   Ascending means going up. Ascending order sorts alphabetically, from A to Z. It also sorts numerically, from the smallest number to the largest number. (Lesson 9.6)

attachment   a file or object that is attached to an e-mail message (Lesson 14.2)

Back button   a button that you click on to go back one page in a Web browser (Lesson 15.2)

Backspace key   a Windows® and IBM® PC key that deletes characters to the left of the cursor (Lesson 6.3)

bold   a style that makes characters look darker or thicker (Lesson 8.4)

border   a frame around text or art on a page (Lesson 12.1)

browse   to search data for specific information

Browse mode   a view on the screen used to enter data as well as add, edit, delete, copy and sort records (Lesson 9.3)

browser   a program that allows you to view Web sites on the Internet (Lesson 15.2)

byte   the amount of memory or space one character takes up (Lesson 5.2)

Cancel button   a button that you click on to close a dialog without doing any commands (Lesson 3.2)

case sensitive   this indicates that the computer will recognize the case (uppercase or lowercase letters) of the word or phrase (Lesson 7.3)

CD   compact disk; a type of portable storage disk; a CD-ROM is read only; a CD-R is recordable (Lesson 5.3)

cell   a place where a row and a column meet in a spreadsheet (Lesson 10.1)

Central Processing Unit (CPU)   hardware that directs how information flows in, out, and through a computer (Lesson 1.2)

character   a letter, number, word, punctuation mark, or symbol on a keyboard (Lesson 2.2)

Chart button   a button that you click on to create a chart in a spreadsheet (Lesson 11.5)

click   to press and release the mouse button (Lesson 1.2)

client   a personal computer connected to a server in a network (Lesson 14.1)

clip art a piece of art that is already drawn (Lesson 12.1)

Close command a command that closes a window of a file or folder (Lesson 3.1)

column a section of text that runs from top to bottom on a page (Lesson 12.2)

column layout Shows database records in a table with records shown in rows and fields shown in columns. (Lesson 9.7)

command an order you give to a computer to do a job (Lesson 3.1)

Command key the key on a Macintosh® that helps open menus and gives commands when it is used together with other keys (Lesson 3.1)

compact disk (CD) a type of portable storage disk; a CD-ROM is read only; a CD-R is recordable (Lesson 5.3)

computer an electronic machine that stores information and instructions, performs calculations, and organizes data (Lesson 1.1)

computer virus a small program that can make copies of itself and be spread from one computer to another (Lesson 5.1)

Copy command a command that copies text and stores it to be pasted elsewhere (Lesson 6.5)

CPU Central Processing Unit; hardware that directs how information flows in, out, and through a computer (Lesson 1.2)

currency another word for money (Lesson 10.5)

cursor a blinking vertical line that shows the place on the computer screen where text is being entered; it also refers to a mouse pointer (Lesson 2.1)

Cut command a command that removes text and stores it to be pasted elsewhere (Lesson 6.5)

database software that stores similar information in an organized way (Lesson 9.1)

default name the name a computer will give to a file or folder if you do not name it; examples are Untitled 1, Document 1, or Workbook 1 (Lesson 3.3)

defragment to rejoin parts of files that are stored in different places on the hard disk, using special software (Lesson 5.1)

delete to remove something from a document, such as text or art (Lesson 6.3)

Delete key a Macintosh® key that deletes characters to the left of the cursor; a Windows® and IBM® PC key that deletes characters to the right of the cursor (Lesson 2.2)

descending Descending means going down. Descending order sorts alphabetically, from Z to A. It also sorts numerically, from the largest number to the smallest number. (Lesson 9.6)

desktop the background on the screen where icons and windows are shown and can be arranged (Lesson 2.1)

desktop publishing using a personal computer to combine text and art on a page (Lesson 12.1)

dialog box a window that asks for more information, then finishes the command (Lesson 3.1)

disk a thin, flat, round plate on which data can be stored; also short for "portable disk" (Lesson 5.1)

diskette a thin plastic disk that stores information (Lesson 1.3)

document any work done on a computer with applications software, such as a letter, report, budget, newsletter, or presentation (Lesson 6.1)

drag when you move an item with the mouse by clicking on it and holding down the mouse button (Lesson 2.1)

drive a part of the hardware that stores data and instructions (Lesson 4.1)

drop when you place an item that is being dragged by letting go of the mouse button (Lesson 2.1)

e-mail electronic mail; a way to send written messages and files between computers (Lesson 14.2)

edit to change text that is already entered (Lesson 6.3)

Edit menu a menu that lists commands that can make changes to text, numbers, or art in a file, such as Cut, Copy, or Paste (Lesson 3.1)

End key a key that moves the cursor to the end of a line, page, or document (Lesson 2.2)

Enter key a Windows® and IBM® PC key that moves the cursor down one line; a key that enters data in a cell (Lesson 6.2)

entry bar see *formula bar* (Lesson 10.2)

field a place in a database where specific groupings of data are entered and stored (Lesson 9.2)

file a set of information or instructions that is named (Lesson 3.1)

File menu a menu that lists commands that can do jobs with files, such as Save or Print (Lesson 3.1)

Find command a command that opens the Find dialog box (Lesson 7.1)

Find mode used to search for a record or group of records in a database. (Lesson 9.3)

Find Next button a button that you click on to find the next place a word or phrase appears in a document (Lesson 7.2)

floppy disk a type of portable storage made of a thin, bendable plastic disk that may be inside a hard plastic case (Lesson 5.3)

flowchart a diagram that shows the steps needed to do a job (Lesson 1.3)

folder a place where you can save and organize files (Lesson 3.2)

font the design of the text characters (Lesson 8.3)

Font menu a menu that lists fonts (Lesson 8.3)

format the way text looks on a page (Lesson 8.1)

formula cell content that does calculations in a spreadsheet (Lesson 11.1)

formula bar a box to enter or view information that goes in a cell; also called entry bar (Lesson 10.2)

Forward button a button that you click on to send a copy of an e-mail message to someone else; a button that you click on to go forward one page in a Web browser (Lessons 14.3 and 15.2)

freeform a way to draw your own objects without using shapes made by the computer (Lesson 12.4)

function a built-in shortcut formula that does calculations in a spreadsheet (Lesson 11.4)

gig short for gigabyte; about 1,000 megabytes (Lesson 5.2)

gigabyte (GB) a measure of computer memory equal to exactly 1,073,741,824 bytes; about one billion bytes (Lesson 5.2)

grammar the proper rules of language (Lesson 7.5)

Grammar command a command that starts the grammar checker in a word processing program (Lesson 7.1)

handouts documents with information printed from a presentation (Lesson 13.1)

hard disk a thin, flat, round metal plate on which data can be stored (Lesson 5.1)

hard drive a tool, built into the computer, for storing data and instructions (Lesson 1.2)

hardware the equipment that makes up a computer (Lesson 1.2)

head a title that is used to separate parts of text on a page (Lesson 12.2)

Help menu a menu that can help you solve problems or find information about ways to do things on the computer (Lesson 3.1)

hit list an index of search results from a Web search engine (Lesson 15.4)

Home key a key that moves the cursor to the beginning of a line, page, or document (Lesson 2.2)

home page the Web page that a Web browser automatically opens first; the starting Web page for any Web site (Lesson 15.2)

HTML HyperText Markup Language; a language used to write files to be read with a Web browser

IBM® International Business Machines Corporation; a company that makes computers (Lesson 1.1)

icon a picture that stands for something else, such as a disk or a program (Lesson 2.1)

icon view a way to view file and folders shown as icons with their names (Lesson 4.2)

Ignore button a dialog box button that gives the command to skip past highlighted text (Lesson 7.4)

inbox a built-in folder that stores e-mail you have received (Lesson 14.3)

indent the extra space as the start of a paragraph (Lesson 6.2)

input the information that is put into a computer (Lesson 1.3)

Internet millions of connected computers that share information (Lesson 14.1)

Internet Service Provider ISP; a company that connects personal computers to the Internet (Lesson 14.1)

ISP Internet Service Provider; a company that connects personal computers to the Internet (Lesson 14.1)

italic a style that makes characters slant to the right (Lesson 8.4)

joystick an input tool with a lever and some buttons (Lesson 2.3)

justified when text is lined up with both the left and right margins (Lesson 8.4)

K short for kilobyte; about 1,000 bytes (Lesson 5.2)

keyboard the set of keys with numbers and letters used to type information into a computer (Lesson 1.2)

keyword a word that describes information being searched for (Lesson 15.5)

kilobyte (KB or K) a measure of computer memory equal to exactly 1,024 bytes; about one thousand bytes (Lesson 5.2)

labels layout used to print labels from a database. (Lesson 9.7)

LAN   Local Area Network; see *network*

landscape   see *orientation*   (Lesson 8.5)

laptop   a small, portable computer

layout   the way fields and records in a database look on the screen (Lesson 9.7)

Layout mode   Used to change how a database record is shown on the screen or printed (Lesson 9.3)

link   a button, text, or image that connects to a Web page (Lesson 15.3)

list view   a way to view files and folders with their names listed in alphabetical order (Lesson 4.2)

Macintosh®   a brand of computers and an operating system made by Apple Computer, Inc. (Lesson 1.1)

mainframe computer   a large computer that can be used by many people at the same time, can store great amounts of information, and do many jobs at the same time (Lesson 1.1)

Make Chart command   command which is used to create a chart in a spreadsheet (Lesson 11.5)

manual feed   to add special paper, such as an envelope or stationery, into the printer by hand (Lesson 2.4)

margin   the space from the edge of the paper to the text area (Lesson 8.4)

meg   short for megabyte; about 1,000 K (Lesson 5.2)

megabyte (MB)   a measure of computer memory equal to exactly 1,048,576 bytes; about one million bytes (Lesson 5.2)

megahertz (MHz)   a unit of measure that tells the speed of a computer's CPU (Lesson 5.2)

memory   the part of a computer system where information and instructions are held for use by the CPU (Lesson 5.2)

menu   a list of commands for doing different jobs on the computer (Lesson 3.1)

Microsoft® Windows®   an operating system made by Microsoft Corporation (Lesson 1.3)

mode   a way a computer enters and displays data (Lesson 9.3)

monitor   the screen that shows information that comes out of the computer (Lesson 1.2)

mouse   a pointing tool that you move with your hand (Lesson 1.2)

network   a group of computers that are connected (Lesson 14.1)

New command   a command that starts a new document (Lesson 6.2)

New Slide command   a command or dialog box found in presentation software that makes a new slide (Lesson 13.3)

newsgroup   a place where people with the same interests can send and read messages (Lesson 14.4)

online   connected to a computer system or to the Internet (Lesson 14.1)

Open command   a command that opens an existing file and the software it was created in (Lesson 3.2)

operating system (OS)   makes up the inside of a computer including the CPU, memory, and system software; also called *computer system* (Lesson 5.2)

orientation the way a document prints on a page. If the top of the document begins at the short side of the page, it is portrait; if the top of the document begins at the long side of the page, it is landscape (Lesson 8.5)

OS short for operating system (Lesson 5.2)

output the information that comes out of a computer (Lesson 1.3)

Page Down key a key that moves the view in a window ahead one page or screen; PgDn key (Lesson 2.2)

page layout the way text and art are arranged together on a page (Lesson 12.2)

Page Setup command the command under the File menu that opens a dialog box where you can choose the page size, orientation, and margins (Lesson 8.5)

Page Up key a key that moves the view in a window back one page or screen; PgUp key (Lesson 2.2)

Paste command a command that places cut or copied text wherever the cursor is placed (Lesson 6.5)

path the address that tells you where to find a file on a computer drive (Lesson 4.1)

PC short for personal computer; usually refers to an IBM®-like PC, not a Macintosh® (Lesson 1.1)

personal computer (PC) a computer that fits on a desk; it is used by one person at a time, at home, in school, or on the job (Lesson 1.1)

placeholder a box with dashed or gray lines that shows where text or art will appear in a document (Lesson 13.4)

point size a measure of the height of characters (Lesson 8.2)

portable storage a disk that stores data and can be removed from the computer (Lesson 5.3)

portrait see *orientation* (Lesson 8.5)

presentation a way to use text and art to communicate information or ideas to other people (Lesson 13.1)

printer cable a cord that connects a printer to a computer (Lesson 2.4)

processor a part of a computer system that operates on data (Lesson 5.2)

publishing the printing of many copies of a book, magazine, newspaper, or other document (Lesson 12.1)

RAM Random-Access Memory; a temporary area in the memory (Lesson 5.2)

random-access memory RAM; a temporary area in the memory (Lesson 5.2)

read-only memory ROM; a permanent area in the memory (Lesson 5.2)

record data about a single person, place, or thing (Lesson 9.3)

Replace command a command that opens the Find and Replace dialog box; also called the Find/Change command (Lesson 7.1)

Reply button a button that you click on to answer an e-mail message (Lesson 14.3)

Resume button a dialog box button that gives the command to start again or continue; also called the Start button (Lesson 7.4)

Return key a Macintosh® key that moves the cursor (or text) down one line (Lesson 6.2)

ROM Read-Only Memory; a permanent area in the memory (Lesson 5.2)

save   to store a document and the changes you make to it on a computer disc (Lesson 3.3)

Save command   a command that saves a new file or saves the changes you make to an existing file (Lesson 3.3)

scanner   an input tool, used to copy a picture of something, such as a photo or newspaper article, into the computer (Lesson 2.3)

scroll bar   a bar along the edge of a window that moves what is in the window up and down, or left and right (Lesson 3.1)

search engine   a program for finding information on the Web (Lesson 15.4)

Send button   a button that you click on to send an e-mail message (Lesson 14.2)

server   a computer that provides information and manages it for a network (Lesson 14.1)

Shift key   A special key used together with other keys. Used with a letter key, it types a capital letter. If used with a key containing two characters, the top character will be typed. (Lesson 2.2)

Shut Down command   a command that tells your computer to turn itself off (Lesson 5.1)

slide   a page in a presentation document (Lesson 13.1)

software   a set of instructions that tells a computer what to do (Lesson 1.3)

sort   to arrange data in a certain order, such as alphabetical, numerical, or by date (Lesson 9.6)

Spelling command   a command that starts the spell checker in a word processing program (Lesson 7.1)

spreadsheet   a table that displays data (Lesson 10.1)

spreadsheet formula   a math expression that shows a calculation (Lesson 11.1)

standard layout   shows database record with each field on a separate line (Lesson 9.7)

Start button   in Microsoft® Windows®, a button used to quickly start a program, find a file, or get help (Lesson 4.4)

status bar   in a Web browser, it shows you what happens as you connect to a Web site or page (Lesson 15.2)

storage   a place where data and software can be held or saved (Lesson 5.3)

storage capacity   the number of bytes that a disk can hold (Lesson 5.3)

storyboard   a series of sketches that shows the order in which slides will appear (Lesson 13.2)

style   the way text characters look—**bold**, *italic*, or underline (Lesson 8.2)

stylus   an input tool, like a pen with no ink, used to draw on a special pad (Lesson 2.3)

submenu   a menu that appears on the monitor when a command from a main menu is selected (Lesson 10.5)

supercomputer   a very, very fast mainframe used to do jobs at the fastest speed possible (Lesson 1.1)

system   makes up the inside of a computer including the CPU, memory, and system software; also called *operating system* (Lesson 5.2)

system software   the type of software program that runs the computer hardware and other software; it creates the desktop and file systems you see (Lesson 1.3)

Tab key   a key that indents or moves text next to the cursor leaving a space; a key that moves the cursor from cell to cell or field to field (Lesson 6.2)

table   a framework for displaying data made up of rows and columns (Lesson 10.1)

task   pieces of work to be done (Lesson 6.1)

thumbnail sketch   a rough drawing that shows the text and art layout of a page or slide (Lesson 12.2)

title bar   a bar across the top of a window that shows the file's name (Lesson 3.3)

toolbar   a row of buttons you click to give commands to a computer (Lesson 3.1)

trackball   an input tool that moves the cursor when rolled (Lesson 2.3)

typeface   the appearance of the characters

underline   the style of text where characters have a line below them (Lesson 8.4)

Uniform Resource Locator (URL)   an address of a particular page or document on the Web (Lesson 15.1)

URL   an address of a particular page or document on the Web; it means Uniform Resource Locator (Lesson 15.1)

utilities software   software program that helps a computer run properly; virus protection is one type of utilities software (Lesson 1.3)

View menu   a menu that lists the commands for displaying files, folders, or documents in different ways (Lesson 3.1)

virus   see *computer virus* (Lesson 5.1)

WAN   Wide Area Network; see *network*

Web browser   a software program used to view documents and move from site to site on the World Wide Web (Lesson 15.2)

Web site   a collection of documents on a World Wide Web server (Lesson 15.2)

window   an area on the screen where information and icons appear (Lesson 2.1)

Windows®   see *Microsoft® Windows®* (Lesson 1.3)

word processing   computer software, or program, used to type and change text (Lesson 6.1)

word wrap   the automatic movement of text to the next line after filling the current line (Lesson 6.2)

World Wide Web   a collection of documents or files connected together on the Internet; the Web (www) (Lesson 15.1)

Index

A

Address bar, 308
Alignment, 150, 152
All button, 52
Apply button, 269
Area charts, 233
Arrows, 45
    choosing paper size, with, 155
Art
    adding, into document, 245
    arranging on page, 244
    drawing your own, 250
    inserting, from file, 275
    moving, 275
    placeholders for, 271
    resizing, 275
    in storyboards, 267
    using, in presentation slides, 264, 265
Automated teller machines (ATMs), *57*

B

Back button, Internet, 309, 319
Backups, 91
Bar graphs, 233–234
Barnaby, Bob, 123
Berners-Lee, Tim, 307
Bold, 144, 248
Browse mode, 171, 186, 188
Built-in storage, 88
Bytes, 88

C

Camera, 31
Cancel button, 45
Case sensitive, defined, 127
CDs, 83
Cells, 197. *See also* Spreadsheets
    active, 198, 219, 229
        deleting entries from, 198
        entering information into, 198
        in formulas, 225
    copying contents of, 205
    mistakes in, 206
    cutting contents of, 205

deleting contents of, 205
editing data in, 207
moving from cell to, 199
names of, 197, 198, 222–223
pasting data from, 205
selecting, 205
working with multiple, 205–206
Cells command, 209, 211
Change All button, 127, 130
Change button, 127, 130, 133
Chart button, 232
Charts, 233
    comparing data, with, 233
    making, 232–234
    for presenting data, 236
Chip, computer, 84
Circuit, computer, 80
Clear button, 184
Clients, network, 288
Clip art, 251–253, 275
Clip Art Gallery, 251, 275
Close button, 251
Column charts, 233
Columns, 197, 222, 229. *See also* Spreadsheets
    adding, to text document, 247
    in Format menu, 247
    names of, 202
    spreadsheet, 197, 201–202
    text, 246, 250
        in slides, 267
Commands
    alignment, 150
    Cells, 209, 211
    checking and editing, 123
    Close, 46
    Copy, 113, 176
        for drawing, 255
        using, for data in cells, 205
        using, to copy an object, 255
    Cut, 112, 176
    Delete Record, 176
    Duplicate Record, 176
    File, 48
    Find, 72, 122–123, 124–125

Find/Change, 126, 128
Font, 144, 208
Go, 313
Grammar, 122–123, 136
History, 313
inactive, 47
Insert Chart, 232
Make Chart, 232
Move to Back, 257
Move to Front, 257
New, 48, 254
    (Microsoft® Windows®), 69
New Folder (Macintosh®), 68
Number, 209, 211
Open, 42, 44, 47
Page Setup, 155
Paste, 112–113, 205, 255
Print, 47, *52*
problems with, 47
Replace, 122–123, 126, 128, 129, 136–137
Save, 48–50
Save As, 50, 58–59
Send to Back, 257
Send to Front, 257
Size, 208
Sort Records, 182–183
Spelling, 122–123, 130, 135, 136–137
Common functions, 228
Computer freezes, 93
Computers, 20, 245
    antivirus utility software for, 82
    circuits in, 80
    in digital cameras, 245
    hardware of, 7–9
    household machines containing, 14
    job-related uses, examples
        account assistant, 75
        bank workers, 216
        building contractor, 204
        car dealer, 164
        computer operator, 120
        computer technician, 87
        customer service representative, 111
        desktop publisher, 250
        graphic artist, 20
        invitation maker, 153
        message board operator, 35
        reporter, 99

        sales assistant, 299
        TV newswriter, 100
    mainframe, 4
    making pages on, 250
    mini-computers, 65
    online library catalog, 185
    organizing, 64. *See also* Files; Folders
    personal (PC), 4–5
        microcomputers, 123
    projectors controlled by, 265
    proper shut-down steps for, 83
    supercomputers, 5
        for weather forecasting, 167
    systems, 84, 94
    systems components of, 84–85
    taking care of, 82–83
    VCR, 40
Computer virus, 82
Copy button, 113
Copying text, 113
CPU (Central Processing Unit), 7, 84
    changes in speed, timeline, 86
    output sent back by, 10
    software and, 11
Cross-hair pointer, 255
Cursors, 23, 104, 271, 272. *See also* Pointers
    using, for cutting and pasting, 112
    using, for editing data, 173
    using, to edit formulas, 225
Cut button, 113
Cutting text, 112

D

Data, 173, 175
    analyzing, with spreadsheet, 218
    identifying kinds of, 168
    planning, for database storage, 168
    for spreadsheets, 196
Database book, 175, 178–179. *See also* Databases
Databases, 166–168. *See also* Records
    adding a new record to, 172
    computer, library, 185
    diagram of partial, 172
    of names and phone numbers, 190
    Find form, 179–181
    layouts of, 186
    for making labels, 190

modes of, 171
to present information, 190–191
programs for, differences in, 175
records of, 171
uses by car dealers, 164
using, 179
Date field, 169
Date order, 182. *See also* Sorting records
Default names, 49
Define Fields dialog box, 169
Defragment, 82
Delete button, 131
Delete Record, 172
Desktop, 24, 36
Desktop publishing, 244
combining text and art in, 258
to present information, 258
for school newspapers, 242
use of digital cameras in, 245
Details view, 66
Digital cameras, 245
Discussion groups, 289
Disks, 82, 89
Documents, 102. *See also* Text
checking, 121–123
editing, 122–123
linked, on Internet, 307, 312
starting new, 104, 106
tab settings in, 151
using computers to design, 140
Drawing, 254–256
moving objects to front or back, 257
Drawing pad, 31
Drive, 65
Duplicate Record, 172

E

Error message, 181, 231
on Internet, possible reasons for, 321
Errors, 130–131, 133
finding and correcting, 135, 136

F

Field List, 188
Field name, 168, 169
Fields, 168–171, 182
choosing, 169. *See also* Databases

in Field List, 188
useful names for, 168
in column layouts, 186
deciding on, to sort records, 182
deleting, from a layout, 188
moving to other, 173
selecting, 173
in standard layouts, 186
File menu, 251
Files, 44
backup, 91–92
copying, 58, 91
finding, 72–73
HTML, 307
importance of entering names for, 49–50
make and save new, 51
making copies of, 50
moving, to new folder, 76
organizing, 62–64, 76–77
renaming, 58
views, 66
with similar names, 71
Find button, 72, 126, 178
Find/Change command, 126, 128
Find/Change dialog box, 126–127, 129
Find dialog box, 72, 124–125
Find form, 179, 181
Finding text, 124
Find mode, 171, 178–179, 186
Find Next button, 124–129
Find what, 124, 129
Floppy disks, 83, 89. *See also* Portable disks
Flowcharts, 10, 16, 17, 287
Folders, 44
finding, 74
icon view, 66
list view, 66
making new, 68–70
moving files to new, 76
opening, 46
organizing, 62, 64
views, 66
Font command, 144, 208
Font dialog box, 144–145
Font list, 148
Font menu, 148
Fonts, 147
changing, 148–149

solving problems by, 157
choosing, 248
Format Cells dialog box, 208
Format menu, 143, 144, 208–209, 211, 241
    Columns, 247
    dialog box, 209
    Equal Width, 247
    Number of Columns box, 247
Formats, 142
    changing, 154
        solving problems by, 157
    changing number, 210
    changing numbers, 209
    currency, 208, 211
    dates, 208, 211
    Font command, 208
    Format menu, 208
    of Internet text documents, 307
    numbers, 208, 211
    Size command, 208
    special, in spreadsheets, 207
    uses for, 142, 158–159
Form Design view, 171. *See* Layout mode
Form mode, 186
Formula bar, 198, 212, 219, 225
Formulas, spreadsheet, 218–221
    to analyze information, 236
    editing, 225–227
    fixing errors in, 231
    writing, 222
Formula symbols, 218
Forward button
    e-mail, 294
    Internet, 309
Functions, 228–229
    using, 230, 236

G

Gigabyte (GB), 85, 88
Grammar check, 133–134
Grammar dialog box, 133
Graphs, 233. *See also* Charts
Grow Font button, 145
Gutenberg, Johannes, 103

H

Handles, 252, 255, 271
Hard disks, 82

backups for, 91
built-in, 88
Hard drive, 7, 88
Hardware, 7
Heads, 246–247, 250
    formats for, 248
Help feature, e-mail, 197
Highlighting, 109, 126
    errors, in spell check, 131
Home button, Internet, 309
Home page, 308
Horizontal ruler, 151
HTML (hypertext markup language), 307

I

Icons, 23
    for computer disks, 88
    database book, 175
    finding commands for, 55
    New Folder (Microsoft® Windows®), 69
    organizing, 36–37
    for toolbars, 55
    Untitled Folder (Macintosh®), 68
Icon view, 66–67
Ignore All button, 131
Ignore button, 131, 133
Inbox folder, 294
Indent, 105, 151
Input, 10, 14, 22
    using mouse for, 12
Input tools, 20, 22, 26, 31–32. *See also* Keyboard; Mouse
Insert button, 275
Insert menu, 251
Insert Record, 172
Internet, 185, *285*, 307
    newsgroups, 297–298
    uses for, 289
Internet Sevice Providers (ISPs), 289
    newsgroups available through, 297
Italic, 144, 248

J

Joystick, 31, 43
Justification, 150

K

Keyboard, 8, 26
  braille, 43
  entering text to slides, with, 271
  entering text with, 105
  input received by, 10
  moving from cell to cell, with, 199
  nonfunctioning, 93
  using
      to choose command, 42
      for input, 12
      for presentations, 277
Keys
  Alt key, 8, 42
  arrow keys, 12, 278
      moving between cells, with, 199
      using, for presentations, 277
  Backspace key, 26, 28, 67, 107, 173, 205
  Character key, 26
  Command key (on Macintosh®), 42
      shortcut keys using, 43
  Command-Option-Esc, for computer
    freezes, 93
  Control key (in Microsoft® Windows®), 43
  Ctrl-Alt-Delete, for computer freezes, 93
  Delete key, 28, 67, 107, 173, 188, 205
      to remove placeholder, 271
      removing objects in drawing, with, 255
  End key, 27
  Enter key, 28, 115, 198, 205, 219, 226, 272
      use of, for Web sites, 309
      using, to move one cell down, 199
  Home key, 27
  Letter key, 26
  Movement key, 26–27
  Number key, 26
  Numeric key, 27
  Page Down key (PgDn), 27, 277, 278
  Page Up key (PgUp), 27, 277, 278
  Punctuation key, 26
  Return key, 28, 198, 205, 219, 226, 272
      use of, for Web sites, 309
      using, 199
  Shift key, 28
      for use in drawing, 254
  Special, 28
  Symbol key, 26
  Tab key, 105, 115, 151, 173
      moving one cell to right, with, 199

Keywords, 318–319
Kilobyte (KB or K), 85

L

Landscape orientation, *155*
Layout menu, 187–188
Layout mode, uses for, 171
Layouts, 186–189
  types, 186–187
Library, 275
Light pen, 32
Lincoln Memorial, 241
Links, 312–313, 319
List view, 66–67
Local area network (LAN), 288
Lowercase, 129

M

Mailing labels, 187
Manual feed button, 33
Margin, 154
Mars Global Surveyor mission, map, *163*
Match case, 127
Mauchly, J. W., 6
Megabyte (MB), 85, 88
Megahertz (MHz), 84
Memory, 84–85
  RAM (random-access memory), 84–85
    upgrading, 87
  ROM (read-only memory), 84
Menus
  Arrange, 257
  Drawing, 254
  Edit, 42, 112–113, 124, 126, 128, 176, 205
  File, 42, 47, 52, 251, 254
  Font, 148
  Format, 143, 144, 208–209, 211, 247, 269
  Help, 42
  Insert, 251, 269, 275
  Layout, 187–188
  meaning of gray items in, 47
  opening, 42
  Order, 257
  pop-up, 45, 72
  shortcut (Microsoft® Windows®), 69
  Start, 83
  Style, 144
  View, 42, 277, 279

Message board, 35
Microphone, 31, 43, 143
Micropro International, 123
Mini-computers, 65
Modes, database, 171
Monitor, 8, 10, 12, 25
Motherboard, 87
Mouse, 8, 22–24
    in multimedia projector remote control,
      265
    clicking, 23, 30, 36, 44
    dragging items with, 24–25, 30, 36, 188
    dropping items with, 24–25, 36
    first, 32
    input received by, 10
    nonfunctioning, 93
    opening a menu with, 42
    pointer, for freeform drawing, 255
    pointing and clicking in cells, with, 199
    problems with, 15
    resizing windows with, 30
    scrolling with, 45
    using
        to cut and past text, 112
        by dragging, 109, 112
        for input, 12
        for Internet, 307, 312
        for presentations, 277
        to select text, 109
Mouse pad, 15
Move button, 188
Moving objects, 257
Moving text, 112–113. See Copying text;
    Cutting text; Edit menu; Pasting text

N

National Weather Service, 167
Networks, 288
New button, 104
New document window, 104
New Field dialog box, 169
New Layout, 187
New Layout dialog box, 187
New paragraph button, 115
New Record, commands to adding, 172
Newsgroups, 85, 297–298
New Slide dialog box, 269
Newsreader, 297
Next Record, 172

Nonprinting characters, 115
Number command, 209, 211,
Number field, 169

O

OK button, 52, 209, 247, 269, 275
Online shopping, 311
Open button, 104
Open dialog box, 44–45
Orientation, changing paper, 155
Output, 10, 14, 33
Output tools, 33

P

Page layouts, 246, 249, 250
    for newsletter or yearbook, 258
    planning, 246, 250, 259
    for slides, 267
Page margins, 154, 156–157
Page Setup command, 154–155
Page Setup dialog box, *155*
Paragraphs, starting new, 105
Parentheses, in functions, 228–229
Paste button, 113,
Pasting text, 112, 114
Path, 65, 73
Pie charts, 233
Placeholders, 271–272, 275
Pointers. *See also* Cursors
    Internet, 312
    cross-hair, for drawing, 255
    differing looks of, 23
    hidden, 12, 15, 22–23
    mouse, for freeform drawing, 255
Point size, 145, 157
    choosing, 248
Portable disks, 83. *See also* Floppy disks
    copying files onto, 91–92
    storage capacities, 89–90
Portable storage, 88–89, 91
Portrait orientation, 155
Posters, using formats in, 158–159
Presentations, 262, 264
    adding art to, 275–276
    making interview, about yourself, 274
    organizing information for, 266, 268
    planning, 280
    showing, 278

using mouse or keyboard for, 277
using multimedia projectors in, 265
Presentation software,
    265, 269, 275, 277, 279
    slides, made with, 264
Presentation window, 271–272
Preview area, 154
Previous Record, 172
Print button, 52
Print dialog box, 52
Printer, 8, 33
    parts of, 33–34
    output printed by, 10
Printing, 53
Printing press, first, 103
Processor. *See* CPU (Central Processing Unit)
Projectors, for viewing presentation slides,
    264, 265
Publishing, 244

R

RAM (random-access memory), 84–85, 95
    upgrading, 87
Records, 171, 178. *See also* Databases
    active, 175
    changing, 175, 177
    copying, 176–177
    deleting, 176–177
    finding, with Find mode, 178. *See also* Find
      mode
    hidden from view, 179
    modes to view and work with, 171
    moving through, 175
Records, sorting. *See* Sorting records
Renaming files, 66–67
Replace All button, 127
Replace button, 127
Replace dialog box, using, 127, 129
Replacing text, 126
Reply button, e-mail, 294
Resizing windows, 30
Resume button, 131
Return button, 115
ROM (read-only memory), 84
Rows, 197, 222, 229. *See also* Spreadsheets
    names of, 202
Rubinstein, Seymour, 123
Ruler, 151

S

Save button, 48
Save dialog box, 49
Saving, 48, 50
Scanner, 31, 32
Scroll bars, 45
    to bring database field into view, 173
Search button, in search engines, 315
Search engine, 315, 318
    clicking on popular subjects, 319
    using, on World Wide Web, 322
Search results index, Web, 315
Server, network, 288
Set Field Order dialog box, 187
Show All Records, 179
Shrink Font button, 145
Size button, 145
Size list, 145
Slide Layout dialog box, 269
Slide layouts, 269, 275
Slider, 45
Slides, 264
    adding art to, 275
    adding text to, 265, 267, 271–273
    rearranging, 279
    title, 267
    using art, in, 265
    using storyboard to show order of, 266
Slide show, 264. *See also* Presentations
Slide Sorter, in View menu, 277, 279
Software
    applications, 11
    database, 102, 166, 175, 178
    desktop publishing/presentation, 102
    drawing tools, 254
    presentation, 241, 264–265
    programs, installing, 94–95
    spreadsheet, 102, 196
      doing math with, 218
    systems, 11, 24, 85
    for use with photographs, 245
    using, for tour guides, 241
    utility, 11, 82
    to view Web pages, 307
    voice recognition, 143
    Web, first, 307
    word processing, 99, 102

desktop publishing, in, 244–245
Sort buttons, 182
Sorting records, 182–184
Sort Records dialog box, 183
Space bar, 115
Spell check, 130–132.
Spelling dialog box, 130–131
Spreadsheet formulas, 217
Spreadsheets, 196
   cells, 197
      active, 198, 202
   changing font size and style in, 208
   charts linked to, 233
   columns, 196–197, 201–202
   entering data into, 198
   everyday uses for, 234
   example, 201–202, 204
   formula bar, 198
   formulas, 218, 220–221
   organizing information for, 201–203, 212–213
   rows, 197, 201–202
   using formats in, 208
   using, like calculator, 218–219
Start button, 131
Start menu, 83
Status bar, 312
Status bar messages, 309
Stop button, Internet, 309
Storage, 88–89, 91
Storage capacity, 88
Storyboard, 266–267, 269–270, 274, 280
Style
   choosing, 248
   text, 144
Style buttons, 144
Style menu, 144
Stylus, 31, 65
Submenu, 208
Suggestions box, 133
Supercomputers, 5, 6, 167, 199
Surge protector, 83
System software, 85–87

T
Tab settings, 151
Tasks, word-processing, 102–103

Text. *See also* Documents
   adding, 107
   alignment, changing, 150. *See also* Alignment, 152
   arranging on page, 244
   changing appearance of. *See* Formats
   changing formats for, 248
   changing selected, 109
   copying, 113–114
   cutting, 112
   deleting, 107, 110
   editing, 102–103, 107, 108
   entering, 103–104, 110
      for slides, 271
   finding, 124
   moving, 112–114
   pasting, 112–114
   replacing, 126
   selecting, 108
   size, changing, 145–146
   style, changing, 144, 146
   using, in presentation slides, 264–265
Text field, 169
Thumbnail sketch, 246–247, 249–250, 253
Title bar, 50
Toolbars, 54, 104, 113, 205, 208
   buttons on, 150, 309
   for drawing, 254
   format commands on, 143
   icons for, 55
   Sort buttons on, 182
   using buttons on, 56
Touchpad, 7
Trackball, 7, 31, 43

U
Underline, 144, 248
Uppercase, 127
URL (Uniform Resource Locator), 308–309
   of linked Web pages, in status bar, 312
   typing errors in, 321

V
Viewing files. *See* Files, views
Viewing folders. *See* Folders, views
View menu, 67
   ruler in, 151
   Slide Show, in, 277
   Slide Sorter, in, 277, 279

W

Washington, D.C., 241

Web, 307. *See also* World Wide Web
  index of search results, 315
  links, 312
  search, 318. *See also* Links; Search engine
    narrowing, with keywords, 318

Web browser, 308, 310
  following links with, 314
  information search, 317
  keyboard search, using search engine
    and URL, 320
  window, 308

Web pages
  address bar on, 308
  loading, 309
  moving among, 313
  Rock and Roll Hall of Fame and Museum,
    306

Web sites, 308

  home page, on, 312

Wide area network (WAN), 288

Window, 23
  arranging, 36
  horizontal ruler at top of document, 151
  new document, 104
  resizing, 30, 37
  use, for Internet, 307

Word processing
  for organizing information, 116–117, 274

Word processing programs, 102–103
  drawing tools, 254

WordStar, 123

Words to know, 3, 21, 41, 63, 81, 101, 121,
  141, 165, 195, 217, 243, 263, 287, 305

Word wrap, 105

World Wide Web, 285, 289, 304, 306. *See also*
  Web
  first software, 307, 311
  information search, 323

Photo Credits